BETWEEN THE COVERTS

The Shooter's Bedside Book

To Jody and Clare

With *many* thanks for giving me the opportunity to stalk the game that is Laverstoke Park! I do hope that you find something of interest in here.

With very best wishes

[illegible]

DEDICATION

In their wilder teenage moments, I used to tell both of my sons that if they were gundogs I would write 'Not For Breeding' on their pedigrees. I am happy to say that I was very, very wrong, and at 6:44 a.m. on 26 September 2015 James and Rachel proved by how much. So this book can only be:

For Teddy

The family .410 is waiting for him as soon as he's big enough.

BETWEEN THE COVERTS

The Shooter's Bedside Book

Charles Smith-Jones

Illustrations by Will Garfit

Quiller

First published in the UK in 2016
by Quiller, an imprint of Quiller Publishing Ltd

British Library Cataloguing-in-Publication Data
A catalogue record for this book is available from the British Library

ISBN 978 1 84689 225 7

Design by Arabella Ainslie
Edited by Kirsty Ennever

Illustrations by Will Garfit
Cover painting by Ben Hoskyns

Printed in Malta

Quiller
An imprint of Quiller Publishing Ltd
Wykey House, Wykey, Shrewsbury, SY4 1JA
Tel: 01939 261616 Fax: 01939 261606
E-mail: info@quillerbooks.com
Website: www.quillerpublishing.com

CONTENTS

Anecdotes, Unusual Facts, Curiosities
and Keeper's Tips appear throughout

INTRODUCTION

This is not a text book. Its purpose is not to make you a better shot, although I hope that you may find a useful tip or two in it. Likewise, the A-Z of species is not intended as a detailed natural history, but rather as an affectionate look at some of the birds and animals that both delight and exasperate us – with a few facts I hope you find interesting about each one along the way. I thought long and hard about whether to include their scientific names but eventually did so, just in case an overseas reader might be unsure of an English name. I had to make up one Latin name, though – you'll see why when you come to it. You may find yourself looking in vain for a few species (for instance, there were certainly too many ducks to include them all) but I had to draw a line somewhere.

It is worth emphasising that where I mention some of the laws that relate to our shooting sports in the UK, these are only correct at the time of writing and are of course subject to change.

There are a few little oddities here and there which do not directly relate to sporting shooting but I hope that they fit in well enough with the overall theme. I have deliberately steered clear of deer and deer stalking as much as possible; there was enough of that in *The Deer Stalker's Bedside Book*. Instead I have tried to keep the focus on the shotgun rather than the rifle.

The Glamorgan Fusiliers are not a real regiment, but readers may recognise a few familiar eccentricities if they were fortunate enough to serve in one with a similar sporting ethos. I regret to say that I have not had to search too hard for some of the incidents described, and Diana the buzzard (her real name was Bramble) as well as many of the other animals actually did exist, though I'm afraid that in real life the Adjutant had to put his foot down when it came to a ferret. The ill-fated character Second Lieutenant Teal is based on a number of people I have come across. The name of one of them is on the front of this book.

Glen Garron does not exist either, and if anyone thinks that they recognise either themselves or anyone else I can only apologise – it is totally unintentional. Instead the stories feature an amalgam of a wonderful array of people, places and experiences from over the years, and it has been great fun arranging the stories around them.

Included in the book are quite a few quotes from one of my favourite sporting authors, Robert Ruark, as well as short biographical pieces on both him and one of the ultimate shooting heroes, Jim Corbett. I do hope you decide to have a look at some of their works, which are still reprinted over forty and sixty years after their respective deaths – they are as thrilling today as they ever were, and I don't think that you will be disappointed.

In The Deer Stalker's Bedside Book, *I included an outrageously untrue 'fact' for readers to look out for. As the idea went down quite well I have done the same again somewhere in the pages that follow. So, if you want the fun of trying to find the 'fact', read on, but beware – there may be one or two red herrings as well and, incidentally, it has nothing to do with the piece called Hyperion, which I hope is obvious once you spot some of the references! If you would rather know what it is in advance, the answer is revealed on the back page of the book.*

I very much hope that you enjoy dipping in and out of these pages. I have certainly had great fun putting it together.

ACKNOWLEDGEMENTS

It is always difficult to know where to start (or end) with the thanks, so in no particular order and with apologies to anyone I might have inadvertently left out, I would like to express my gratitude to Andrew Johnston at Quiller Publishing for his encouragement, along with his eagle-eyed editor Kirsty Ennever and design genius Arabella Ainslie, who between them have once again assembled a jumbled mass of material into an attractive and coherent volume. I also have to give Andrew credit for a very clever title for a bedside book, and can only wish that I had thought of it myself.

I must of course thank artists Ben Hoskyns and Will Garfit whose talents add so much attraction and atmosphere to the finished product.

I am also very grateful to Joe Dimbleby, editor of *Shooting Times*, for allowing me to use some early material originally used in his magazine. A host of sporting friends, some dating across many years and others made through my more recent second career at Sparsholt College, are sadly too many to mention individually. I would, however, like to single out Tony Lowry and sporting agent Howard Day of Outside Days; I'd also like to thank Charles Skeffington of Fulham Interiors for some fascinating statistics. My colleague Matthew Norris-Hill from Sparsholt is owed special gratitude for wading through my rough copy to check that there were no inadvertent howlers in the text. Whilst I have used a number of sources to check my facts, I would like to name three particularly useful volumes. James Marchington's *The Natural History of Game* and Brian P Martin's *Sporting Birds of the British Isles* have been truly invaluable sources of authoritative and accurate information, while Dr Stefan Buczacki's magnificent *Fauna Britannica* has at times confirmed some fascinating, unusual and occasionally downright bizarre facts.

Finally, I must thank my long-suffering wife Sara for her good-humoured tolerance when faced with a kitchen table constantly covered in reference material, coupled with an uncommunicative and preoccupied husband. Once again, I am indebted to her for her encouragement and honest criticism and, not for the first time, couldn't have done it without her.

Charles Smith-Jones

AN A–Z OF QUARRY SPECIES

ALIENS

I'm not talking about little green men with antennae here, rather some bird species that might cross your barrels in the course of a shooting day. With a few exceptions, they are not covered by an open season or a General Licence (see page 154) to shoot them, so it is worth being aware of a growing number of non-indigenous species that are becoming established in the wild in the UK.

Wildfowl collections are very popular, so it's not surprising that most of the newcomers are ducks and geese. Among the ugliest must be that popular farmyard bird now turned feral, the muscovy duck, a large black and white bird with a distinctive red growth (or 'caruncle') above the beak. Despite their name they come from South America rather than Moscow, and were domesticated in Colombia and Peru long before the arrival of Europeans. A small pouch under the beak produces a musk-like smell, hence the name.

Unlike the muscovy, the little mandarin duck, about the size of a teal, is undeniably attractive and becoming widespread across the south of England. They don't seem to cause any economic damage, though, and have little impact on other wildlife. The nest is usually many feet off the ground in a hole in a tree trunk; the ducklings have to jump for it when they leave the nest, floating almost like thistledown to the ground.

Another pretty little duck is not so welcome. After a number of ruddy duck escaped from the Wildfowl Trust in Slimbridge during the late 1950s, there was initially no problem until they started to mix with white-headed duck in Spain and it was realised that they were interbreeding. Considered a major threat to the genetic integrity of the already rare white-headed duck, the ruddy duck quickly found a price on its head. A government programme reduced numbers to a handful after being launched in 1999, and it is estimated that by the latter stages it was costing something like £4,800 a brace to bring them to account. Who says that driven grouse are expensive?

There are still more escapees from collections that might turn up occasionally. Black swans (Australian natives) have been here since the first introductions in 1791 and occasionally crossbreed with our native mute swans. Bar-headed geese (from Asia) can sometimes be seen mixing with

Canada and greylag geese, and the brightly coloured red-breasted goose (Siberia) with brent and barnacles. Non-natives also confirmed as breeding here include the swan goose (eastern Asia), wood duck (north America), ruddy shelduck (south-eastern Europe) and red-crested pochard (western Europe), and who knows what else will establish itself here next.

You cannot raise your gun to any of the preceding species, but by all means shoot the Canada goose; it's currently on the General Licence (so there is no close season) and so abundant now that you'll find it covered elsewhere as a legitimate and important quarry species. It has been joined by the Egyptian goose, which comes from Africa, on the General Licence. Despite the name, the latter is not really a goose but more closely related to our familiar shelduck. Like the Canada, though not yet in such vast numbers, it is spreading fast and has now reached a point where some observers consider further spread to be virtually unstoppable.

Then there are parakeets. Two species, the ring-necked and monk, have also been recently included on the General Licence. Their origins are the stuff of urban myth; some say that they escaped from Ealing Studios when Humphrey Bogart and Katherine Hepburn were there filming *The African Queen* in 1951, others that rock star Jimi Hendrix released them in Carnaby Street during the Swinging Sixties. It is more likely that they originated from multiple escapes over the years before establishing themselves firmly in south-east England. Whatever the case, they are now breeding in such numbers that there are fears they are displacing our native birds which also rely on holes in trees for nesting.

It's a bit surreal to see flocks of parakeets flying screeching across London parks or dangling off bird feeders in urban gardens, and although they are undeniably attractive they need to be seriously controlled. The chance, perhaps, for a special Macnab of invasive aliens – how about parakeet, muntjac and signal crayfish?

Keeper's Tip: Lay out your shooting kit the night before or keep a check list handy – it is easy to forget something if you are in a morning rush.

BLACK GROUSE

Tetrao tetrix

Once experienced, a black grouse lek is never forgotten. In early spring, in the dawn light, the peak of activity occurs when the males, or blackcock, come together in the traditional displaying sites which are used year after year. Here they compete furiously to outdo each other as they strut, wings drooping and air sac in the neck inflated to make them seem even larger than they are. The characteristic lyre-shaped tail is extended above the brilliant white under-tail coverts, fluffed out in distinct contrast to the deep black of their bodies whilst the vivid red skin flaps are engorged with blood to stand vibrantly above the eyes. Whilst a certain amount of sparring can take place, blood is very rarely shed and the display is everything. Every bird wants to be in the middle of the lek, at the centre of attention, as this increases his chances of attracting a mate.

Meanwhile the females, or greyhens, gather at the edges of the activity as they decide which of the males is to be granted the privilege of breeding with them in this particular year. Smaller, plainer birds, their plumage is a mottled mix of browns and greys, and they have only a slightly forked and rounded tail compared to the magnificence of those of their male counterparts. Seen side by side, it can be difficult to appreciate that the male and the female even belong to the same species. Sometimes the blackcock gather to lek alone, but the arrival of the greyhens drives them into a special frenzy. The background to all this activity is a loud, bubbling call made by the males as they endeavour to attract the attention of a potential partner. This is one of the most dramatic courtship displays in the bird world, and certainly the most magnificent you are likely to see in Britain.

The term lek, by the way, is thought to come from the Swedish *leka*, meaning 'to play'. Black grouse are not the only species to use this stratagem for attracting a mate; many other creatures do so as well, mainly birds, but also some mammals, insects and amphibians.

Sadly, the sight of lekking blackcock is not as common as it once was across the country and you'll have to travel north to witness it. Perhaps 150 years ago the species was common across Britain, reaching as far as the south coast (it was known as the heath poult in Hampshire), but by the end of the nineteenth century it was already in decline – though old shoot records show that black grouse were still featuring in Home Counties bags after the First World War. Population reductions are attributed variously to habitat loss, egg collecting and over shooting.

Over the last hundred years the breed has retreated northwards, and today your best hope of seeing one is in Scotland, where it is still fairly widespread if low in numbers, the northern Pennines or upland areas of Wales. There are estimated to be some 6,500 breeding males left across the country.

There remains a legal open season for the species, which may be shot from the 20 August in most places, though not until the 1 September if you happen to be in Somerset, Devon or the New Forest. These last three places are only included within the law, though, as a throwback to a once more widespread population – sadly the birds are long gone, and the last one to be seen in Somerset was in 1981. The start of the season was deliberately set later than that for the red grouse (which of course comes in on the 12 August) as the young black grouse are slower to mature. In truth the black grouse is no longer deliberately shot. Indeed, should you mistake a greyhen for a red grouse on a driven day, expect to pay your host a serious fine for the offence. The species can be hunted with an easier conscience in their northern and eastern European strongholds where a much healthier population, estimated at over three million pairs, exists. There are still even a few to be found, albeit in isolated pockets, in France, Germany, Belgium and the Netherlands, though they have disappeared from Denmark.

Only a few years ago I actually experienced driven black grouse whilst in the Cairngorms. The blackcock are impressive, a good third larger in size than their red cousins and unmistakeable, though the greyhens are smaller, and the overall experience was something to behold. They fly high for a game bird, their rapid wing beats punctuated by long glides, and it would have been a question of heavier shot and more tightly choked barrels than usual. I am glad to report, though, that I was armed not with a shotgun but a notebook and pencil – this was a census in support of the ongoing conservation drive to preserve these magnificent and delightful birds. What a triumph it would be if their decline could be reversed.

BLUE HARE

Lepus timidus

Laying the strongest claim to being the only true British native among the family *Leporidae*, the hares and rabbits, the blue hare's ancestors were once widespread before competition from their introduced brown relative forced them into the more remote upland areas. Though also found in Ireland, in mainland Britain the breed is now truly common only in the Scottish Highlands. Relocations to other parts of Scotland and northern England, mainly for shooting purposes, have established other populations, but it is highly possible that it has already disappeared from the parts of Wales where it was introduced.

Also known as the mountain, hill, Irish or white hare, it is not a particularly valuable sporting species. While hare shooting is enjoyed in its own right on some estates, most seem to be shot as incidental opportunities when grouse shooting. Many Guns, aware of the disadvantages of having to carry an extra three kilograms in the game bag when a long day's walking stretches ahead, can be prone to letting them depart unsaluted. I recall a walked-up grouse day years ago when all of the Guns shared this frame of mind. After about half-a-dozen had been allowed to get away scot-free, an exasperated shout from the keeper of 'Will you no' bliddy shoot them?!', accompanied by a thumb jabbed over his shoulder, to alert us to the fact that his assistant was following half a mile behind in an Argocat to periodically collect the bag. From that point on we were not so reluctant.

The reason our keeper was so keen to see hares shot was that, where grouse suffer from high tick burdens and the tick-borne louping ill virus, hares are considered to help sustain these high tick levels. Reducing hare numbers is therefore seen as a way of suppressing the disease. Some keepers also regard them as competitors for food with the grouse. The hares themselves are susceptible to a gut parasite, *Trichostrongylosis*, which itself controls numbers much in the same way as the strongyle worm causes grouse densities to fluctuate.

The blue hare lives above ground, sheltering in a form made among rocks, tussocks of heather or other available vegetation. They have been known to dig burrows, which can be up to two metres long, but the leverets are born and raised above the surface. The reason for the tunnels is unclear but one theory is that they are maintained as an emergency sanctuary from eagles.

Smaller and with shorter ears than the brown hare, the blue hare's summer coat is grey with the bluish undercoat that gives it its name. In winter, in common with the stoat, the coat turns mostly white although a variable area of the back usually remains a light grey. The tips of the ears are always brown. The Irish subspecies does not, however, change colour in winter.

They are good to eat, although most writers seem to regard the meat of the brown hare as superior. Their main food item is heather, so land managed for grouse shooting with its mosaic of various stages of growth is beneficial to them. Although the blue hare tends to be solitary, very large groups can gather in the same place to feed and up to seventy have been recorded together. In numbers, they can be detrimental to commercial interests on the lower slopes of the hill; one of my most memorable experiences was being taken out on a lamping expedition at the end of a day's stalking to control damage to newly planted conifer plantations. Shooting from the back of a Land Rover, the keeper took great delight in lighting up targets up to 300 metres away (no hand-held rangefinders in those days), which I was expected to hit with my deer calibre rifle. I like to think that I didn't entirely disgrace myself, and an abiding memory is the keeper's small son being directed rather like a human labrador as he ran backwards and forwards, accompanied by shouts from his father, to collect the bodies lying hidden in the furrows between the new plantings.

Keeper's Tip: Check beforehand in case a shoot day is likely to include a duck drive, for example, when you will need non-toxic loads.

Shooting clay targets is a very cleansing experience. It's very relaxing. It takes a lot of concentration. It's also very social, since you're usually shooting with friends. You can talk and forget about almost anything else that's on your mind. **Tom Selleck, actor**

BROWN HARE

Lepus europaeus

The brown hare has a legion of local names: Aunt Sarah, fuddie, malkin, old aunt, Katie and Sally are but a few of them, and irrespective of sex we tend to think of the hare as a 'she'. Weighing as much as fifteen pounds, the animal is one of the largest Lagomorphs and greatly prized as a quarry species on the Continent, whereas in Britain it is less highly regarded. Indeed, many shoots forbid the taking of ground game of any kind for reasons of safety.

Mystery surrounds how the brown hare found its way to Britain. It's a common assumption that the species was introduced by the Romans, but archaeological evidence points to them being with us since the Iron Age. There is very little to suggest, however, that they were here before that. If they were deliberately introduced, then, the question is by whom? We'll probably never know the answer to that question but the hare has definitely imprinted itself into our culture and folklore. Early Anglo-Saxons associated the animal with fertility and reproduction, a belief which transferred easily to the Easter association with life and rebirth. The 'Easter bunny' has only supplanted the hare in very recent times. The spring goddess Eostre held the hare her sacred animal; the later pagan festival of Eastre undoubtedly derives from this, and it's not difficult to see how the word has passed onwards from paganism and into Christianity. At one time, hare hunts were traditionally held at Easter in much of Britain, the origin of modern children hunting for Easter eggs. There is also a strange link to cats; one popular name for the hare is 'puss', while the Welsh 'cath' also means cat. Both species were once considered to be the familiars of witches, so this may offer an explanation.

'Mad as a March hare' is a common phrase springing from the hare's frantic courtship behaviour every spring, when animals chase, leap, and jump vertically for no apparent reason, 'box' with each other and generally act abnormally as the bucks compete in spectacular fashion. Their antics can in fact be seen well beyond the end of March, and were noted in a line from a poem of 1500, which describes people being 'as braynles as a Marshe hare'. The March Hare is, of course, a character in Lewis Carroll's *Alice's Adventures in Wonderland*: '... as this is May, it won't be raving mad – at least not so mad as it was in March.' To call someone 'hare-brained' comes from the same behaviour.

The brown hare's table qualities are excellent, though Mrs Beeton notes that 'its flesh is considered dry, notwithstanding that it is deemed, in many respects, superior to that of the rabbit, being more savoury, and of a much higher flavour'. Excellent, if frequently misquoted, advice is offered over a century earlier by Hannah Glasse in her 1747 *The Art of Cookery Made Plain and Easy*. To her is often attributed the phrase 'first catch your hare' when offering a recipe for jugged hare. In fact, what she really wrote was 'take your hare when it be cas'd' (i.e. skinned). 'Jugged', by the way, means enclosed or imprisoned (as in the slang 'in the jug') in the language of the day, so the hare is cooked in a closed pot as opposed to being roasted on the fire.

Hare coursing, which was probably first brought to Britain by the Romans, has of course been illegal here since 2005 but that doesn't mean that it has stopped completely. Large amounts of money can be gambled and its practitioners are frequently violent towards those who challenge them, while fields and property are damaged indiscriminately. Some farmers unfortunately see the best solution to the problem as simply eradicating the hare from their land. Elsewhere, if hares are numerous, farming interests can be threatened and organised walked-up shoots are held to reduce numbers. I've attended one or two in the past but prefer not to these days; people who seldom shoot in the company of others are rather too prone to taking uncomfortably dangerous shots in their excitement.

Many who are otherwise keen Shots prefer not to shoot the hare. I recall a hard lesson learned many years ago on a walked-up day on Salisbury Plain, where the rule was 'you shoot it, you carry it'. With several miles of rough going ahead, I took two within the first few hundred yards and quickly learned that their weight doubles, at least psychologically if not physically, for every mile walked. It's also easy to underestimate the pace at which a hare is moving: flat out, it can reach speeds of up to forty miles an hour, so to ensure a clean kill you need to allow the sort of lead you might apply to a bird in flight. The cries of a wounded hare are both piercing and distressing, so it is easy to understand why some choose not to raise their gun in the first place.

BROWN RAT

Rattus norvegicus

You are never more than six feet from a rat, or so runs the urban myth. In truth this 'fact' has been conclusively debunked, and seems to stem from a very old Ministry of Agriculture campaign aimed at promoting hygiene through hyping up the fear factor. Another much-quoted suggestion is that rats outnumber humans in the UK; again, this is probably not true. Of course we have no way of being sure, but some observers estimate the rat population to be about ten million, with humans outnumbering them by six to one. According to the British Pest Control Association, Birmingham has the highest rat population in the country.

Whatever the case, *Rattus norvegicus* is invariably an unwelcome neighbour. The brown rat is only one of many other introductions to our shores, but probably the least desirable. It is believed to have arrived from China (not Norway, as was originally believed and resulting in its scientific name) aboard sailing ships in around 1730. You still hear people speak very occasionally of the Norway rat and, even more rarely, of the Hanoverian rat. The latter name reflects another misbelief about its origins in this country, as it was mischievously (and no doubt politically) suggested that the animal arrived in this country with George I. The brown rat certainly rapidly supplanted the black, the latter now so rare in this country as to be virtually extinct. Another native of the Far East but brought over much earlier by the Romans, the black rat quickly succumbed to its bigger, more aggressive cousins and now the only known wild population is in the Outer Hebrides.

Indisputably a major pest species, among its many crimes is the effect the brown rat has on ground-nesting birds and their eggs, hence its listing among the enemies of our quarry species. An excellent climber, swimmer and burrower, it is intelligent and adaptable, and almost effortlessly seems to defy most methods of control. Chemical poisons are the main method used today to limit the numbers, but even here the species seems to have a natural ability to develop resistance to them. Now inhabiting every continent apart from Antarctica, brown rats are universally accepted as one of the most successful animals on this planet, probably eclipsed only by Man himself. A true omnivore, the breed can survive on a wide variety of foodstuffs; in some parts of the world, populations have adapted to a true hunter's existence, stalking and killing birds as large as ducks, whilst others have learned to catch small fish or dive for molluscs.

A social animal, the rat prefers to live in large, hierarchical groups. They will dig their own tunnel systems but also use man-made underground spaces such as cellars or sewers. Breeding is rapid. A female can produce up to five litters, consisting of as many as fourteen young, every year, and the young rat is capable of producing its own young by the time it is only two months old. Average body weights for adults are about 350 grams for males and 250 grams for females, but larger specimens are not unusual. In 2014 a particularly large animal, weighing one kilogram and dubbed Ratzilla by the media, was caught in Sweden.

It's a common myth that a cornered rat will go for your throat, although if you are crouching and there is no other escape route it may try to jump over your shoulder. Until as recently as the early nineteenth century, the 'sport' of rat baiting was enormously popular, and huge wagers would be placed on how quickly a dog could kill the greatest number. Professional rat catchers could make a good living supplying the baiting pits, of which there were over seventy in London alone at one point. Wagers usually revolved around whose dog could kill the most rats within a minute. In 1862 one celebrated dog, 'Jacko', a bull terrier, set the record of killing 100 rats in the space of just 5 minutes and 28 seconds – that's a rat every 3.3 seconds.

The last public rat baiting took place in Leicester in 1912, resulting in the promoter being prosecuted and fined. Rat baiting is not to be confused with today's perfectly legal practice of ratting, an efficient method of pest control which usually involves small dogs like terriers being let loose in an enclosed area, such as a barn. It can be remarkably effective and, I have to say, enormously exciting.

At the other end of the rat spectrum I do have to end on a much more positive note, at least from the rat's point of view – domesticated varieties can make charming, intelligent and responsive pets. A mid-nineteenth century professional rat catcher, Jack Black of Battersea, is credited with starting the trend by keeping any unusually coloured animals he caught and breeding them to produce different colour strains. I have even come across claims that he supplied Queen Victoria and her court ladies with pet rats, which were kept in gilded cages. Another rather more likely customer was Beatrix Potter, who based her *Samuel Whiskers* on a rat obtained from Black. Whatever the case, rats are certainly far more rewarding pets than the more usual rabbits and guinea pigs allowed to children, although I'm sure that some parents might be rather less than enchanted by the idea.

> **Keeper's Tip:** When you get to your peg, especially in wooded areas where visibility is poor, always give your neighbouring Guns a wave before the drive starts and check where pickers-up and other people might be. Knowing where everyone is helps to ensure safe shooting.

A hunk of beef raised on Scottish moorland has a very different ecological footprint from one created in an intensive feedlot using concentrated cereal feed, and a wild venison or rabbit casserole is arguably greener than a vegetable curry. **Tristram Stuart, environmental campaigner**

CANADA GOOSE

Branta canadensis

Sportsmen tend to divide geese into two main categories. One covers the grey geese of the genus *Anser*, which have pink or orange legs and feet and include the greylag, pink-footed and white-fronted. The other group contains the darker-legged black geese of the genus *Branta*. Most of the latter, including the barnacle and brent, do not feature on our lists of legal quarry, but there is one very notable exception – the Canada. Indeed, the latter is so unwelcome that it joins the woodpigeon and other pest species on the General Licence, and is not even afforded the protection of a close season when it may not be shot. Canadas are very much the subject of pest control and, while admittedly offering the wildfowler sport, must be pursued with this in mind.

First introduced into this country as an ornamental species for country estates as far back as the seventeenth century, the Canada goose is, as the name implies, a native of the northern Americas. Its spread since then has been rapid. It adapts better than most others of its kind to living in close proximity to humans, and is the only one of the black geese that is likely to be encountered inland. The Canada is guilty of many crimes in human eyes. A large flock can devastate cereal crops (just fifty birds can destroy an acre of barley in one day), and the fouling of public areas such as parks and sports fields is a major concern. A single goose consumes its own body weight in food every four days, defecates every twenty minutes, and produces around one and a half pounds of faecal material daily; research indicates that goose droppings can carry a large number of diseases harmful to humans. It is also a particularly large goose, with the average gander weighing in at almost twelve pounds, whilst some are even larger. They have been known to bring down electricity lines, and airport authorities are especially concerned by the potential for catastrophic bird strikes. Heathrow Airport, in close proximity to a profusion of man-made lakes and a burgeoning Canada population, has special cause to be worried.

Added to these hazards must be the aggressive behaviour of nesting birds undeterred by a normal fear of humans: a hissing, territorial Canada standing erect with wings outspread before coming at you to attack with wings and beak is a fearsome creature indeed, and woe betide the walker or fisherman who gets too close to a nesting bird or its goslings. Even the shooter has to take good care to stand clear of a falling goose if he does not want to risk a serious and potentially lethal impact.

Opinions vary regarding the culinary value of the Canada goose. While some say it is hardly worth the effort of cooking, I have found that a young bird makes for excellent eating – although an old one, in all fairness, can sometimes be better suited to resoling your shoes if not treated with respect and may benefit most from a long session in the slow cooker. To tell them apart, look at the primary feathers – those of mature birds are rounded, while worn and faded ones indicate an immature bird. Likewise pointed, rather than indented, tips of tail feathers indicate an adult bird. By all means pluck and roast the entire goose, but many people don't go to all the bother and simply remove the breast meat.

Of all the geese, the distinctive honking clamour of a skein of Canadas is the most likely to be encountered when standing on your peg on a driven day, and great excitement it can cause. Despite their general licence status, remember that lead shot is prohibited for shooting any goose whether you are on the foreshore or in a Hampshire field. As you fumble for your bismuth cartridges to replace the pheasant loads in the chambers, have a mind to height and speed. The Canada is a tough bird and needs to be hit hard, so take care that your target is within range and that your loads are up to the job. It will also be going faster than you might imagine, so you'll need to make at least as much allowance as you would for a pheasant if you want shot pattern and target to coincide. Shoot away, though, if you can – you're doing your part in the name of pest control.

Tonight we'll be talking to a gunsmith who's invented a sage and onion bullet that shoots the goose and stuffs it at the same time. **BBC Television Programme, *The Two Ronnies***

CAPERCAILLIE

Tetrao urogallus

By rights the capercaillie shouldn't be on this list as it has not been legal quarry for the British sportsman for a long while now. Given that it's our largest resident grouse, though, it would be wrong not to include it. Memorably described by Duff Hart-Davies as 'the jeroboam of British birds' the sight of one, whether in flight or on the ground, is simply unforgettable. Head to tail the bird measures almost a metre and gives the impression of a flying turkey. A fully-grown cock bird can weigh as much as five kilograms although the hen, as is the case with most game birds, is considerably smaller. He has a striking, slate-grey body with a dark blue tinge, reddish-brown wings, a long rounded tail and the typical grouse red eye-liner; she is a rather more understated mixture of buffs and browns, far better suited to concealment when incubating eggs on the forest floor. It's impossible to mistake a capercaillie of either sex for anything else, thanks to their size.

The source of the name is unclear. One suggestion is that it is derived from the Gaelic *cabhar coille*, meaning 'cock of the woods', while another is *capull coile*, or 'horse of the woods', which refers to the whinnying, equine sound that the lekking cock bird is reputed to make.

The capercaillie became officially extinct in this country by the end of the eighteenth century. It used to be a fairly common bird, not just in Scotland but also present in northern England and Ireland. The last Irish birds probably disappeared in the 1760s, and it is suggested that the species may have hung on until as late as 1815 in Scotland when an old cock bird was reputed to have been shot near Fort William. The decline is probably attributable more to a mixture of the extensive felling of their pinewood habitats and a series of damp and cold summers, since described as a 'Little Ice Age', rather than the shooting of them.

The story did not end there, though. In 1837 the species was reintroduced to Perthshire using Swedish stock and rapidly recolonised the new conifer plantations there with such success that by the 1970s there was thought to be a population of about 20,000. Sadly, the success ended there and numbers dropped rapidly, blamed variously on overgrazing by sheep (which depleted the blueberry, a major food source for the birds), collisions with deer fences, increasing predation by foxes and crows, and human disturbance. Another major factor may well be that the pine marten, largely exterminated as a perceived pest by the time of the 1837 reintroduction, is now thriving again in Scotland. By 1999 the capercaillie population was estimated as a mere 1,000, and today a second extinction seems almost inevitable, although Scottish National Heritage remains hopeful that numbers have stabilised in their core areas of Deeside and Speyside.

Although technically a legal quarry until only comparatively recently, for many years before that the capercaillie's decline was recognised and there was a voluntary ban on shooting them in any case. Sadly this did not have the desired effect, and in fact some observers noted in 2001, when the species was formally removed from the legal quarry list in Scotland, that this would probably do more harm than good by removing a major incentive for preserving its habitat. Interestingly, the capercaillie has never really been classified as a game bird because, by the time that the 1831 Game Act was passed, they had already been designated as extinct in Britain for several decades. The capercaillie has featured on British menus for millennia, as evidenced by the study of prehistoric cooking sites, but more modern man has seen the bird rather more as a trophy than a gastronomic delight. It has the reputation of tasting of turpentine. Discussing the future of the capercaillie in a 1999 House of Lords debate, Lord Thomas of Gresford reported that 'a ghillie on the Glen Tanar estate told me that as a boy his mother would stuff a capercaillie, when one had been shot, with potatoes in order to take away the pine flavour. She would make sure to throw the potatoes away, but even so he was not a fan of what he ate because the taste was something resembling an air freshener'! It is very likely that much had to do with the season in which the bird was shot and the diet available to it; on the one occasion I have tasted capercaillie (shot, I hasten to add, in Sweden) the flavour was reminiscent of very fine and tender fillet steak.

Happily, while the capercaillie has declined in Scotland, it remains a widespread species elsewhere with sub-species found across northern Europe and Russia, and scattered populations as far south as the Pyrenees of France and Spain. It is an important sporting quarry in Scandinavia, where the bird is stalked rather than driven, often by being 'treed' by a trained hound. The bird is unconcerned by the presence of the dog, which it knows cannot reach it; the skill lies in the hunter's ability to approach close enough for an accurate shot with a small bore rifle.

Hunting in the Americas 1

A two-year Army posting to Canada offered, I hoped, some shooting opportunities and I didn't waste any time before booking myself onto a hunters' awareness course that would lead on to the grant of a licence, essential before I would be allowed to venture out into the woods. As I was in Québec the whole course was conducted in French and my 1970s O-level in the language had not really prepared me for that. Although in time I came to terms with the heavy accent and unfamiliar words (in general terms, Québecois is to European French as broad Geordie is to southern English), I spent most of the day uncomprehending and simply looking at the pictures on the projector screen. I worried that I would not be remotely capable of taking the test at the end of the day. Fortunately the instructor took pity on me and provided the final examination paper in English. The first question asked the candidate the best way of demonstrating his shooting ability to friends. To my very great relief, the test was the multiple choice type and possible answers offered were roughly: 1) on a rifle range 2) shooting the cones off telegraph poles or 3) shooting beer bottles off the top of a wall. Fortunately the paper was simply looking for a small degree of common sense, and I was duly issued with a licence.

As soon as the season was open, I had tremendous fun wandering the woods behind the camp where I was stationed in search of duck and spruce grouse around the multitude of small streams and small lakes. Armed with a single-barrelled, non-ejecting 20 bore, I had to be careful to make every shot count. On the advice of the Canadian Army captain who had lent me the gun I also carried a couple of rounds of solid slug – 'just in case', I was told. The Canadian woods can get quite daunting and eerie, especially if you are alone, and one afternoon I disturbed something large, which went crashing off through the bushes. Moose, deer, or bear? I didn't know, but at such times the imagination can go into overdrive. I'd been assured that black bears are not usually dangerous, but as I proceeded along the dirt track I started to get the feeling that I was being watched and could actually feel the hairs on my neck start to stand up. After a while I could stand it no longer and the cartridge containing No 5 shot was exchanged for one of the solid slugs. I decided to head back and after a short distance rounded a bend: superimposed over my bootprints before abruptly turning off the track was a set of pad marks, each easily eight inches across, rounded and with clearly defined claw prints. They hadn't been there when I had passed that way just a few minutes earlier. It was a very interesting half-hour before I made it back to the car, nerves at screaming pitch. Back home my Canadian captain friend made light of my experience. 'Don't be worried, the bear's only curious!' From then on, though, I made a point of never hunting alone.

CLAY PIGEON

Columba terra

No list of quarry species would be complete without the humble clay pigeon. True, it makes for rotten eating, but it affords a great deal of pleasure and essential practice to us all, so it has to be included. Besides, the origins of this sporting target are fascinating in their own right.

As sporting firearms became more efficient in the nineteenth century, so the concept of shooting live birds trapped and then released for the purpose, as opposed to the hunting of wild game under natural conditions, grew. The practice usually revolved around a set number of pigeons being released individually on the call of the shooter; the usual format was that to count, the shot bird had to fall within a marked grid. It became a highly popular pursuit and could attract large crowds of spectators, with huge wagers often being made on the outcome. Somewhat controversially, live pigeon shooting even featured in the 1900 Paris Summer Olympics, for the one and only time in the history of the competition. Unsurprisingly, as attitudes became more enlightened this 'sport' eventually declined but was not finally banned outright in Britain until 1921, although it goes on in some other countries still.

The first alternative to shooting a live bird was a glass ball, although this was expensive, ungainly and difficult to launch with considerable limitations on the range that could be achieved. These balls were sometimes filled with feathers, dust or even shredded paper for added realism when they were hit; they were usually launched from a catapult resembling a medieval siege engine. The design of the disc-shaped clay pigeon we know today is attributed to American George Ligowski, who came up with the idea in 1880 as he watched boys skimming clam shells or flat stones across a lake (some sixty years later, Barnes Wallace found similar inspiration for the 'Dam Busters' bouncing bomb). The clay pigeon is a compromise between strength and fragility, needing to resist the stresses of launching while retaining the ability to shatter when hit by a few shotgun pellets. Early ones were made of clay, but modern targets are mainly manufactured from a composition of pitch and limestone.

We get a lot of our modern terms from the old live shooting

practices. The 'trap' was originally the basket that contained the live pigeon and the command 'pull' the instruction to pull the cord to open the trap to release it. We still refer to inert clay pigeons as 'birds' today, even though they look nothing like them, and a hit is a 'kill' whilst a miss is a 'bird away'.

Clay pigeon shooting is a massively popular sport in its own right, and those who wish to distance themselves from the practice of killing live animals and birds often talk of clay 'targets' rather than pigeons, which are 'scored' instead of 'killed'. A wide variety of disciplines is available, though more importantly for the sportsman's purposes the clay can be thrown to mimic a number of realistic targets and is a fun and valuable form of practice before the season opens. You can even get explosive attachments which cause the clay to break up with a bang, flash and puff of smoke when hit – a bit unnecessary perhaps, but undeniably great fun.

The driven clay day is becoming increasingly popular, and is a great way of sharpening skills before game shooting starts in earnest. Run as a formal shooting day, including the drawing of pegs, participants can be faced with a variety of targets thrown to resemble a real drive, though in far greater quantity, and it is possible to go through more than ten times as many cartridges as you normally would. You might move between driven pheasant and grouse butts, with tiny mini-clays occasionally thrown in to represent snipe. Beware, though, to reduce your cartridge loads and thus the kick of your gun, or it can get painful. On one hot day, with everyone in shirtsleeves, I shot with a lightweight 16 bore and was praying by lunchtime for the punishment to stop. The bruising took days to go down.

One great advantage of 'driven' clays is that the Guns can deliberately behave badly (within, of course, the bounds of safety) and get away with it. Poaching your neighbour's birds, a cardinal sin on a real day, is great fun and a source of amusement and friendly rivalry. One of my favourite drives on a recent day was the rabbit stand. Teams of four Guns were faced with rabbit clays bowled along the ground in all directions in front of us, with the warning that a set number of them would be fluorescent orange. For every one of these that was missed, each Gun would have to pay the trappers an agreed fine. This concentrated the mind wonderfully as we tried to ensure that one gun remained loaded and ready at all times, while the trappers did their best to provoke the opposite. Unsurprisingly, we ended up parting with our cash.

COOT & MOORHEN

Fulica atra & Gallinula chloropus

Some might find it strange that these two duck-sized birds are included in a list of quarry species, and even more so to learn that they have open shooting seasons (apart from in Northern Ireland). The uninitiated may consider them to be ducks and it's an understandable error, as both spend much of their lives swimming on the water. Ducks, however, they most certainly are not, belonging to the family *Rallidae* which also contains the secretive water rail and now very scarce corncrake.

Similar at first glance, the two are easily told apart. The coot (*Fulica*) is the larger bird, about the size of a teal. It is black all over apart from a white frontal shield to its beak, hence the expression 'bald as a coot'. The moorhen (*Gallinula*) is a couple of inches smaller with white edges to the folded wing and a red and yellow bill. When swimming the coot's tail is not obvious, whereas the moorhen's is tilted at a jaunty angle, white underneath, and constantly jerking up and down as it swims. Neither bird flies particularly well or willingly – take-offs can be a prolonged affair as they patter along the surface before actually getting into the air – but they are excellent divers, staying submerged until danger has passed, with just their beaks held out of the water.

Whilst most of our British coot and moorhen are year-round residents, they are joined every winter by migrants from the continent, and some coot even arrive from as far away as Russia. The designation 'coot' is thought to have its origins in Middle English, as an imitation of the bird's sharp, loud call. The moorhen has nothing to do with moors – its name is actually a derivation of mere, or lake. Both can be aggressive towards others of their species, with beaks and powerful legs used freely in fights. The moorhen seems to be the more aggressive towards its fellows, and serious body damage, even deaths, have been known to result from territorial arguments.

Both are common and, although not often shot deliberately today, occasionally end up in the bag. Coot drives used to be annual public events and whole communities would join in. The most famous was held on Hickling Broad in Norfolk every St George's Day, 23 April (which would not be possible today as that is well after the end of the open season). Guns would be divided into boat and land parties: the boats would spread out in a line to drive the coots whilst the remaining participants would line the banks at the place to which it had been decided to drive the birds. Brian Vesey-Fitzgerald recorded in his 1946 book *British Game*:

'... the birds would come swimming along in front of the boats. Then finding themselves trapped between two lines, they would rise and fly wildly round in all directions. The shooting I understand, was inclined to be dangerous. But the bags were enormous. The record for a public shoot at Hickling seems to be 910 coot in 1901, but on 25 February 1927, 1,175 coot were killed by twenty guns.' (The 1927 record may be impressive, but it is still considerably less than the 1,700 coot, once again to twenty guns, shot at Slapton Ley in Devon in January 1891.)

While neither coot nor moorhen might be justly considered a widespread pest species, both have been known to take the eggs and chicks of other birds amongst their otherwise mainly vegetarian diet. The moorhen in particular has been accused of serious crop damage in places where numbers are high; as they uproot plants while feeding, the effects of their presence can be more severe than the grazing of ducks.

Once popular table birds, both have fallen from favour in recent times. The coot in particular has been accused of having a strong and sometimes muddy flavour, especially if it has been feeding in estuaries, and birds which have been taking grain or grass are considered the best. The moorhen has a better reputation as table fare and even Mrs Beeton herself stated that young ones made for very good eating. The flesh is somewhat rich, though; in my falconry days I would avoid feeding up a hawk on too much of a moorhen kill as it would put it out of flying condition for much longer than, say, a similar amount of rabbit or partridge. In the gentlemen's clubs of 1940s wartime London, beset by rationing, moorhen was frequently substituted for plover on the menu – so much so that it became common practice to serve plover with the feet attached so that the diner could easily spot any trickery.

People never lie so much as after a hunt, during a war, or before an election.
Otto von Bismarck, statesman

DEER

While I've deliberately tried to avoid making this a 'deery' book, they are often to be seen when shooting, whether disturbed from their couching places during an informal walk around, driven past the Guns on a formal day, or materialising by the flight pond as you wait silently for the first mallard to drop in. Therefore it is worth having a quick look at the various species that you might encounter.

The most common example to see bursting through the line of pegs on a driven day is the **roe** (*Capreolus capreolus*). Its scientific name means 'little goat', which is a fair indication of its size. From a distance, all deer tend to look bigger than they actually are, because their relatively long legs create a false impression of height. A rich, foxy red during the summer, the roe's coat changes to a much duller grey-brown by the time pheasant shooting starts but the antlers are not cast by the buck until as late as December in some cases. It differs from all other deer by having no visible tail, but its white rump patch consists of erectile hair which is fluffed out when the animal is alarmed.

If any deer runs at you, it's best to get out of the way pretty quickly. Even a small, antlerless specimen can cause a nasty injury if it hits you! I have met one lady beater who spent the entire season with her arm in a cast after being struck by a roe doe running flat out. That the deer seems to be coming at you is not malicious intent on its part, though – it's almost literally blind panic. On one shoot I attended, a roe buck ran straight into a tree and broke its neck.

Smaller than the roe, at about the size of a springer spaniel, the **muntjac** (*Muntiacus reevesi*) resembles a small, hairy pig and has shorter legs than the average deer. It does have a short tail which is raised vertically when the animal is alarmed, revealing the white underside. Muntjac are notoriously reluctant to leave cover unless they absolutely have to, instead doubling back inside the dense bramble beds in which they prefer to shelter. Sometimes they can become trapped in wide mesh fences of the sort that usually surround areas of plantation. If this does happen, approaching it from the head side can sometimes persuade the animal to back away and escape unharmed. If the deer is injured, though, it's far kinder to euthanise it – but do beware of the sharp canine teeth that it is quite capable of using in self-defence. I always carry thick gardening gloves if I am called out by the police to deal with deer injured in road accidents, just in case I have to handle a live one.

Unless you live in Bedfordshire, the fen country of Cambridgeshire or the Norfolk Broads you are unlikely to encounter the **Chinese water deer** (*Hydropotes inermis*), although its range is slowly increasing. Similar in size to the muntjac, it is unique among our deer in that the males never grow antlers (their scientific name means 'unarmed water drinker'). Instead they grow impressive canine tusks which they use for competing with other bucks and defending themselves. Females have tusks too, but these are small and not visible on the live animal. The CWD is declining in its native China and Korea and estimates suggest that the introduced English population comprises at least ten percent of the world total.

The first of the three larger deer species is the **fallow** (*Dama dama*). Like the red and the sika, it is a herding rather than a solitary species as many a motorist has discovered to their cost when, assuming that the deer that has crossed their path is alone, they have been unprepared for the thirty more which follow behind it. Coming in several colour varieties which include black and white, the common fallow is a reddish-brown with white spots that disappear as the darker winter coat comes through. The antlers of a mature buck are palmated, making them easy to tell apart from other deer. The fallow is far ahead of other deer in evolutionary terms; stalkers consider them a real challenge, as the deer are quick to recognise regular human activities and change their own movements to avoid whatever they perceive to be a threat.

Of a similar size to the fallow is the **sika** (*Cervus nippon*). Originating in Japan, it is locally very common within restricted ranges which include the Poole Basin of Dorset, parts of Cumbria and much of the western side of Scotland. Its name means 'deer' in Japanese. In Scotland there is a particular concern that sika are interbreeding with the closely related red deer, potentially endangering the genetic integrity of the latter. One issue with sika is that they have a reputation for aggression; most stricken deer are only concerned with getting away from humans and their dogs, but the sika may attack if it is able. For this reason, do take great care if you have to deal with an injured one.

Finally we come to the **red deer** (*Cervis elaphus*), the original

Monarch of the Glen and Britain's largest wild land mammal. It and the roe have the distinction of being truly native to these shores, whilst the other four have all been introduced at one time or another. You may well encounter the red deer in the process of pursuing grouse on the Highland hill, but they are to be found in other places across the UK as well. An East Anglian, West Country or New Forest stag will dwarf its Scottish counterpart, even though the two are the same species. The Scottish animal has been forced to adapt to ensure its existence in a harsher environment with poorer feeding, and has done so by becoming smaller. Wherever you are, though, the red deer rut, which takes place between September and November, is an iconic countryside event as stags roar and fight to determine the right to breed.

> **Keeper's Tip:** Aim to arrive early for organised shoot days. Keepers and shoot captains are always anxious to move off at the appointed time, and late guests hold everyone else up.

FOX

Vulpes vulpes

I have a sneaking regard for the fox and suspect that many keepers, pest controllers and Masters of Foxhounds do too if you could but get them to admit it. In competition with, and as a result persecuted by man since the latter gave up his hunter-gatherer ways and took to farming, the fox has done rather better than the lynx, wolf and bear that have edged their inevitable way towards British extinction. Instead, the fox has flourished, a sure sign of its adaptability and resourcefulness. Paradoxically, it is man which has assisted the fox's spread in many cases – witness their export as far afield as Australia to satisfy home-sick huntsmen. You could forgive the fox much were it not for the habit of surplus killing: large numbers of trapped prey items in release pens or chicken sheds can be destroyed by a single animal, which needs to take no more than one or two.

There are in fact some dozen species of fox worldwide of which ours, the red fox, is but one, although *Vulpes vulpes* has the widest distribution across the northern hemisphere. An opportunistic omnivore with a widely varied diet and a willingness to live near to the presence of man, the fox has chosen to move ever closer to built-up areas. The urban fox started to appear in Bristol and London only as recently as the 1940s but can now be commonly encountered in other towns and cities across the country. As a fox will eat just about anything that a human will, they have flourished, sustained by those who deliberately encourage them by putting out food. Regrettably, as foxes have become so tolerant of close human proximity, instances of them entering houses have increased. In 2013 a baby's finger was bitten off by a fox which dragged the infant out of his cot and in 2010 nine-month-old twin girls were mauled by a fox as they slept. Both incidents occurred in London, where there are estimated to be some 10,000 urban foxes alone.

In the countryside such occurrences are thankfully rare, but then the fox is treated more realistically. The Game and Wildlife Conservation Trust estimates that the British fox population totals almost a quarter of a million animals, and that gamekeepers probably account for 80,000 of these every year. Man is the only real predator in Britain thanks to the demise of the wolf and the lynx, although golden eagles are said to take foxes occasionally. In urban areas, the motor car is probably the biggest killer; shooting is not practical under such circumstances, and live trapping more often than not simply results in the animal being relocated.

The fox remains well entrenched in folklore, not just in this country but worldwide, with a reputation mainly based on its cunning and trickery, and goes by many names – Charlie, Tod and Reynard are perhaps the most familiar. It is noteworthy that in children's literature the fox is usually depicted as roguish rather than simply evil, as is the lot of the wolf; this may form much of the basis of our love/hate relationship with the animal, and indeed some of the deeply entrenched camps which vie over how it ought to be treated. The Japanese take fox mythology to a deeper level than European folk culture and the *kitsune* is believed to possess a higher intelligence, magical powers and even an ability to assume human form. Some can apparently grow as many as nine tails – the more tails, the more powerful the fox.

In August 2015, as a refreshing diversion from the usual media circus surrounding the Glorious Twelfth, a fox was pictured in a national newspaper sleeping soundly on the second floor windowsill of a house in Notting Hill. As foxes can't climb sheer brick walls or fly, one has to wonder how it got there. Were it not for a series of photographs showing it in different positions it might have been tempting to suspect the assistance of a taxidermist with a sense of humour.

Hunting in the Americas 2

The moose season in Québec was short, only three weeks, so it was with great excitement that I looked forward to taking part. Three Canadian soldiers from the base I was working at were making up a hunting party for a week in the woods, living in a small caravan, and had invited me to join them. We met at the prearranged rendezvous at the start of a vast wilderness of swamps, forest and lakes some forty miles to the north of Québec City. Dressed in my habitual Salisbury Plain stalking kit of camouflage jacket and trousers with hat and face veil, I rounded the corner to be dazzled by three figures dressed head-to-toe in blaze orange. They took one look at me, burst out laughing and explained why: common sense and state laws both demanded high visibility hunting clothing. Somewhat abashed, I quickly accepted the offer of some loaned kit – they had anticipated this and brought extra with them.

The game plan for the week was simple. Our hunting block was divided into four areas, and we would rotate among them, either sitting and waiting at a suitable point or 'still hunting'. The latter is a wonderful North American phrase which describes perfectly the art of stalking on foot – although you are not actually still, you are moving so slowly, stopping frequently to watch and listen, that you might as well be. Each night, we would meet back at the caravan for a simple meal and a few bottles of Labatt beer before going out again at first light the next day.

For the first three days I elected just to sit and watch. A clearing at the edge of a swamp offered several hundred yards of visibility in three directions, so I built a temporary hide on the wood line that the SAS would have been proud of. It was so well disguised that once, having left it to answer a call of nature, I had difficulty finding it again myself. It fooled some other wildlife just as easily; at one point a porcupine decided to join me in it, and man and animal exited the enclosed space in opposite directions at speed. A fisher, a relative of the martens and looking something like a mink on steroids, made its cautious way not ten yards from me, and a great white heron flew in to spend most of each morning immobile on the swamp edge. On several occasions white-tailed deer, one a magnificent buck with huge, forward-swept antlers, passed through the clearing but the open season for these was still some weeks away. Of my intended quarry, a cow or bull moose, there was no sign however.

By the fourth day I was getting impatient with sitting in a hide, so decided to still hunt instead. When you literally can't see the wood for the trees, it is all rather anonymous finding your way around, but I had a good map showing a number of marked tracks, so I decided to stick to these. I must have covered several miles on this particular day when the track simply wasn't there any more. Puzzled, I examined the map closely but with all the trees it was impossible to see more than a hundred yards in any direction to pick out any landmarks. With a sinking feeling I realised that I had somehow strayed off the mapped track onto a deer trail, and that I was well and truly lost. It is a daunting and rather scary thing to be lost in such a vast area of forestry and swamp, knowing that in every direction bar south there is nothing but hundreds of miles of... nothing, unless you are lucky enough to stumble across an isolated settlement. Besides, this was not a kind country, with plenty of chances to sprain an ankle or worse – what would happen if you injured yourself, or met something large and unfriendly? At such times there is nothing for it but to stop, try to think clearly, and come up with a plan. My salvation lay in my backpack. I had got into the habit of carrying a whistle and Silva compass with me when stalking on Salisbury Plain, itself a bleak and disorientating place when the light fails and all the familiar landmarks disappear. Taking the compass, I set it for south and determined to march on that bearing no matter what. Eventually, I hoped, this would get me to civilisation. To cut a long, tiring and worrying story short, the little compass came up trumps, and hours after skirting endless swamps and fallen trees I heard the unmistakeable sound of a motor vehicle somewhere ahead. Cresting a small rise, the sight of a road brought almost unbearable relief, and better yet I recognised where I was. Half an hour later I was back at the caravan, where I determined to keep mum about my adventures of the day. I decided to return to my original ambush tactics for the remainder of the week, which produced neither sight nor sound of a moose but at least it meant that I knew where I was. The Silva compass remains an essential part of my stalking kit to this day, over thirty years on.

Very few moose were shot in the area that year, by the way, and certainly nothing fell to my rifle. The closest I ever came to one then was in the Québec Zoo; it was to be many more years before I was successful, even if it was on the other side of the Atlantic in Estonia when I finally got my chance. The limited hunting season for moose may be fixed in Canada, but the weather is certainly not, and this particular year was unseasonably warm. This meant that the moose stayed up in the cooler, high woods rather than descending to the swamps where they would have been easier to locate. I know that at least one animal succumbed to a local hunter's bullet though. A close neighbour on the military 'patch' where we lived drove around with a cow moose's head on the roof of his car for a couple of weeks until, presumably, the smell got too much for him. Try that in Hampshire and see where it gets you.

GADWALL

Anas strepera

The gadwall is often overlooked. You have probably seen them but dismissed them as mallard. Look a bit harder though and you will note that they are very different – the drake is smaller and greyer, and while the ducks are similar, the female gadwall lacks the blue speculum (or wing patch) of the mallard. Look also for the white wing patch on the bird in flight. The drake may seem nondescript from a distance, but closer up it is a picture of understated elegance, with a finely barred variety of greys, blacks and browns in its plumage. The gadwall goes by many local names: 'grey duck' is self-explanatory, but in the south-east of the UK they were once known as the 'bastard duck', reflecting an early belief that they were a cross between wigeon and mallard.

Whilst British breeding numbers are not high, you might encounter these birds anywhere across the south and east of England and more locally in eastern Scotland, Wales and Ireland. Numbers swell considerably when the winter migrants arrive to join the residents, not just on the coast but inland too. The gadwall may just as easily feature in the wildfowler's bag as on the game cart at the end of a day involving a visit to the duck pond.

It may be surprising to hear such a dapper little duck being described as a pirate, but the gadwall has a special reputation for snatching food items from the beaks of diving ducks as they surface. Stealing from coots is also widely documented. As the gadwall is a dabbling duck, suited only for feeding just below the surface, this behaviour allows them to exploit habitats which would otherwise be too deep for them to feed in normally.

Apart from times of courtship, the gadwall is one of our quiet ducks, so it's surprising that the Latin word *strepo* from which it gets its scientific name means 'to clamour'; the name 'gadwall' itself dates from the seventeenth century and is said to be imitative of their chattering call. Of all the duck the gadwall is said to be the best eating by far; in *Sporting Birds of the British Isles*, Brian P Martin describes it categorically as 'the most delicious of all duck at all times'.

Originally only a winter visitor, the first records of the gadwall breeding in this country are not until as (comparatively) recently as 1850, when a pair was caught in a Norfolk duck decoy, pinioned and released. These in turn attracted other winter migrants which stayed to nest. Assisted by escapes from collections and more deliberate releases, numbers have grown gradually and the gadwall is still considered to be thriving today.

> **Keeper's Tip:** Don't forget to turn off your mobile phone unless it is absolutely necessary to keep it on during a shoot day. It is annoying and distracting to other guests, and besides you will enjoy your day more without it.

GOLDEN PLOVER

Pluvialis apricaria

Only three wading birds appear on our quarry lists across the UK, the golden plover, the snipe and the woodcock (plus the jack snipe in Northern Ireland), but it is the first of these that seems to be targeted the least. In days gone by this was not the case, and the professional wildfowler might take as many as seventy birds with a single shot from his large bore punt gun, stalking the birds as they fed in their thousands on the tidal mud flats. Today, the golden plover does not exist in the huge numbers of over a century ago, and there is not much public appetite for these little birds, so the numbers shot are tiny in comparison.

The golden plover nests on the upland moors in the summer before moving to lower ground and coastlines for the winter where resident birds are joined by migrants from the north. It is one of many species which benefits from grouse-moor management, and breeding pairs on moors where intensive predator control is carried out are much higher in number than in those places where it is not.

Golden plovers are small waders, about the size of a mistle thrush. In summer plumage, the bird is unmistakeable for anything else and has to be one of the most beautiful of our upland birds. Its upper parts are a rich, speckled gold and black extending up onto the cap; the underparts and face are black. During the winter shooting season, a bit more care has to be taken over identification, though, as these colours become somewhat more nondescript. The flight is fast and manoeuvrable, and the shooter who can identify regular flightlines can have great sport with contour-hugging flocks, which often travel in tightly packed V or W formations. Waiting at their feeding areas, on the other hand, can test the most skilful of Guns as the parties drop out of the sky with dazzling speed. If you are lucky enough to hit one, you'll find it delicious (although you'll need more than a single bird to satisfy anything but the most frugal appetite).

The mournful, melodious, single note call of the golden plover is truly one of the most evocative sounds of our wild places. An old Cheshire name for the bird is 'sheep's guide', arising from the belief that it warns sheep of impending danger, while in other places its call has been compared to the wail of a lost soul.

It's a little known fact that the golden plover was instrumental in the creation of the book series *Guinness World Records*. In 1951 Lord Beaver, then managing director of the Guinness Brewery, became involved in an argument as to which was the fastest in flight, the golden plover or the red grouse. Discovering that nowhere in print was there anything that might settle the argument, it occurred to him that a book containing such information might be popular. In 1954 he commissioned twin brothers Norris and Ross McWhirter, who ran a fact-checking agency in London, to produce the first *The Guinness Book of Records* later to become *Guinness World Records*, which became an instant bestseller, and a publishing tradition was born.

Fesaunt exceedeth all foules in sweetness and wholesomenesse and is equal to a capon in nourishing ... it is meate for princes and great estates and poore schollers when they can get it. **Thomas Cogan, *Haven of Health* (1584)**

Keeper's Tip: A hat with a brim doesn't just keep your head warm and dry, it shades your face and makes it less obvious to your quarry.

GREY PARTRIDGE

Perdix perdix

How the fortunes of the grey partridge have fluctuated over the last century or so. Once abundant across much of Britain, their numbers have declined alarmingly as gamekeeping and farming practices have changed; today, to maintain a harvestable surplus of birds, land management has to pay very special attention to the needs of this species. Without suitable food, cover and, above all, protection against predation, there is no surplus. As recently as the 1980s I recall walked-up shooting on Salisbury Plain resulting in large bags of wild, sustainable birds; last season (2015), in the very same area and thanks to increased predation and changes in land use over the intervening thirty or so years, there was just one known covey. We are pleased to host them and leave them well alone. In fact the shoot rules are that no partridges are to be shot at all, just in case someone mistakes a grey for a redleg (of which many are released locally).

The grey partridge has always been held in high esteem as a sporting quarry as well as on the table. Henry VIII gave them special protection on his land between Westminster and St Giles-in-the-Fields, issuing a proclamation that: 'Any person, of any rank, who should presume to kill or in any wise molest these birds was to be thrown into prison and be visited by such other punishments as the king should seem meet.'

A century ago it was the grey partridge rather than the pheasant that dominated game shooting. Between 1870 and 1930 it is estimated that about two million were shot every year in Britain alone. After the Second World War, however, there was an alarming drop in numbers, attributed to the advent of pesticides (which killed off the insects that their chicks depend on), a reduction in predator control, and finally the loss of nesting cover as hedgerows and grassy banks were removed to enable more intensive agriculture. The population is thought to have declined by over eighty percent between the years of 1970 and 1998. Before the advent of the driven shoot, partridges were walked up and some astonishing numbers were shot. In 1870 a team of ten Guns shot 376½ brace in the course of a single day in Forfarshire. A move towards driving pushed bag sizes higher yet, and one day at Holkham in Norfolk in 1905 produced 835½ brace. That partridge numbers could sustain such levels of shooting speaks volumes for the success of this little gamebird under the right conditions.

Part of the grey partridge's decline has been due to the fact that they cannot be put down, or released, in the way that pheasants and the more recently introduced redleg can be. You can indeed tip greys out into the countryside, but without the right habitat they will not do well. They are not a mass-produced gamebird; rather, the partridge needs time and space to pair up and hold a territory, producing naturally reared broods. The gamekeeper, doing his counts in the spring, takes a great interest in the established pairs, their territories and the number of chicks they have produced, for it is from this information that a judgement can be reached on what kind of realistic surplus will be available for the coming shooting season. Partridges make good parents and, under the right conditions, can be prolific breeders; indeed, a clutch of sixteen eggs is fairly common and more than twenty-three have been recorded, placing the grey among the most fecund of the bird species. The serious partridge shoot is undoubtedly a wild bird shoot in the true sense of that phrase, and every effort will be made by the landowner to give the birds the conditions that they need to succeed. Such efforts are to be admired and encouraged; to the grey partridge *aficionado*, it will always be a case of quality over quantity.

If there is a lot of affection for *Perdix perdix*, it's not surprising. With his plump round body, understated dapper plumage of grey and brown, and distinctive orange face, he is often referred to as a proper little English gentleman (although not by a Scottish colleague of mine, who takes great exception to the English having the effrontery to claim ownership: 'it's a bliddy grey, no' a bliddy English partridge!').

To many, the grey is *the* partridge, and the more recently introduced redleg is no more than a flashy, foreign interloper. An important and popular member of the British countryside, it is no accident that he features as the logo of the Game and Wildlife Conservation Trust.

A gun is a tool, Marian; no better or no worse than any other tool: an axe, a shovel or anything. A gun is as good or as bad as the man using it. Remember that. **Alan Ladd, actor, as *Shane***

GREY SQUIRREL

Sciurus carolinensis

You can't be friends with a squirrel! A squirrel is just a rat with a cuter outfit.
Sarah Jessica Parker

Despite the strenuous claims of its apologists – and it's surprising how many there are – the grey squirrel simply doesn't belong here. Imported from its native North America and deliberately released into parks in the 1870s as, believe it or not, an 'ornamental' species, it has now spread to just about every corner of Britain and only a few places remain free of it. Its crimes are legion; bark stripping, stealing eggs and young chicks, and, of course, carrying the squirrel pox virus, which is largely responsible for the devastation of our native red squirrel population. The grey also loves to chew just about anything it can get its long and capable teeth into, causing considerable damage on the shoot alone to hoppers, water pipes and feed bins. I don't think that there is one plastic seat or foam-covered shooting bar among my high seats which hasn't received such attention. A recent report suggests that the damage caused by these beasts costs the UK economy something in the region of £14 million every year.

We have no way of being sure, but one estimate of the UK grey squirrel population is well in excess of 2.5 million compared to no more than 15,000 or so of our poor beleaguered native reds. (There are hopes, though, that the number of the latter has finally stabilised and may even be on the increase.) Trapping, poisoning and shooting are all brought into play in an attempt to control the number of greys. Where both squirrel species are present, live trapping is probably the best option, to avoid killing the protected red. Be aware, though, that it is illegal to release a grey back into the wild. In 1931 a government initiative introduced a bounty system, paid on every squirrel tail submitted, with free cartridges given to squirrel shooters. The scheme was not as effective as had been hoped and was eventually scrapped in 1958. It seems that some less scrupulous individuals were maintaining sustainable populations as a source of income, whilst others trapped and released animals to carry on breeding – having first chopped off their tails. One way of reducing the number of grey squirrels is catching them at home in their nests, or dreys. These football-sized constructions are made out of twigs and lined with moss, grass, bark and other materials to create a safe and warm refuge. One squirrel may build several, but during the winter they are often shared for warmth. Poked out with a long, extending pole, the result can be a veritable explosion of squirrels when an occupied drey is disturbed. The shooting that follows can be fast, furious and testing of the very best of shots.

If you have a mind to, you can eat squirrel, and our American cousins set great store by the meat as a delicacy. Not so long ago, some game dealers were offering more per shotgunned carcase than they would for rabbits (and these must be ferreted or rifled, mind, with no lead shot in the body to worry the cook or gourmand) and there was a thriving market for these amongst the trendier London gastropubs. This market, sadly, seems to have dried up somewhat of late.

I opened with a quote from Sarah Jessica Parker, and would like to end with a tale that illustrates the point she makes. Many years ago a friend found a newborn grey squirrel in the remains of a drey which had been blown down by a gale. The infant rodent was only a day or so old, and was little more than a pink, blind squib of a thing. Stan took it home and successfully reared it to maturity. It became a pet, living in its outdoor run during the day but coming into the house every evening. It was a charming little creature, and would sit on your shoulder quite happily accepting nuts, raisins and other treats offered between fingers. It was gentle, affectionate and adored being stroked. When the animal was about a year old, it was as though some malign power suddenly flipped a switch in its head and the gentle pet became, in the space of seconds, an evil fiend. In between shrieking squirrel profanities at the world in general and Stan's family in particular, it managed to bite every one of them before they evacuated the drawing-room where it proceeded to do an amazing amount of damage for something so small. Stan, ever a practical man though never famed for his subtlety, added considerably to the destruction with several cartridges from his 12 bore in the course of bringing this now extremely wild and aggressive animal to account. He explained afterwards that opening the window and releasing such an ill-tempered creature with no ingrained fear of people onto an unsuspecting public simply wasn't an option. He also added that he could have done with a much more open choke and that it was surprisingly difficult to develop an effective swing onto a fast-moving target in a small enclosed space. So please don't be tempted – they may look cute, but looks can be deceptive. Ms Parker is right; you really can't be friends with a squirrel.

If the partridge had but the woodcock's thigh, T'would be the best bird that e'er did fly. **C E Hare, writer**

GREYLAG GOOSE

Anser anser

The largest of our 'grey' geese, the greylag is the only one that is truly native to our shores rather than just a winter visitor. Once restricted to the far north, it has spread and can be encountered just about anywhere within the country, although the truly wild breeding population is still really only found in Scotland. The ancestor of the familiar domesticated goose, feral populations have now established themselves further south to help with the spread. Native birds are joined by migrants from Iceland and northern Europe every winter; in fact at this time the entire Icelandic population comes to Britain. Where the name comes from has been disputed. Some claim that it 'lagged' behind when the other winter goose species had departed on migration, others that 'lag' is simply an old name meaning goose. It is also possible that the name derived from the 'leys' or fields that the birds grazed.

The greylag was once considered the most numerous of our geese, and though that honour has now been claimed by the Canadian interloper, it remains an immensely important quarry species and a mainstay of the wildfowler in particular. The clamour of a far-distant flock has been likened to that of a pack of hounds in full cry and can be heard from a very long way off; just the thing to quicken the heartbeat of anyone crouching in concealment, hoping for them to pass overhead. Connect with your target and you'll need to take care not to be in the way when the bird falls to earth. A big gander can weigh as much as ten pounds and has a wingspan of almost six feet. Drop one onto the water, especially where there is a current, and you'll need a strong and determined dog to retrieve it.

Long before the turkey became popular, a goose was (and still is for many) traditional fare for Christmas Day. The practice goes back a long way and probably has origins in tenants bringing their landlords a goose when paying their annual rents. Anecdote has it that Queen Elizabeth was eating goose on Michaelmas Day (29 September) when news of the demise of the Spanish Armada reached her; thereafter she resolved to eat goose on every Michaelmas to honour the event. Whatever the truth in this story, the eating of goose at Michaelmas was a tradition long before Elizabeth took the English throne: and the transfer to a Christmas traditional meal probably came much later.

Greylag, like most geese, are excellent parents, both helping to take care of their young. This is in direct contrast to most duck, where the drake takes no interest in rearing the brood. Greylag also have a particular reputation for being faithful to their partners. Birds pair for life, a devotion reinforced every year by a 'triumph ceremony' when the male employs a ritualised display in which he launches a mock, or sometimes real, attack on another gander. On the completion of this, both male and female display together to reinforce their existing bonds. This ceremony is not just confined to the greylag, but has been observed in most of the true geese species.

There is a common belief that a skein of geese is always led by an old gander, which should never be shot as it will be too tough to eat. This theory has been disproved; the truth is that the point position is regularly changed so that all members can share the benefit of the slipstream produced by those in front. Nor do flocks of geese on the ground post guards to look out for predators while the remainder concentrate on feeding.

In the farmyard, the greylag is probably the most aggressive of all the poultry you might encounter, and these birds have been employed as sentinels for centuries. Legend has it that a flock of geese, kept in the Temple of Juno on the Capitoline Hill in Rome, saved the city from a night attack by the Gauls, by alerting the sleeping population with its loud alarm calls.

A 'wild goose chase' is today taken to mean any undertaking that is doomed to failure. The phrase's origins, however, actually lie in horse racing, where horsemen followed a lead horse at set distances in a formation that mimicked the V of a skein of wild geese in flight. 'Esteeme a horse, according to his pace, but loose no wagers on a wilde goose chase' wrote Nicholas Breton in his 1602 work *The Mother's Blessing* – sound advice even today.

Hunting in the Americas 3

A brief stopover in New York found me staying with American friends Peter and Diane on Long Island. The weekend coincided with the opening of both the duck and the deer season. Would I like to go and try for one or the other, Peter wondered? It didn't take long to come to a decision as I had always wanted to try for a whitetail buck, and said so. 'Before you decide,' said Peter, 'let me tell you a few stories first.' He then proceeded to recount some hair-raising tales of opening day in New York State: these included accounts of hunters shooting at moving bushes which turned out to contain their buddies, a man who shot his wife after mistaking her for a bear, and of the woods alive with blithe spirits all desperate to bag a deer during the short open season and careless of where their bullets might end up. He finished with a description of a Jersey calf being brought into a weighing station on the bonnet of a Chevrolet by one triumphant hunter, an inner-city man who clearly had no idea what a deer looked like. Peter said that he had witnessed this episode himself and swore that it was true. I was beginning to get the impression that he didn't want to send me home in a box.

We agreed that it might be a better idea to go duck shooting instead. A few hours later we had driven to a lake towards the eastern end of Long Island, a surprisingly remote part of such a highly populated area. Peter insisted that I wore a shooting jacket in blaze orange. 'For safety – we don't want you getting shot by mistake, and besides, it's the law.' As we carried the gear to one of Peter's regular hides by an inlet on a large lake, he assured me that I would see plenty of duck. I wasn't disappointed. The duck, mostly mallard, kept coming and coming; Peter reminded me to restrain myself or we would reach our limit far too quickly, so we agreed to try to shoot drakes only. I was using a borrowed 12 bore and Peter had a single barrelled muzzleloader – he liked the tradition and challenge, he explained.

As a flight of duck crossed us at head height, there was a bang from the far side of the lake some hundred yards away, and a charge of shot from a hunter opposite us kicked up a multitude of splashes just in front of our hide. Peter leapt to his feet. I waited for him to complain loudly across the water, but apparently that wasn't the New York convention. Instead, Peter threw his gun up and, with a colourful curse, let drive with it towards the offender.

Clearly our antagonist didn't get the message and, before the smoke from Peter's black powder load had even begun to clear, gave us both barrels in return. The water to our front erupted again, this time even closer to us, and a few pellets rattled off the front of our wooden hide. I got the distinct impression that he had aimed off to allow for the fall of shot. I looked across to Peter, only to see him reloading his percussion gun from a powder horn. 'More powder, more shot' he muttered between clenched teeth, a determined expression on his face. He fired again and appeared satisfied with the result. Our enemy didn't waste any time in returning fire, and what I can only describe as a peppering match ensued. I am ashamed, or should that be pleased, to say that I did not take part; I spent my time keeping well under cover behind the stout logs of the duck blind. Peter seemed a bit disappointed by this at the time, but said later that he put it down to good old-fashioned British politeness. The chap the other side of the lake gave up first – maybe he'd run out of ammunition – and we saw a flash of blaze orange through the trees as he vacated his hide and scurried off.

Peter looked at me with an expression of deep satisfaction. 'I guess that showed him! Say, I'll bet that you do things a little different in England?' I found myself at a bit of a loss for words. 'Too bloody right!' was the best that I could come up with. By the time I took off my blaze orange 'safety' jacket back at the car, though, I couldn't help but find the whole business ridiculously funny, in a perverse sort of a way.

MALLARD

Anas platyrhynchos

It is difficult not to use the word 'ubiquitous' when considering the mallard, as this duck has one of the widest distributions of all the wildfowl. Its natural range encompasses the northern Americas, Europe, Asia and North Africa, and where it doesn't occur naturally, man has introduced it. If you visit a park with a lake anywhere in the world, the chances are that you'll find a mallard or two on it waiting for a free meal. In fact, this bird is so versatile that it doesn't necessarily need water close by to thrive. It adapts readily to a wide variety of habitats, including urban areas, and has been known to nest in trees and on high buildings as well as at its more traditional waterside sites.

It's also very numerous, and very much the mainstay of wildfowl shooting. As the species that most domestic ducks are derived from, it is easy to rear in numbers and is in fact the only type which is produced commercially for shooting. Numerous breeds are derived from it, but the typical curled-up tuft of feathers of the tail is a giveaway as to a duck's origins. The pure white birds that are often seen are especially striking – they were bred originally as decoys, to attract wild birds for sport or for trapping. For some reason these frequently breed true to type and can still be seen on the rivers and flight ponds in many parts of the country decades after their use as decoys has ceased. Otherwise, domestic mallard breed freely with their wild brethren, and some interesting colour variations frequently turn up in a wildfowler's game bag. When man first domesticated the mallard is not known, although the Chinese were keeping them at least 2,000 years ago.

The scientific name *platyrhynchos* is taken from the Greek *platús* meaning wide or flat, and *rhúnkhos*, a beak. Mallard is thought to have derived from the Latin *masculus*, male, and Old German *art*, meaning hardy or bold. From this the Old French *mallart*, or wild drake, developed, and the English word 'mallard' has been in use since the Middle Ages. Of all the ducks, they are believed to be among the longest lived, even though predation and other natural factors mean that most usually expire much earlier than the twenty-nine-year-old ringed bird recovered by researchers.

Opportunistic feeders, they are truly catholic in their tastes and will take everything from seeds and aquatic plants to molluscs, earthworms and even small rodents. The female is an excellent mother to her brood of up to twelve, occasionally more, but high levels of predation mean that only a fraction of the ducklings, perhaps only one or two in the majority of cases, make it to maturity. The drake's behaviour at mating time is, however, not admirable. Mating itself is forceful and can be extremely stressful for the female, who might be pursued aggressively by a number of unattached drakes who take it in turns to mount her. At times it has been known for the unfortunate duck to be drowned. Even when they have established pairs, it is quite usual for drakes to be promiscuous, abandoning the duck as soon as she is on the nest to seek another partner.

The mallard is our most numerous resident wild duck, and numbers are boosted still further by migrants, which flood in from Iceland and northern Europe every autumn and winter. They feed mostly at night, so waiting at the flight pond offers exciting and challenging shooting at dusk as the birds drop in, seemingly out of nowhere in the fading light. Do not, though, be tempted to over-shoot a flight pond. Fed well and shot sparingly it will produce duck throughout the season. If you shoot it too often it will produce little to nothing. If you are able to identify flight lines onto the September stubble this can be especially productive, and produces what are probably the best-tasting birds for the table.

Reared duck can, I'm afraid, become ridiculously tame if allowed to grow up with too much human contact. I'll never forget one occasion on a south of England early season shoot when the Guns were told that we were 'going on to have a crack at the ducks'. One or two of us wondered why the keeper and a couple of beaters had pulled on waders; the consequent sight of watching them in the water trying to chivvy the duck off the surface and into the air was embarrassing. Some of us couldn't bring ourselves to shoot, as the mallard circled low as they attempted to get back onto the water. Properly reared duck are a different matter, shy and jumpy, especially so if they have been joined by wild birds. Great care then has to be taken getting Guns into position if the birds are not to depart before the drive can start, gaining height rapidly and soon reaching a point where they are way beyond shot. On one momentous drive on a Welsh shoot, I recall the Guns creeping in to hedgerows far from their pegs, with instructions to 'run like hell to them when the horn blows'. The ensuing scene was a bit like something from

Dad's Army as we dashed, shotguns at the high port and game bags flapping, to get into position before the duck lifted. We earned our shooting that day, and the duck certainly didn't hang around to give us a second chance.

Keeper's Tip: Beaters and others who contribute to the day's sport always appreciate it if Guns seek them out at the end of the day to say a simple 'thank you'.

You see I'm against hunting, in fact I'm a hunt saboteur. I go out the night before and shoot the fox. **Tim Vine, comedian**

PHEASANT

Phasianus colchicus

He looks like he is two yards long, and he looks mighty slow. But when you subtract his neck and his tail you are shooting at a pretty small target. He flies faster than a bobwhite, or so I am told, and he sheds shot like a duck. I'd lead him pretty far and then double it. No man ever killed a cock pheasant by shooting it in the tail. All you get that way is feathers.

Robert Ruark, *The Old Man and the Boy*

The mainstay of organised shooting in the UK as well as so many other countries, the pheasant holds the dubious honour of being our most popular game bird. It has been estimated that something like 15 million are shot annually between October and January, many of them deliberately released or 'put down'. It is the pheasant's pure bad luck to be a large, attractive bird that flies well (most of the time), is easy to rear and is, to cap it all, delicious. Thomas à Becket reputedly dined on pheasant the night before he was murdered in Canterbury Cathedral in 1170.

It is generally accepted that the first pheasant were introduced to this country by the Romans; records certainly show they were here well before the Normans arrived and a popular theory suggests that they were specially bred for the table by Roman officers after being originally brought to southern Europe from Asia. It's also possible that Phoenician traders had a hand in importing them. The name 'pheasant' supposedly has its origins in the Middle English *fesaunt* or the Old French *fesan*; the Latin *phasianus*, 'Bird of the Phasis', refers to the River Phasis (now the Rioni) in the Caucasus. *Colchicus* is for the ancient city of Colchis, now Kutaisi, the legislative capital of Georgia, which lies on the banks of the Phasis.

The first arrivals certainly reflected their eastern European origins and were what we see as the Old English Blackneck today. The familiar Ringneck, with his distinctive white collar, was not introduced to Britain from the Far East until much later. There are some forty-nine species of pheasant worldwide, many of them found naturally in Asia, and most of them interbreed easily. Man has since taken advantage of this ability, to produce any number of varieties – but most are based on the original import of *Phasianus colchicus*. They can also hybridise with some other birds including domestic fowl, as Charles Darwin noted in his *Origin of Species*.

If you live in the right area you might also be in for an unexpected surprise. The golden pheasant from China (*Chrysolophus pictus*), a magnificent bird with gold crest and rump and red body, still breeds in selected parts of the country, mainly Breckland, East Anglia, but there are still said to be small populations left in Hampshire and Dumfriesshire.You are unlikely to see one in the air, though: they are notoriously reluctant to leave the ground, and much prefer to take refuge in dense cover rather than fly. They are rather clumsy in flight and certainly not on your quarry list. Nor is their close relative, the equally stunning silver and black Lady Amherst's pheasant (*Chrysolophus amherstiae*), another natural Chinese resident that was successfully released in the Woburn area during the nineteenth century. Once numbering some two hundred pairs, the species has declined catastrophically thanks to predation by foxes and loss of habitat. In 2015 there were press reports saying that birdwatchers were flocking to the area in an attempt to glimpse the last remaining bird, a cock, before the species disappeared for good in Britain. Re-establishing the Lady Amherst's is very unlikely, as the introduction of non-native species is forbidden by the Wildlife and Countryside Act. Once the last one is gone, it will be seen by many as a sad loss to our countryside.

The popularity of the pheasant rose sharply as the breech-loader, with its ready-made cartridges, replaced the time consuming muzzle-loading shotgun in the latter half of the nineteenth century. This in itself allowed a move from traditional, walked-up shooting over setting or pointing dogs to the driven *battue*, which demanded greater numbers of birds as the fashion for ever larger bags became the norm. The pheasant, among all the gamebirds, was unfortunate in being the most amenable to rearing in sufficient quantities to meet this demand, and its pole position as the sportsman's quarry was thus assured.

Today the gamekeeper has a bewildering variety of pheasants from which to choose. While the Old English and Ringneck remain popular, strains such as the Michigan Blueback, Bazanty, Scandinavian or Manchurian are readily available. The very length of the list can be disconcerting: each strain is reputed to have different qualities regarding size, flying ability, resistance to disease and, importantly for the gamekeeper, willingness not to stray far from their release area. The Michigan Blueback has a special reputation as a wanderer; on my own shoot, our bag one day comprised almost fifty percent Bluebacks. To the keeper's knowledge, nobody within at least a fifteen-mile radius was putting them down. Of course not all of the birds shot have been released. The pheasant has happily made a home in the British countryside, breeding readily and successfully. Where their predators are controlled they flourish, and 'wild bird' shoots, where quality rather than quantity is appreciated, are increasing in popularity. Much prized is the wild pheasant of the fens of East Anglia, smaller than most, but with cunning and superlative flying abilities to test the best of Guns. Some enlightened gamekeepers have reverted to the old-fashioned method of raising pheasant chicks under broody hens, which teach them survival skills and natural feeding; these birds, once released, supplement the wild stock and have a much higher chance of surviving to breed themselves.

The pheasant is something of a paradox. When out stalking, I've noticed time after time that if you stealthily enter a field containing a wide variety of wild creatures such as deer, rabbits, fox or hares, it's always the pheasant that notices you first and makes for cover. On the other hand, a gamekeeper friend despairs of them. 'From the moment they leave the egg,' he complains, 'they are constantly looking for new and innovative ways to kill themselves.' You do have to wonder at times how this species has managed to prosper so well.

PINK-FOOTED GOOSE

Anser brachyrhynchus

To be perfectly honest, I can't really remember my first pheasant properly, but I do recall every detail of the first pinkfoot. I must have been about fourteen, and even today I can still see myself kneeling by a dry stone wall in the dark waiting for the first rays of dawn to creep through. It was bitterly cold and the borrowed over-and-under 12 bore felt unfamiliar in my hands. As the light came up, I also clearly remember my dilemma as a fox followed the line of the wall up to within ten yards of me, only to wheel and make off across the root field at speed as soon as it recognised my silhouette. Our host, however, had been quite specific about patience and concealment, so Charlie was allowed to leave unsaluted.

The light came suddenly and as I wondered if the geese were ever going to arrive, an extraordinary sound reached me. I'd never heard it before but knew instantly what it was – that unforgettable cackling clamour of geese on the move. I risked a careful look over the wall; the sky, empty a moment ago, was suddenly full with skein following skein, some losing altitude and heading in my direction. Heeding the advice given to me and heart pounding, I ducked down and gripped the gun as the noise grew until I could hear the distinct 'wink wink wink' of individuals. By pure luck I judged the right moment to stand up; as my head appeared over the low stone wall, what seemed like hundreds of flying shapes flared over the decoys. Urging myself to pick just one, the gun found its way into my shoulder and went off. More used to my single-barrelled gun, safe in the cabinet back at home, I clean forgot to fire the second shot but it didn't matter. A dark shape lay among the decoys, a bird that I'll never forget and, despite a lifetime of shooting since, a very special prize among my memories. It was delicious, but I wish in retrospect that I'd got it set up by a taxidermist instead. Such choices are always simple in hindsight!

The pink-footed goose is one of our smaller geese and is dwarfed by the much larger Canada and greylag. A large specimen may weigh a little over seven pounds. The body is grey-brown, the head darker. It has a noticeably shorter neck than other geese, and is the only one of our grey geese to have a pink beak and legs. The bill itself is short and shallow, giving rise to the scientific name taken from the Greek *brachy* (short) and *rhynchos* (beak).

Something like 200,000 arrive from their northern breeding grounds in Greenland and Iceland to spend the winter with us, around half of which descend upon Norfolk and the Broads. Fifty years ago the picture was rather different, and maybe only a quarter of this number overwintered in Britain, but now the pinkfoot is far and away our most numerous quarry goose: good news for the wildfowler, not so good for the arable farmer.

The pinkfoot arrives with us every October to graze in estuaries and farmland. Cereals and stubble grain are popular foods, followed later by roots and brassicas. Sugar beet is especially popular and is felt to be a good source of energy to prepare them for the long flight back to the summer breeding grounds. Flocks can be thousands strong but break up as the winter progresses and food sources change. As noted above, the most popular and perhaps most important wintering grounds in Britain lie in Norfolk, where as many as 70,000 birds have been estimated in recent years. These Norfolk birds represent some twenty-five percent of the world population; considering that the pinkfoot was considered scarce in Norfolk during the 1970s, this is a good indication of the bird's recovered population. (The UK wildfowl count for 1977 recorded just 69,000 for the whole of the country.)

Noted for its fidelity to regular feeding grounds, the pinkfoot can be relatively easy to exploit once you know its habits. It is up to shooters not to be too greedy, and to recognise that it can take only one poor breeding year to have a serious effect on numbers. We have the species in trust, so we must all ensure that it continues to thrive, to provide sport and spectacle for the years to come.

Keeper's Tip: Try to be quiet on your way to the peg and once on it. Game birds are not stupid, and too much noise can ruin a drive.

Death doesn't worry me – what really worries me is dying first, and my wife selling my guns for what I told her I'd paid for them. **Anon**

David Niven – Pheasants and Pigeons

In his bestselling memoir *Bring on the Empty Horses*, British Hollywood actor David Niven relates the story of being invited to shoot pheasants by the 10th Duke of Marlborough during the last week of January. A listening Humphrey Bogart was greatly impressed by Niven's connections until it was pointed out that it wasn't that much of a compliment, the end of January being when all serious shooting was finished and that it would be a low-key affair, and probably cock birds only at that. Niven records Bogart's outrage at this slight, giving the hapless Duke what might today be described as a 'wedgie' whilst roaring: 'Now get this Dook... get this and get it straight... you quit insulting my pal with your goddamn *COCKS ONLY!*'

There is, however, one story that David Niven did not include in any of his books, which was related to me by the son of one of his pre-war contemporaries between drives on a shoot day in Wiltshire. It seems that Niven, a somewhat unsuccessful soldier before he turned to acting, had been consigned to an observation post in the roof of a farmhouse during a long Army exercise, equipped only with a basket of homing pigeons and instructions to despatch one if he saw anything worth reporting.

After several days of no activity whatsoever, Niven got bored. He wrote a brief message, attached it to the leg of a pigeon, and released the bird. Shortly afterwards it arrived at Battalion Headquarters where the Adjutant retrieved the message and read it to himself. The Commanding Officer demanded to know what it said.

'I don't think you'll like it, sir,' the Adjutant replied, but the CO was insistent. 'Very well, sir,' said the Adjutant. 'The message reads: "I have been sent home for shitting in my basket".'

PINTAIL

Anas acuta

Very fine bird, the pintail. He doesn't cheat, which is more than you can say of some people. He won't eat fish on you, like a mallard will ... And he's the best looking duck in the business.

Robert Ruark *The Old Man and the Boy*

The mallard may be gaudy, the teal a charming jewel, the gadwall is dapper, but Robert Ruark's Old Man sums the pintail up perfectly. Of them all, the best word to do him justice is simply 'handsome'; in Hampshire he's known as the *sea pheasant*, in Ireland the *lady bird*, or in Wexford the *cracker*. To top it all, he comes with the reputation of being the fastest-flying of all our duck. It's just a shame that he is just not as numerous over here as some of the other species – although that, I suppose, would make him less of the prize that he is. Slightly larger than the mallard, the pintail drake is unmistakeably elegant with his chocolate brown head, white neck and grey flanks. The long, black, central tail feathers that give him his name make up about a quarter of his overall body-length. The duck is, inevitably, less striking but just as easy to distinguish in flight, being long-necked, slender and agile, with a noticeably pointed tail. Only a handful of pairs breed in Britain, but around 30,000 birds visit us each winter from their breeding grounds in Scandinavia, Iceland and northern Russia. Occasionally birds can turn up from unexpected sources; one ringed in Labrador, Canada, was shot in England only eleven days later. You are most likely to encounter rare resident birds in eastern England and central Scotland, while the largest overwintering flocks are to be seen in the Dee and Solway estuaries, or on the Ouse Washes.

The pintail sits high in the water and has a distinctive silhouette; it often mixes with other ducks, especially wigeon. It does have the reputation among wildfowlers of being particularly wary, usually being the first to take flight if any danger is suspected. Unlike other ducks, it sometimes flies in V-formation flocks, and large rafts are occasionally encountered on the water looking from a distance for all the world like pheasants (hence the Hampshire name). The birds much prefer to feed at night, when their long necks allow them to reach deeper underwater; days are spent at rest, preening and dozing.

You might be fortunate enough to witness courtship displays, which can take place early in the New Year. Several drakes may compete over the attentions of an individual duck, crowding around her with heads lowered as they whistle continuously and softly. The display may also include drakes rearing out of the water before flicking their beaks to splash water towards the duck, or reaching backwards with their heads in an apparent attempt to touch their tails. Aerial chases can also occur, as several drakes fly in pursuit of a duck until only one of them is left.

Once considered to outnumber even the mallard in worldwide populations, pintail numbers have fallen badly over the last half-century. In North America the decline has been a great cause for concern and between 1966 and 2010 was estimated at around 2.6 percent per year. Climate change, drought, the drainage of wetlands to make way for agriculture and over-hunting have all been blamed. The pintail is one of the earliest ducks to breed, and their preference for nesting in dry locations, often well away from water, can attract them to stubble fields where they are seriously affected by farming operations such as mowing, ploughing and harrowing.

PTARMIGAN

Lagopus mutus

It has been suggested that when the sun's fire burns low and ice creeps further across the earth the ptarmigan will be the last bird left alive, and indeed there is a great deal in this for the species has evolved to live at inhospitable altitudes which would soon kill most creatures.

Brian P Martin *Sporting Birds of the British Isles*

Toiling up the path from the Ranger Base towards the summit of Cairn Gorm with a dozen students, we had left the heather far below us: now we were in an arctic-alpine landscape of granite scattered with a few hardy plants. A pair of grey and white birds suddenly appeared just a few yards in front of us. Both ignored our group of walkers; the male, with his distinctive red flash above each eye, stood proudly on a rock and opened his beak to proclaim his presence to the world with a call that has been likened to running a stick down the posts of a picket fence. The birds were completely unfazed by our presence and there was plenty of time to set up a tripod and take a number of photographs. Despite the muted conversation of the students increasing in volume once they realised that they weren't disturbing the birds, still the pair remained unbothered. These were ptarmigan, totally unconcerned by close human proximity, and it was difficult to relate them to their close cousin the red grouse, which would have been up and away long before we had begun to get close to them.

The ptarmigan is distinguished by a number of characteristics, not least its hardiness. Although it occasionally overlaps with the red grouse on lower ground, it is rarely seen below heights of some 2,500 feet above sea level where conditions are harsh, a bird of the very high tops where other animal life is scarce. For this reason it is seldom bothered by predators which tend to seek easier pickings elsewhere. Dark-bodied, though retaining white bellies and wings during the summer, the birds are perfectly camouflaged against the patchy snow that lies at such heights throughout even the summer months. By the time the real winter snow arrives, their plumage becomes all white and you have to be very sharp-eyed indeed to spot them. The search for sustenance frequently demands an ability to burrow into deep snow. Their feet are perfectly adapted for a wintry existence, being thickly feathered all the way to the toes as an adaptation to walking on snow – their Latin name, *lagopus*, means 'hare foot'. The name 'ptarmigan' is itself thought to derive from the Gaelic *tàrmachan* or 'croaker', after the call characteristic of the species.

Some sportsmen claim a reluctance to shoot the ptarmigan because of its reputation for tameness, and even Mrs Beeton commented in 1861 that '… at Hudson's Bay they appear in such multitudes that so many as sixty or seventy are frequently taken at once in a net. As they are as tame as chickens, this is done without difficulty.' In reality, the challenge of shooting ptarmigan is reserved for the very fittest, given the elevation and rocky nature of the ground that the pursuit demands must be visited. Expect steep, lung-bursting climbs in terrain where slips and trips can have serious consequences; one sporting writer of a century ago went to great pains to stress the need for every shooting party member to carry a pocket compass against the sudden losses of visibility which so often occur at great heights. Even then, bags are unlikely to be high, and most would consider themselves lucky to achieve just a couple of brace of birds at best from a day's sport. It is easy to miss a fleeting chance when you are struggling to regain your breath. The personal bag of 122 ptarmigan made by the Hon Geoffrey Hill in 1866 was highly unusual, and one suspects the assistance of a large team of beaters in a particularly good breeding year. For the true ptarmigan hunter, it is the achievement and not the size of the bag that counts, and such sportsmen invariably develop a deep respect for their quarry.

Some say that the flesh of the ptarmigan is similar to that of the red grouse. Naturalist Thomas Bewick felt differently: in 1797 he wrote that the birds feed '... on the wild productions of the hills, which sometimes give the flesh a bitter, but not unpalatable taste: it is dark coloured, and has somewhat the flavour of the hare.'

Shooting is not a real threat to ptarmigan numbers today, although we cannot discount the dangers of commercial greed, but sadly other pressures are taking their toll. While an increase in the popularity of skiing, hiking and other activities in previously unpressurised high places has brought with it a build-up of the human debris that attracts crows and other potential predators of eggs and chicks, the real enemy is climate change. Global warming, along with an associated habitat loss and greater exposure to predators, is pushing the ptarmigan's range ever northwards. As long ago as the turn of the eighteenth century, it could still be found in northern England, but may now only be encountered in the Highlands of Scotland. Far from being to the species' protection, the hardiness so admired by Brian P Martin (quoted at the beginning of this piece) may yet work against it in the long run.

Keeper's Tip: Pigeons can be very tempting but don't shoot at them until game birds have started to flush over the Guns.

Spirit of well-shot woodcock, partridge, snipe; Flutter and bear him up the Norfolk sky. **John Betjeman, *Death of King George V***

QUAIL

Corturnix corturnix

Like the capercaillie, the quail may not be on our quarry list but it still earns its right to be included here as a member of the Galliformes, the largest of the families of game birds and containing some 178 species worldwide. Only six of these are native to Britain while the pheasant and red-legged partridge are introduced, but of them all the quail is by far the smallest. To be more precise we really should speak of the common quail *Corturnix corturnix*, as there are many species spread around the world, including the very distantly related bobwhite quail so beloved of American sportsmen.

A tiny game bird, the shape of a partridge but the size of a starling, the quail is only about seven inches in length and weighs just a few ounces. Being so small, and having a fairly nondescript and sandy-coloured plumage, it is very difficult to spot and seldom seen. It avoids flying unless really necessary, crouching if threatened, and flushing only at the very last moment. Given any option, the quail simply prefers to creep away on the ground. The best sign of its presence is usually the call, an evocative and liquid three-note 'wet-my-lips', most often heard at dusk.

Unlike the capercaillie, which was not covered by the 1831 Game Act because it was extinct in Britain at the time the law was made, the quail did not make it onto the quarry lists because of all our game birds it is the only migratory species. Prior to modern game laws a few may have been taken by sportsmen at stubble time, but by the time that the autumn shooting truly began the quail would have long since left these shores. Travelling at night in small coveys, the quail overwinters in northern Africa and returns to Europe to breed in the spring. At this time it is very vulnerable; flying low, it is easily snared in long nets and large numbers are still killed on passage through the Mediterranean region. The quail has never been an abundant species in this country anyway, although the occasional bumper breeding year can cause populations to fluctuate considerably, and its habit of nesting in fields leaves it very vulnerable to modern harvesting machinery.

The quail has always been reputed to have an especially amorous nature, sadly not truly the case, although that didn't stop the term 'quail' being used to describe a prostitute in seventeenth and eighteenth century

England. It does have happier connections though: the Book of Exodus describes how the Israelites, fleeing Egyptian enslavement, asked God for meat and were rewarded with a huge flock of migrating quail. It is also said that Jane Seymour, pregnant in 1537 with the future King Edward VI, developed a ravenous craving for quail. This resulted in huge diplomatic efforts being ordered by her husband King Henry VIII, to obtain sufficient supplies from Calais and Flanders to satisfy the Queen's appetite.

Today, the quail is a popular table bird but those you find at the butcher or supermarket are almost certainly not of the common variety; rather they are the larger, though closely related, Japanese quail instead. They share the family's ability to breed rapidly, and from hatching to sexual maturity and laying eggs of their own can take no more than just five or six weeks when conditions are right. Beware, though – the ancient Greeks recognised as early as the fourth century BC a condition known as *coturnism*, an illness featuring muscular tenderness and breakdown caused by eating quail that had themselves eaten poisonous plants. Fortunately, modern breeders know better than to feed their birds on hemlock, hellebore or woundwort, variously reputed to be the source of the condition.

RABBIT

Oryctolagus cuniculus

It may come as a very great surprise to many people that the rabbit is, in evolutionary terms at least, a relatively recent arrival in the British Isles: but just how they got here has been the subject of debate for years. Until fairly recently a lack of any written references predating the thirteenth century was used as negative evidence that it was the Normans who introduced them as a source of fur and food; this theory seemed to be backed up by a lack of any archaeological proof from before the twelfth century, and the fact that the rabbit is not even mentioned in the Domesday Book. In 2005, however, an archaeological dig at Lynford, Norfolk, produced the butchered remains of a rabbit alongside fragments of pots dating from the first or second century AD, proof at last that the Romans had brought at least some to these shores.

The natural range of the European rabbit is south-western Europe;

the source of ours was probably Spain. Originally the term 'rabbit' was more correctly applied to the younger animal, probably coming from a Norman French term of endearment for the young, *rabbet*. The proper name for an adult was a 'cony' or 'coney' (deriving from the Latin *cuniculus*), and they were maintained in 'coneygarths' or warrens. These would often be situated on islands, not just to contain the rabbits – the species dislikes swimming – but to protect them from predators such as foxes. Warrens were valuable commercial resources and jealously protected; warreners were employed to guard against theft. Artificial burrows and underground runs were provided for the inhabitants in past times, for it seems that then the rabbit was not so inclined to dig its own as it has become accustomed to doing today.

By the eighteenth century, thanks to escapes, releases and warrens falling into disuse, the rabbit had multiplied to the point of becoming a major agricultural pest. No longer a luxury food item for the nobility, it became a freely available and cheap meal for those of more limited means. By the 1950s the British rabbit population probably numbered in excess of 100 million, and the myxoma virus, endemic to rabbits in South America, was deliberately but unofficially introduced via France to Britain by those keen to reduce numbers. Despite legislation prohibiting the deliberate dispersion of the disease, it spread quickly and perhaps ninety-nine percent of the rabbit population was killed by myxomatosis. Rabbit numbers eventually recovered as animals developed a natural resistance to myxomatosis and, despite the appearance of viral haemorrhagic disease in the 1990s, have probably reached well beyond 30 million despite the animal being a major prey item for just about every predatory animal or bird capable of taking it. With the ability to breed at just four months old, and then produce as many as four or five litters of up to seven kits at a time every year, predation has not held the species back. If this grieves the farmer and others who suffer from the depredations of the rabbit, the sportsman who finds his pleasures with ferret, dog, net, hawk or gun has much for which to be grateful. For a great many people, the rabbit offers more accessible sport than the expensive driven pheasant, and some shooters even come to prefer it, given an honest choice. There is, of course, no close season.

Forget the bland, farmed animals offered for sale in the supermarket – the flesh of a wild rabbit is delicious and infinitely versatile. It is very low in fat, delicately gamey and particularly good when casseroled. A traditional rabbit pie takes some beating, or use the meat instead of chicken in the slow cooker – you'll find that it doesn't fall apart as readily, and still holds its flavour well. Young animals are of course the most tender, whilst an old buck will definitely benefit from a longer cooking time.

Of all our birds and animals, the rabbit is one of the foremost as far as folklore is concerned. It is a long-standing symbol of fertility and rebirth, as well as of innocence: witness its association with Easter. The animal is also a symbol of playfulness and tricks, from the *Br'er Rabbit* of the old Afro-American folktales to the *Bugs Bunny* cartoons. Just why carrying a rabbit's foot is considered to bring good luck is not clear, although this custom occurs in a number of cultures worldwide and long pre-dates Christian times. The idea of a rabbit's foot as a talisman to bring good luck goes back as far as 600 BC, probably stemming from ancient beliefs that humans descended from animals and that carrying a part of your animal ancestor brought protection. It certainly isn't lucky for the rabbit though.

One rather darker belief comes from the Isle of Portland in Dorset, where the mere mention of the word 'rabbit' came to be considered bad luck and was never uttered aloud. This probably comes from the undermining of quarries by systems of burrows, resulting in cave-ins causing injuries or death when an unfortunate miner dug in the wrong place. At the butcher's you would simply point, or ask for a 'furry thing' or 'underground mutton'. If 'rabbit' was ever found scrawled in jest on a boat or other machinery it would not be used that day. When Cockney pop duo Chas & Dave released their hit record 'Rabbit' as recently as 1980, a pub put it onto their juke box and suddenly found that it had lost all of its customers. The superstition persists even today.

'As we stood in front of the fire, steaming out our wet clothes, after having risked death by drowning, exposure and pneumonia, after having been up since black night, after having rowed and poled miles, after having frozen fingers setting out decoys and having frozen feet from inactivity – after having been uncomfortable constantly in the quest for a few pounds of bird meat that I didn't like to eat too terribly well, I concluded one thing: if you have to be crazy to hunt ducks, I do not wish to be sane.' **Robert Ruark, *The Old Man and the Boy***

The Great St James's Park Shoot

There is a story often told in the Officers' Messes of the British Army which, beyond the assurances of those with family members who swore that they were there at the time, does not seem to figure in any official records and its truth cannot be verified. Perhaps that is for the best.

With Buckingham Palace at its western tip and Horse Guards Parade on the eastern side, St James's Park is a little oasis of green at the very heart of London. Like any good oasis, it has a plentiful water supply in the form of a long, narrow lake, which accounts for about a third of its fifty-eight acres. The park has changed considerably over the years; in the days long before the modern Buckingham Palace was a mere gleam in its architect's eye, the area housed a deer park and duck decoys where wildfowl were lured in and killed for the royal table. Much later, King James I kept a collection of exotic animals there, Charles II courted Nell Gwynn in its gardens, and today it is home to a large collection of ducks, geese and other waterfowl. The first pelicans of many to occupy the park were presented by the Russian Ambassador in 1664.

Not that far off lies Chelsea Barracks, home to a succession of Guards regiments. One such was stationed there during the 1930s when a new subaltern, recently commissioned from Sandhurst, was posted in to command a platoon in one of its four companies. He was welcomed into the Officers' Mess by his brother officers, who were quick to apprise him of the coming draw for the annual invitation to shoot in St James's Park. The draw, he was informed, was granted by the monarch of the day to whichever of his Guards battalions was stationed in Chelsea Barracks and affording him royal protection; this was his way of showing appreciation whilst also achieving an annual cull of the prolific waterfowl. Because of the small size of the park, only the lucky winner of the draw would be invited actually to shoot, while his brother officers would provide the beating team. The names of all officers in the battalion would be entered and the winner informed by the beginning of September.

Thus it was that the young subaltern received, with great delight, an envelope postmarked 'Buckingham Palace' containing an exquisitely engraved card inviting him, in the name of the King, to be that year's Gun for the shoot. The invitation set the date and strict shooting times, while inviting the bearer to take 'all legal quarry of the day' though expressly forbidding the taking of any pelican or other exotic species.

The day of the shoot dawned bright, and the subaltern took his allotted peg at the Horse Guards end of the park, accompanied by his batman who was to act as loader. It was early morning and there was little traffic moving – this was, after all, the London of the 1930s. At the far end of the lake the beating line, masquerading as a group of dawn walkers with unusually unruly dogs, started off. At first slowly, and then with gathering momentum, packs of wildfowl started to lift from the lake and circle the park. As the subaltern started shooting, more and more were disturbed and, passing his peg before circling back to the far end of the lake, started to fall to his gun. The shooting came thick and fast and the pile of ejected cartridges behind the peg began to grow.

After some five minutes there was a faint sound of sirens in the distance which our hero, deafened by the sound of his own gunshots, only became aware of as they drew closer. By the time the police reached him it is said that he had accounted for some forty head of duck and geese, though happily no pelicans. Unsurprisingly, of his batman and beating team there was no sign.

RED GROUSE

Lagopus lagopus scotica

Mention the red grouse and the keen shot's thoughts tend to turn to Scotland or North Yorkshire, where indeed the main populations are to be found; but in fact the most southerly driven grouse moor in England is Crag Estate, tucked away at the tail end of the Pennines with the urban sprawl of Stockport and Manchester only some ten miles off to the north-west. There are also significant but localised populations in Wales, where the main strongholds are the Brecon Beacons, Snowdonia and the Cambrian Mountains. The species is also found across Ireland as long as a suitable habitat of heather moorland exists to support it.

There are a few birds left elsewhere. Introduced to Shropshire in the 1840s, a small but viable population of red grouse can still be found there even though none are shot these days. Dartmoor also saw similar introductions about seventy years later and a core population remains. There were once shootable numbers on Exmoor but numbers declined to the point that shooting ceased to take place there after the early 1970s. Poor breeding conditions and human disturbance caused further population reductions to the point that the Exmoor National Park Authority declared them extinct there in 2013. Nevertheless, rumours persist that Exmoor may still hold at least a few birds.

The red grouse is a relative newcomer to the shooting scene compared to the pheasant and partridge. Its widespread popularity dates back to the advent of the railway and the breech-loading gun in the second half of the nineteenth century, both of which made shooting more easily accessible to Victorian sportsmen. From that point on, a good grouse moor started to take on a special value, and owners found that letting the shooting was more lucrative than the rents they made from sheep farmers.

The Glorious Twelfth of August is the legal as well as the traditional start of the grouse-shooting season, a date largely dictated by the breeding season. In 1915 there was an attempt to bring this date forward to allow Members of Parliament to shoot during recess. A bill was passed in the Lords allowing the shooting of grouse from 5 August, but rejected by the Commons, apparently to cries of 'we want to shoot Germans not grouse!'.

Whilst the grouse forms an essential part of a modern Macnab, namely the feat of shooting a brace, stalking a red deer stag and landing a salmon in a single day between dawn and dusk, the bird is a more recent addition. In the original 1925 novel by John Buchan, *John Macnab*, only the stag and the salmon feature in the challenges undertaken by the three successful but bored gentlemen who set out to poach them from their neighbours' estates. To make the task even more difficult they forewarn the owners of their intentions in a letter signed simply 'John Macnab'.

Wild grouse populations can fluctuate wildly from year to year, and a spell of cold weather at the critical period for hatching can kill whole broods, leaving a moor containing nothing but barren adults. This can mean years when there are few shooting opportunities, for no responsible landowner would want to destroy his breeding stock. There have been attempts to breed the red grouse in sufficient numbers to release and supplement the wild birds over the years, but these have not proven successful. The main difficulties revolve around the grouse's reliance on ling heather as a major food item; even where captive bred birds have been successfully reared on artificial foods, they experience considerable difficulty in switching to a natural diet and mortality rates have tended to be catastrophically high where releases have been attempted. As a result the red grouse can only be, unlike the pheasant and to a lesser extent the partridge, a totally wild bird and in this lies a great deal of its attraction for the sportsman, along with the wild places where it has to be sought.

Good moor management is accepted as the key to maintaining a healthy wild grouse population. A three-pronged approach concentrates efforts on providing a suitable habitat, reducing predators to a minimal level, and keeping internal parasites and diseases in check. The rotational burning of heather is the traditional method of ensuring that there is a constant supply of young shoots as food while older growth remains available for cover and roosting. Burning also has a useful side benefit by keeping down the number of ticks, an important carrier of disease. Predators such as the stoat and fox are not tolerated. Medicated grit helps to controls the parasitic strongyle worm that lives in the bird's gut and, in high infestations, affects breeding success and debilitates to the point of death. Recently a new threat in the form of *cryptosporidium* has emerged; this causes the bird's sinuses to swell, and the increased pressure within the head has led to the horribly descriptive name of 'bulgy eye'. There is currently no known treatment for this and prevention is the name of the game.

Grouse keepers are constantly facing new challenges – it is a question of being alert, making frequent and regular checks, and staying proactive. Meanwhile owning a grouse moor is not a sure-fire money-spinner, and you have to take the good years with the bad. One keeper I met neatly described grouse moor ownership thus: 'If you want to get a real feel for it,' he grinned, 'just stand under a cold shower and tear up fifty-pound notes – that just about sums it up!'

> **Keeper's Tip:** Once a drive starts, pay attention to what is going on in front of you and don't spend too much time watching your neighbouring Guns – you will miss a lot of chances if you do.

RED-LEGGED PARTRIDGE

Alectoris rufa

Looked down upon by some sportsmen as a poor relation of the native grey partridge, the red-legged or French partridge is nevertheless a hugely important part of the British shooting scene. The name 'French' is in fact a bit misleading. While the species is indeed not a native of these shores, its origins lie further across south-western Europe into Spain and not just exclusively France, and it is more closely related to the rock and Barbary partridges of southern Europe and north Africa, and the chukar which ranges from Greece and Turkey across central Asia and as far as the eastern coast of China.

The redleg, also known as the Frenchman, red partridge or even sometimes green partridge, was first brought to Britain as a sporting bird as long ago as 1673 using stock from France, hence one of the most commonly used names. Whilst not immediately successful as a breeding species in the wild, a colony eventually established itself in Suffolk where the dryer, sandier conditions more closely resembled its home habitat; it is nowhere as successful where the ground tends to be wet. East Anglia remains a major stronghold today although successful breeding has been recorded as far north as Cumbria and eastern Yorkshire. The British climate does not suit the bird well at times, and cold, damp, breeding seasons can have a very negative effect on wild broods. When conditions suit, however, it can breed prolifically, producing average broods of fifteen or so (up to twenty-eight have been recorded) not uncommon. Unusually, the hen will often lay two successive clutches of eggs during the breeding season, which both parents will share the duty of incubating. Predation can, of course, take a very high toll on both eggs and chicks.

One of the reasons that sportsman hold the grey partridge in higher regard is that the redleg is not considered to fly as well. It certainly prefers to run if that remains an option and is capable of very high speeds while still on its feet. As the shooting season progresses and birds become wilder, they also become much more shy, and many an incautious beating line has seen birds which are disturbed too early leaving cover long before they were intended to, usually in the wrong direction. Getting the birds into the air can often be a major challenge, and in heavier clay soils they might collect so much soil on their feet that they find it hard to take off. It is generally agreed that the redleg is not a suitable species for walked-up shooting. They either run too far ahead of the guns, or, if they do take to the air, they are usually much too far off for a shot to be possible. Driving is without doubt the best way to show the redleg to its best potential.

Whilst the redleg, with its boldly barred flanks, white chin surrounded by a distinctive black eye stripe and bib, and red legs (obviously the source of the common name) is easily distinguished from the grey at close quarters, it is not always easy to tell the two apart in flight. Greys tend to come at the line of Guns in coveys, redlegs in ones and twos, but the novice may have difficulty telling the species apart. For this reason, on some shoots where there are greys present and efforts are being made to preserve them, the shooting of any partridge is discouraged and redlegs are not released.

With the decline of the grey partridge, the redleg took on an increased popularity as a sporting bird in the 1960s. Thanks to its habit of laying two clutches a year, game farmers found it easy to produce redlegs in large numbers. They also experimented with more prolific chukar and chukar/redleg crosses, but the release of these was banned in 1992, a move mainly driven by the desire to preserve the genetic integrity of the redleg. Behind this was a mounting concern about declining populations in France and Spain, which placed new importance on the established British birds.

It is difficult to assess just how many red-legged partridge there actually are in Britain today (2016). While there may be as many as 250,000 pairs according to the Game and Wildlife Conservation Trust, these wild birds are supplemented by the release of perhaps as many as six million birds a year by shoots.

While it is easy to dismiss the redleg as a poor second-best to the grey partridge, we should be grateful to have it here. Its appeal is wildly underestimated by many who don't, or won't, understand or appreciate the species, and the redleg is a supremely sporting bird when released sympathetically and driven with proper regard to its true potential. Despite occasional assertions to the contrary, it does not compete with the grey and we should embrace it as a welcome addition to our quarry species. Long may it thrive and receive the respect that it deserves.

Before beginning a Hunt, it is wise to ask someone what you are looking for before you begin looking for it. **A A Milne, *Winnie the Pooh***

SHOVELER

Anas clypeata

A mid-sized duck somewhat smaller than the mallard, the shoveler is immediately distinguished from similar species by a unique flattened, spoon-shaped beak with a comb-like interior, which it uses to sieve small insects and plant material from the surface of the water. The green head, white chest, chestnut flanks and blue wing patches make the drake unmistakeable; in his work *The Magic Skin*, French novelist Honoré de Balzac described him well: 'Stay, that is the shoveler – that fat, brownish black rascal, with the greenish neck and that coquettish iridescence on it.' The female, as with so many other ducks, is drabber in colour but still easily distinguished by her rather less prominent blue wing patches. She, too, has the same distinctive beak. Said to be more inclined towards monogamy than some other dabbling ducks, pairs do seem to remain together for longer. One curious habit that the duck is said to have is that, if flushed from her nest by any perceived predator, she will sometimes defecate on the eggs, presumably to make them less attractive as a food item.

The shoveler may not feature as heavily in the wildfowler's game bag as some of the other ducks, but it is not uncommon. Swimming as though front-heavy, with the bill held not far above the surface of the water, it tends to be shy of man and seems especially uncomfortable when close to the shore. The flight is deceptive, and many mistakenly think that this species offers a relatively easy shot. In fact it is very agile in the air, able to twist and turn with strong and rapid wing beats, even though it is a little slower than the mallard. Shovelers are occasionally seen in large groups, but more usually group together in smaller parties or just pairs. Shallower, fresh or brackish water is preferred for feeding in; they don't 'up end' as much as other dabbling ducks, but they will dive readily if disturbed.

Shovelers can be seen in much of Britain all year round, though the majority are centred in the south and east of England between the Thames estuary and the Wash. Smaller, more localised populations can be found elsewhere. The summer breeding population has been estimated at around 1,000 pairs, but numbers are boosted to around 18,000 individual birds in the winter when migrants arrive from Iceland, northern Europe and even from as far off as Russia.

Of all the dabbling ducks, the flesh of the shoveler has the most mixed reputation for edibility. Some, such as the naturalist Thomas Bewick, rated it very highly indeed, writing in 1804 that it was 'inferior to none'. Others have not been so kind, some considering it not even worth shooting, or muddy in texture and taste at best. Much has to do with what the individual bird in question has been feeding on, and the proportion of animal content within its diet seems to have a direct effect on palatability. Birds that have been taking primarily plant matter tend to taste better.

Keeper's Tip: Only load your gun when you are ready to start shooting, and unload the moment a drive is finished.

SNIPE

Gallinago gallinago

But the houlet cry'd frae the Castle-wa'
The blitter frae the boggie
The tod reply'd upon the hill
I trembled for my Hoggie
Robert Burns

As Burns laments the passing of his young sheep, to the accompanying calls of the owl and the fox, the 'blitter frae the boggie' joins in. Blitter, heather bleater, or bog bleater – the snipe drumming has given rise to a number of local names which reflect its goat-like bleating sound. In France it is sometimes known as the 'flying nanny goat'. In fact the noise is not even a call, rather an effect created by the vibration of the two outer tail feathers in flight. Just why it is referred to as 'drumming' is difficult to understand, as the sound bears little resemblance to a drum. It can be heard all year round, but most frequently at dawn and dusk during spring and into early summer, a time of courtship and the marking of territory, as the bird ascends to a height before falling into a steep, often vertical, dive.

'The boggie' is the snipe's preferred habitat, providing wet feeding areas with plenty of cover where it can hide, perfectly camouflaged in a cryptic assembly of buffs and browns. Like its close relative the woodcock, it has a long, pliable and probing beak with a sensitive tip for locating food items such as worms. Prey is often swallowed without withdrawing the beak from the mud, and eyes set well back at the side of the head allow good, all-round vision while the bird is head down and feeding.

The collective term for a small group of snipe flushed from cover, a wisp, is one of the most delightful, and reflects the flickering nature of the flight. You generally don't see large groups of snipe, and they tend to come singly or in groups of four or five. The zigzagging, rapid flight seems, as more than one observer has remarked ruefully, perfectly suited to avoiding any pattern of shot sent their way. One may often wonder why it seems necessary to expend a cartridge (or, more likely, half-a-dozen or more) to put a tiny bird weighing just a few ounces onto the table, but the answer of course is that any successful shot is a triumph. A walked-up bird, encountered as you struggle through the marshy ground and so often getting up almost at your feet, is an easy bird to miss – more often than not underneath.

The snipe is a resident in Britain, but come the winter it is joined by yet more migrating from Iceland and northern Europe, when the population can swell to well over a million birds. With it comes the less common and smaller, shorter-billed jack snipe, which may only be shot in Northern Ireland; it is said to have a rather less erratic flight than its larger cousin.

The skill involved in finding, then flushing and shooting the snipe has given rise to the military term 'sniper', meaning a highly skilled sharpshooter. To 'snipe' at someone, or make personal comments against them, may not have sprung from this but may actually refer to the bird's long beak pointing at a specific object. To send someone on a 'snipe hunt' is to commit them to an impossible task, rather like a wild-goose chase.

You don't often find snipe at the butcher's, so you'll need to source your own the honest way. In the days before firearms the birds were commonly netted in huge numbers and offered for sale; household records dating from 1512 set the going rate at threepence a dozen. Modern cookbooks often suggest one bird per diner, a ridiculously small meal for a hungry hunter, and you'll need more for anything other than a starter. It is traditional to roast snipe layered in fatty bacon to prevent the breast meat from drying out, with the head twisted round to use the beak as a skewer, and many gourmets insist that the innards should be left intact rather than be drawn before cooking. The plucked bird is placed on a piece of toast in the roasting dish; this soaks up the juices created by cooking and is also served. In her famous work *The Book of Household Management*, Mrs Beeton tells us to:

> 'Place four on a skewer, tie them on to the jack or spit, and roast before a clear fire for about 1/4 hour. Put some pieces of buttered toast into the dripping-pan to catch the trails; flour and froth the birds nicely, dish the pieces of toast with the snipes on them, and pour round, but not over them, a little good brown gravy. They should be sent to table very hot and expeditiously, or they will not be worth eating.'

STOAT & WEASEL

Mustela erminea & Mustela nivalis

The enemies that our quarry birds and animals have to face are far too many to list here, but two ferocious little mustelids are worthy of special mention – the stoat and the weasel. Both have long, slender bodies designed for hunting in confined spaces and burrows; to the uninitiated they may be difficult to tell apart but it is really quite simple (I have no intention of repeating the old cracker joke). The stoat (*M. erminea*) is the larger animal, a male weighing around 250 grams and measuring up to 30 centimetres in length. The weasel (*M. nivalis*) is much smaller at no more than 120 grams and around 20 centimetres long. Furthermore, while the weasel stays the same light brown colour all year round, the stoat's coat frequently turns white (though retaining the characteristic black tip to the tail) in winter. Both, however, have acquired a deserved reputation for a ferocity which is totally out of proportion to their relatively small size.

Not all stoats become white in the winter, and some in the south of the country do not change at all, whereas northern animals almost always do. It is said that a higher proportion of females turn white than males. Wearing robes made from the winter coat of the stoat, known as ermine, was once the preserve of the nobility and can still be seen today adorning British peers on state occasions; the black dots on the white fur are the animal's tails. Rank is defined by the number of bars of ermine used – the highest, four, is reserved for a duke. Although artificial fur is mostly used for new robes nowadays, hereditary peers often pass original ones down through the generations. Folklore has it that the stoat is so proud of its white coat that, rather than see it dirty, it would give itself up to hunters and die rather than risk soiling itself.

Perhaps the stoat's greatest crime is that it is what is known as a 'surplus' killer, and one that finds its way into the chicken house or release pen will often go on a killing spree in the course of which it destroys far more birds than it needs for food. The stoat is also capable of killing prey much larger than itself. Out stalking roe one morning, I once had the privilege of watching a stoat pursue a rabbit up and down a field, constantly changing course over the space of many minutes, with the stoat being kicked off its victim's back several times before it finally obtained a firm hold and delivered a fatal bite to the base of the rabbit's head. I got the impression that the rabbit was not running at anything near full speed but seemed to fatalistically accept that it simply had nowhere to go. The weight ratio between prey and predator must have been around ten to one.

Confusingly, in Ireland the stoat is known as a 'weasel' (the true weasel does not occur there naturally). A much repeated newspaper story from County Donegal in the 1960s told of a woman and her dog who were attacked by a pack of the beasts; the woman escaped, whilst the dog, a collie, was said to have been killed. Such stories of stoats hunting in packs persist even though individual animals are typically more inclined to live apart. Weasels, too, are often believed to hunt in gangs but such suggestions are unproven. It is quite likely that Kenneth Grahame helped to perpetuate the idea through *The Wind in the Willows*, where Toad, Ratty, Mole and Badger do battle with the Chief Weasel and his gang of rampaging mustelids. More probably, sightings of adult animals accompanied by their offspring (weasels can have up to seven young at a time, stoats as many as twelve) gave rise to the belief.

Weasels, for their size, are probably even more aggressive than the stoat and are capable of taking prey items as large as a rabbit (very rarely, they have even been recorded killing capercaillie and hares), although more usually rodents form the main part of their diet. They need to eat around one third of their body weight every day to sustain themselves. By rights British animals should be more correctly termed the least weasel, being the smallest of a family found in the Americas, through Europe and across much of Asia. Occasionally unusually small adult weasels are seen, giving rise to a country belief that there is a separate race of 'mouse weasels'. Those taken in traps are inevitably found to be females (bitches) which usually tend to be more diminutive than the males (dogs) anyway, and the most likely explanation is that these were just particularly small ones.

Both stoats and weasels have been seen 'dancing' in front of their prey to mesmerise it. Sadly, some theorists suggest that this may be more likely brought about by a common parasitic worm causing pressure to the brain which results in fits rather than a clever hunting tactic, but there is plenty of evidence that, whatever the cause, it often seems to work.

The gestation period for a weasel lasts for something between 34 and

37 days, but that for a stoat is a staggering 280, longer even than a human at 266 days. Smaller creatures normally have much shorter pregnancies than larger ones but, in common with some other mammals including fellow mustelid the badger and the roe deer, stoats display a phenomenon known as delayed implantation. After mating the fertilised eggs do not start to develop immediately, but instead float free within the uterus. They do not start to develop properly until some four weeks before the young are subsequently born. For such a small creature, it is surprising that the stoat's gestation period is one of the longest recorded among the mammals, although nothing can match the African elephant's 645 days or 22 months. For the record, the shortest official gestation is that of the opossum at 13 days, although that's cheating slightly given that the young of this marsupial are born immature and carry on developing in a pouch on the mother. The hamster, on the other hand, gives birth to live young at only 18 days.

A Wild Goose Chase

During the 1990s I worked in a well-known military establishment. Its extensive grounds included a number of beautifully maintained sports pitches and two large lakes, and every winter this combination created a conflict.

The lakes attracted Canada geese in huge numbers – not an issue in themselves, you would have thought – but during the day they would wander onto the pitches in search of grazing, producing a mass of goose guano in the process. The rugby players and the Health and Safety Officer were equally unimpressed, so the Adjutant decided that it was time to do something drastic.

Accordingly, the order went out that all shotgun owners were to meet at dawn one morning in mid-October to conduct a cull. A platoon of Gurkha soldiers was also assembled, all of whom were grinning with anticipation, and they were issued with an assortment of 12 bores gleaned from our own armoury and those of local units. As for the rest of us, there was a wide variety of shotguns on show. There were at least two Purdeys present, and one immaculate cavalry captain amazed us all by appearing with a battered old Winchester pump action, in complete contrast to his beautifully tailored shooting suit. Everyone was issued with a few rounds of No 3 shot from the slab of ammunition bought with unit funds for the occasion. The Adjutant briefed the assembly. This was a cull and not sport, he insisted, fixing the tweedier among us with a steely eye. He wanted as many geese as possible shot, so the Gurkhas would commence proceedings with a mass volley onto the water while the rest of us, according to perceived ability, were stationed around the lake to despatch unhit birds as they made off. The geese were, he stressed, to be made to understand that they were thoroughly unwelcome, and persuaded convincingly to spend the rest of the winter elsewhere.

The plan worked, although it wasn't pretty and certainly not sporting. The Gurkhas, who would not have looked out of place in red jackets on the field of Waterloo, lined up at the lake edge, front rank kneeling and rear rank standing, as hundreds of geese, used to being thrown bread, swam in anticipating a free meal. I don't believe that anyone actually gave the order 'Volley fire – present!' but they might as well have done. The sound of thirty 12 bores discharging as one was thunderous, and the water erupted not once but twice as second barrels added to the carnage. Around the lake, the rest of us steadily increased the tally as geese departed in all directions.

As I said, it wasn't sport, but it was certainly effective. A flotilla of rowing boats, commandeered from the fishing club, was then deployed to gather up any birds remaining on the water and to despatch the occasional flapper, of which there were surprisingly few. There must have been well over fifty Canadas laid out at the end of proceedings (along with a single grey squirrel that nobody admitted to) and everyone was instructed to take one home; the Gurkhas claimed the remainder for a communal *bhat*, a Nepalese curry meal. I carefully chose a young bird and put it to one side before taking to a boat to help with the clear up.

There is a postscript. A week later, my goose was plucked and consigned to the oven, and we invited friends around to share it. Unbeknownst to me, a generous spirit among the Gurkhas had decided that it was wrong that the *sahib* had taken such a small goose and, instead, substituted a much larger bird for the one I had so carefully chosen. It soon became clear that we had ended up cooking something very, very old indeed. The final result, its texture not far removed from shoe leather, proved impossible to eat. In the end it was given to the dog, which had trouble enough breaking it down. We sent out for a Chinese takeaway instead.

TEAL

Anas crecca

As you cluster around the game cart to examine the bag after the driving of the shoot duck pond, laid out among the Canada geese and mallard will be the smallest bird of the lot, but the one which inevitably attracts the most attention and admiration. Compact, perfectly formed and exquisitely coloured with a green eye-stripe edged with pale yellow over a chestnut brown head, and flanks of the most delicate grey on white barring, the diminutive teal is a prize valued far beyond its larger brethren. It is a little jewel of a duck, on top of which its powers of flight are prodigious. Prolific sporting writer John Marchington characterises it as 'a jet fighter to the mallard bomber', a very apt description. Besides being quick in level flight, the teal possesses the ability to take off almost vertically from the water before departing with a series of twists and turns capable of outsmarting the most expert of Shots. Walked up, it has a reputation for sitting tight before exploding into the air – you have to be alert and ready if you are to have any chance of connecting with it. The 'springing teal' clay on a sporting lay-out, fired from the trap directly into the sky, is considered to be one of the most challenging of the targets on offer.

Whilst the teal can be encountered anywhere, it is not a numerous visitor to most inland sites. You'll find them in larger numbers on the coast and in wetlands, flickering and turning in small, tight flocks (or 'springs') like waders in a breathtaking display of aerobatics. Come the winter, the British breeding population of around 2,500 pairs swells dramatically as migrants from the Baltic, Siberia and elsewhere join them to push numbers to almost a quarter of a million individuals. When the weather turns really hard, though, the teal shows more sense than many other species that stay loyal to their winter quarters and many may move southwards, usually to France and Spain but occasionally as far as North Africa, in search of kinder climes.

The teal is a vociferous duck: the clear, whistling and far-reaching *cryc cryc* of the drake is the inspiration for its scientific name *crecca*. Female birds have a quieter, bark-like quack, and flocks in flight call almost continuously to each other.

While observers can be divided regarding the table quality of some of the other ducks, there is a wide consensus that the teal stands out as far and away the best of them all. The Romans certainly appreciated them, for their bones have been found at the settlement of Silchester in northern Hampshire, not far from Basingstoke. It is just a shame that they are so small; a male bird weighs no more than twelve ounces, the female slightly less. Mrs Beeton recommends 'two for a dish', also suggesting that the better flavoured birds are to be found once the first frosts have set in. She notes that the cost in 1861 was a shilling each, against four to five shillings for a brace of mallard, but that they are seldom available.

The barred flank feathers of the teal have long been the foundation for any number of anglers' flies meant to imitate small baitfish and other aquatic life, including the Peter Ross, Teal & Green, Teal & Black, Teal & Red. The most famous and productive has to be that superb sea trout pattern the Teal, Blue & Silver. Hugh Falkus, a recognised master among fly fisherman, himself nicknamed it 'The Medicine' for night fishing on the Cumbrian Esk.

Keeper's Tip: When faced by a large pack of birds, whether it is a flush of pheasant or a flight of duck, force yourself to focus on one bird and ignore the rest. Inexperienced Guns often tend to shoot into the middle of the group and fail to hit anything!

WHITE-FRONTED GOOSE

Anser albifrons

One of the true, or 'grey' geese, the whitefront is one of those that does not breed in Britain. There are two distinct races that may be encountered here during the winter months, the European and the Greenland. The first of these, the European, breeds in arctic Russia and Siberia, where it nests on the tundra before travelling to western and southern Europe, sometimes travelling as far down as the Mediterranean coast. Arriving here any time from October until perhaps as late as January (departure from summer grounds is usually dependent on the weather conditions there), it can only be encountered in England and South Wales where it concentrates in very specific locations, such as Slimbridge in Gloucestershire, the Hampshire Avon, Dyfed and the Welsh borders, and a few other highly localised wintering grounds. Elsewhere it is only very rarely seen. Far more do not travel as far as us; many stop in the Netherlands and Germany, where flocks numbering as many as 30,000 have been recorded. In the few places where it may be found it is certainly an abundant and important quarry species to the Welsh and English wildfowler.

The Greenland race does not reach as far south, and is generally only encountered in Ireland, western Wales and western Scotland. It is only very rarely seen in England. In recent years numbers of this race have declined alarmingly, breeding failures being attributed to bad weather and loss of habitat. Human disturbance by visiting tourists from cruise ships has also been blamed. It is not a legal quarry in Northern Ireland, and though it remains on the quarry list on the eastern side of the Irish Sea, there is a voluntary moratorium in place at the time of writing (2016) and full legal protection is expected soon. Ireland is considered to host around half the world population of Greenland whitefronts every year.

The white-fronted goose is easily recognised from the adult bird's boldly barred chest. The beak is edged with very noticeable white feathers around the front of the face (the 'white front' which gives the bird its name), although immature birds possess neither this feature nor the barred chest. All ages have a pink bill and orange legs. In size, it is midway between a greylag and a pink-footed goose, smaller than the former and larger than the latter. Greenland birds are slightly darker and larger than their European cousins. It is considered to be one of the noisiest of the geese, often referred to as the 'laughing goose' for its musical *kow yow* call, pitched rather higher than other species. The calling of a flock has been likened to the sound of bells.

Although gregarious, the whitefront is not necessarily as sociable as other grey geese and can often be encountered in smaller parties or even just as pairs. Sometimes they will mix with greylags or pink-footed geese. Like most geese they are excellent parents, and some observers believe that grandparenting is occasionally practised. Once reared, family parties migrate together, flying high and as fast as fifty miles per hour. Of all the grey geese, the whitefront is probably the most agile in flight, with the greatest capacity for acceleration, near vertical take-off and rapid, spiralling landing.

In *The Sword in the Stone*, novelist T H White had Merlin the magician change young king-to-be Arthur into a variety of creatures to impart lessons to prepare him for his destiny. He chose the white-fronted goose to teach of a society without property or laws where leaders are chosen purely for their ability, where war is unimaginable and the family is all-important. At the end of a wonderfully evocative description of the migration flight, he described the conclusion:

> 'Oh, the whiffling of delight and self-congratulation! They tumbled out of the sky, side-slipping, stunting and even doing spinning nose-dives. They were proud of themselves and of their pilot, agog for the family pleasures which were in store.
>
> 'They planed for the last part on down-curved wings. At the last moment they scooped the wind with them, flapping them vigorously. Next – bump – they were on the ground. They held their wings above their heads for a moment, then folded them with a quick and pretty neatness. They had crossed the North Sea.'

The best example I know, of this astonishingly stupid attitude towards sport, is that of Franz Ferdinand. His, however, was an achievement with the gun. He used to shoot at Konopist with no less than seven weapons and four loaders, and he once killed more than 4,000 birds, himself, in one day. [A propos of statistics and quite beside the point: a Yorkshireman once drank 52½ pints of beer in one hour.] Now why did Franz Ferdinand do this? Even if he shot for twelve hours at a stretch, without pause for luncheon, it means that he killed six birds in each minute of the day. The mere manual labour, a pheasant every ten seconds for twelve successive hours, is enough to make a road-mender stagger; and there is little wonder that, by the time the unhappy archduke had accumulated his collection of 300,000 head of game, he was shooting with rubber pads on his coat and a bandage round his ears. The unfortunate man had practically stunned himself with gunpowder, long before they bagged him also at Sarajevo. **T H White, *England Have My Bones***

WIGEON

Anas penelope

As Brian P Martin says of the wigeon in his definitive *Sporting Birds of the British Isles*, 'this is the sportsman's duck that evokes wild places, wild weather and memorable flights'. We so link it to the arrival of winter migrants that it is easy to forget the few hundred breeding pairs that remain with us throughout the year. The high-pitched whistling *whee-oo* that announces the arrival of a flock is enough to put the hairs up on the back of your neck and raise your heart-rate in anticipation, as you crouch, tense and expectant, in a foreshore gully straining your eyes in the pre-dawn light. The French name for the bird, *canard siffleur*, or whistling duck, is perfectly given.

The wigeon was a mainstay of the early commercial hunters (who shot wildfowl to earn a living), arriving in huge numbers every year when the cold weather sent them southwards. Even today, the winter population is estimated to be as high as nearly half a million birds. The drake has an understated dapper attraction, with his yellow crown, pinkish breast and grey back; inevitably the duck is a plainer brown. In eclipse, that period at the end of the summer after breeding when many duck species moult to replace their essential flight feathers, both sexes look similar.

Presumably because they were killed in large numbers for the table, there was a rather false assumption that wigeon were stupid and easily hunted, and in the eighteenth century the term 'wigeon' was given to a simple-minded person. The fact of the matter is that these ducks, being a highly gregarious species, simply presented a bigger target for the punt gunner. By day they tend to rest on the coastline, flying inland at night to feed.

Whatever vegetable matter is freely available tends to be eaten. The wigeon, like the mallard, teal and others of the sub-family *Anatinae*, is a dabbling duck that feeds just below the water surface but is just as at home grazing on dry land. The marine eel grass *zostera* that grows in estuaries is an important food item but this has declined in availability thanks to disease and possibly sea pollution. Otherwise grasses, roots and seeds are all freely taken. The wigeon, however, will not let you down by eating animal matter, which makes the flesh taste unpalatably strong.

The name wigeon is generally felt to be a reflection of the bird's call; local names include whew, whewer, whim and whistler for the same reason. In Ireland it is known as the yellow poll. You sometimes see the name spelt as 'widgeon', although this, whilst not strictly incorrect, has largely fallen out of use. In the USA the American wigeon, a close relative with which our Eurasian wigeon sometimes hybridises, is commonly known as the 'bald pate' because of the head markings. The delightful *penelope* of the scientific name is derived from the Gaelic *fenella* meaning 'white shoulder' for the distinctive white wing-patch of the drake.

Keeper's Tip: Always carry your gun in a slip between drives, and especially when travelling in shoot trailers or other transport. It is more reassuring for fellow passengers and of course protects your gun against accidental knocks and scratches.

Beware – Men at Play

Grown-ups, I realised quite early on in my childhood, can be a very infantile bunch, and it was probably the members of my father's syndicate shoot who first led me to this conclusion. They were a mixed bunch, which included a member of our local landed gentry, a Justice of the Peace, two farmers, a long-distance lorry driver and the owner of the town's hardware shop. They enjoyed their days greatly and were constantly vying to pull off original practical jokes on each other; I rather think that the atmosphere of these days played a large part in getting me hooked on shooting in the first place. I remember clearly the face of one – I think it was the JP – who'd had cartridges loaded with black powder substituted for his regular modern loads. Standing awed, shocked and speechless amid a huge cloud of smoke, much to the very great amusement of his fellows. Incredibly though, he had hit the pheasant he had shot at as well.

One of the gang had a wilful and badly trained German shorthaired pointed named, rather unimaginatively, Fritz. Fritz had never pointed in his life and had no intention of starting now. He ranged too far ahead, ran in, ate unattended shot pheasants and completely ignored his master. It was generally agreed that the only day he would ever drop to shot was when Fred, his owner, decided that he'd had enough. It took me a while to work out what they meant by that but, anyway, Fritz was in no danger. He and his master were kindred spirits and, whatever their personal faults, were completely devoted to each other. One morning Fritz had played up particularly well, ruining one drive completely, and Fred had reluctantly resorted to a makeshift lead consisting of some thirty yards of baling twine in an attempt to keep him in check when working the root fields. The party retired to the pub for lunch where I was allowed to sit in the corner with a couple of other lads brought out to beat by their fathers.

Fritz was secured to a leg of Fred's chair, and after a while the latter excused himself to visit the Gents. As soon as he was out of sight, three incredulous ten-year-olds watched amazed from their corner table as a dozen or so grown men giggled and sniggered as the baling twine, recovered from the pocket of Fred's shooting jacket, was woven around the room, between chair legs, over a light fitting, round the beer pumps and twice round the barmaid, before being secured to the collar of a sleeping Fritz. A few chairs were laid on their sides on the floor for good measure. Minutes later Fred returned to stand transfixed at the door as he surveyed the scene. His eyes followed the journey of the twine as it wound its way around the lounge bar before ending up at his dog's neck. Eventually he spoke. 'What the hell happened?'

There was a brief pause before, with a straight face, the lorry driver replied: 'Didn't you hear it all, Fred? A cat came in.'

WOODCOCK

Scolopax rusticola

For looks, behaviour and the mythology that surround this unusual species, the woodcock is a truly enigmatic bird and we still have much to learn about it. It was once believed that it flew to the moon during the months when it was not seen in Britain, and the diminutive goldcrest was once known as the 'woodcock pilot', reflecting the belief that it rode on the larger bird's back during migration.

It is, at first sight, a strangely built creature, with its long, probing beak, stout body and short legs. A Senecan Indian myth says that God made its close, and very similar, American relative from the leftover parts of other birds. The beak, though, is superbly adapted, having sensitive nerve-endings for detecting and capturing underground food items, mainly earthworms and insect larvae, whilst the nostrils are located high against the skull enabling the bird to breathe and feed at the same time. The liquid eyes are set at the sides of its head, giving it excellent all-round vision even when feeding. The barred reddish-brown, buff and grey camouflage is incredibly effective as well as being supremely attractive when closely inspected. Put a woodcock among all the other birds on the game cart and it will be the one that attracts the most attention.

Officially classified as a wading bird, the woodcock has adapted for life in fields and woodlands rather than seeking a living on water edges. Whilst some birds remain within our shores all year round, yet more migrate each spring to breed in eastern and northern Europe, returning to Britain in the late autumn, usually around the first full moon of November – still often described as a 'woodcock moon'. They cover some astonishing distances; one, tracked by the Game & Wildlife Conservation Trust as part of their ongoing Woodcock Watch project, travelled over 9,000 kilometres between The Lizard in Cornwall and eastern Russia in 2012.

During spring, if you are incredibly lucky, you may be able to spot the hen on her nest, perfectly camouflaged against the woodland floor. If you are luckier still, you might be rewarded by the sight of a chick being cradled between her legs in flight, once considered a fanciful notion but now accepted as fact. More easily seen is the roding flight: sit quietly at dusk in woodland during April and June and you may be rewarded with sightings of the male as he patrols the air with rapid wing-beats along the tree line, seeking to attract the attention of a female. The preferred habitat is dry, warm and draught-free woods with a good understorey of bramble, rhododendron or similar dense ground cover. Much feeding is done at night, when the woodcock leaves its daytime refuge to feed in the damper and more penetrable open fields.

Easily trapped in light nets and snares, they were once considered stupid birds. Shakespeare wrote in *The Taming of the Shrew*: 'O this woodcock! What an ass it is!' whilst in *Love's Labours Lost* a character describes himself and his friends as 'four woodcocks in a dish' when they all fall in love having vowed not to do so.

The covert feather of the outer primary on the wing has a special cachet among sportsmen, and you can even buy special mounts to set them in your hat. Indeed, among the most traditionally-minded who look down on the wearing of trophies of the chase on your clothing as 'not quite the thing', a woodcock pin feather is perfectly acceptable. Artists also prize the pin feather for painting fine details, among them being the gold stripe down the side of a Rolls-Royce car. The original name for this feather was indeed the 'pen'.

There is nothing that so creates a surge of adrenalin among the pegs during a shoot day as when the cry of 'Woodcock forward!' goes up. The flight is rapid, zigzagging, unpredictable and challenging to connect with. For most sportsmen, to take a 'right and left' (or possibly these days an 'over and under'), namely shooting two birds, one with each barrel, is an achievement in itself, but a right and left at woodcock is something very special indeed. Not only are these birds a difficult target in their own right but to have two in the air in front of you at the same time and offering the opportunity is pretty rare in itself. To hit them both is indeed a triumph. If you manage to, and you have witnesses, you can apply to join the *Shooting Times* Woodcock Club, which earns you a certificate, badge, tie, and an invitation to an annual dinner for fellow-achievers. Once upon a time you also received a bottle of a well-known liquor, but sadly that sponsor has long since moved on.

WOODPIGEON

Columba palumbus

Woodpigeon shooting is not conducted primarily for sport, but is instead all about crop protection. It is important that we get this straight from the very beginning. Every year in Britain alone millions are shot under the terms of the General Licence rather than an open season, and that licence is issued in recognition of the fact that the pigeon is an agricultural pest. Indeed it is a major agricultural pest, and the economic effect of woodpigeon depredations cannot be understated; it has been estimated that a single bird can consume its own weight in food in four days. That it is a wily, fast-flying, manoeuvrable and altogether testing target is very much the good luck of the pigeon shooter, but the fact remains that you are not out there purely for sport – tell that to an onlooker and you could well find yourself in breach of the terms of the General Licence.

The 'woodie' has been described as the poor man's grouse, and certainly a good day over decoys can offer a wide variety of targets, ranging from the relatively easy to the very difficult indeed as birds approach the hide from all angles and directions. A successful pigeon shooter needs to be adaptable and constantly on his toes (metaphorically speaking at least) and many people seek no other quarry. By winter, when resident birds are joined by seasonal visitors, huge bags can reward the Gun with local knowledge who has made a plan, laid out an intelligent pattern of decoys, constructed a suitable hide – and has just a little bit of luck on his side. Lulls in the shooting offer an opportunity to add recently shot birds to the decoy pattern. You need to get it right though; a simple mistake, such as showing a bare face to your quarry, can persuade them to give you a very wide berth indeed.

Outwitting the woodpigeon is big business, as it seems to learn from experience: techniques to get to grips with it continue to evolve. Early plastic decoys and cradles to support the bodies of shot birds have given way to fresh innovations, ranging from mechanical 'flappers', which mimic a pigeon displaying its distinctive white wing-bars landing in front of the hide, to the now ubiquitous 'pigeon magnet'. This rotary device, based on a motor that causes the decoys to circle endlessly, creates movement to attract the attention of incomers and draw them into a wider decoy pattern in the killing area where the Gun waits in ambush. Unsporting? Remember, this is crowd control.

If shooting pigeon over decoys is a daytime activity, roost shooting takes over as the day draws to a close. When the flocks return to their established roosts in the woods, easily identified by the massed droppings on the ground below, the Gun is waiting, taking care not to shoot the first few 'scout' birds that seem to precede the main parties. A windy, dull day seems best, and as ever concealment is essential. Shooting can be at is best when a number of Guns cooperate, covering several woods over a large area and keeping the flocks on the move.

Known as the ring dove until the more familiar name was adopted only a hundred years or so ago, the woodpigeon has long been a source of food for the human table. Its nest is often obvious, and one old, rather heartless country ploy was to secure the squab within it by means of a string around the leg, leaving it to be fed by its parents until grown and at the point of leaving the nest – at which time it would be taken for the pot. Today there is a thriving market for shot birds; pigeon meat is excellent and favoured by many people above any grouse or pheasant. It is one of the few quarry species that can be regularly found for sale in the modern supermarket, and as they have no close season are available all year round. Summer birds, with a higher proportion of fruits and seeds in their diet, are considered the best.

The woodpigeon shooter may well be there to protect the crops. Secretly, though, deep in his heart, lies the fervent and paradoxical wish that they prosper, so as to need serious controlling for a very long time to come.

'A ballistic' said the Old Man 'is sort of hard to explain. Suppose you take the speed of a bird and the angle of flight and the speed of the wind and the direction of the wind and the height of the bird and the size of the shot pattern and the speed of the shot and the strength of the powder, and then you grind them all up in one mill and the right answer comes out. Maybe that ain't the book definition, but it's my definition.' **Robert Ruark, *The Old Man and the Boy***

Loose Talk

As my Army postings took me around the country, I was lucky to belong to a number of military shoots. Some were very formal, some less so, but all were marked by a wide variety of dog training standards. One, a 'beat one, stand one' affair stands out in particular; we were split into two teams, one of which would beat while the others stood at their pegs, swapping roles throughout the day. A member on the opposite team to mine owned a German short-haired pointer, which seemed programmed to head for the line of Guns at speed whenever the start whistle blew and appear in front of then almost before the beaters had moved off. Realising its mistake, it would them work back towards its master, quartering beautifully and flushing any birds that it found to the beating line, which always enjoyed good shooting as a result. This was not popular among my team of Guns.

Years later I recalled the dog over a shoot lunch on the other side of the country and joked about how we would frequently curse the dog's owner. Across the bench, a highly respected retired Brigadier fixed me with a gimlet eye and spoke. 'Yes, I remember that shoot,' he said, 'and that was my dog'.

Keeper's Tip: Once the signal for the end of a drive has sounded, please don't ever be tempted to shoot at any bird which gets up late.

Tales from Glen Garron

A Sting in the Tale

Blue blood isn't always ample protection against a determined adversary

'... and another thing, I want no more of your nonsense this time, d'you hear me?' the Colonel concluded sternly. Willie Cameron sighed. The Laird was wearing his serious face today, and the keeper knew from their long relationship that nothing he could say would change his boss's mind.

The Colonel allowed his features to relax into a smile. 'Listen Tattie, it's only for a week and I'm sure that he hasn't forgotten his lesson from last year.' The use of Willie's childhood nickname, attributed to him by the village schoolmistress who frequently and fairly compared the young Willie's appearance to a *tattie bogle* or scarecrow, was the signal that the laird/head keeper discussion was over. Now the two of them could speak together as the friends they had been since childhood.

Willie had been summoned to the drawing room of the Lodge to be told, to his despair, that the Count would be returning to Glen Garron. During his previous visit the Count, an arrogant, self-important and abrasive man, had been outrageously rude to Willie before being taken to the hill to stalk a stag. Archie, Willie's son, had subsequently contrived to walk the hapless aristocrat into a state of exhaustion during the course of the day, simultaneously managing to ensure that every deer they stalked had been able to spot them and make off long before a shot was possible. The Colonel was fully aware of what had happened that day and did not want a repeat; the Count himself might be a nightmare, but he was married to the Colonel's sister and anyway, the rules of Highland hospitality demanded that he should be treated as an honoured guest.

'Och, okay, boss,' Willie said with a rueful smile. 'I'll do my best, and I'll tell young Archie to do the same. We'll look after the scunner for ye, aye and treat him right. I'll even take him out myself for that gaun buck up in the plantation.'

The Colonel breathed a sigh of relief. 'Thanks Willie, I really appreciate it, and I know that Mary will too. It won't be too bad; your young friend Edward will be staying as well and you can take him up to that loch you keep so well stocked and catch some fish. Come on, take a dram with me before you go home.' Willie brightened at this; Edward, the grandson of the Colonel and Lady Mary, was a pet project of his. Studious, bespectacled and ungainly, the eleven-year-old lad was nevertheless enthusiastic and respectful, and a particular favourite of Willie's. He had taught the boy to cast and arranged for him to catch his first trout, and now looked forward to trying for a grouse with him this year.

The next day Willie, accompanied by an excited Edward, were on the meadow below the Lodge with the Glen Garron child's gun, a short stocked 20 bore with which both he and the Colonel had learned to shoot. Willie was pleased to see how quickly Edward had absorbed his instructions on gun safety, and they had just had their first success hitting a simple clay thrown by the trap, manned by Archie, when the Count appeared from the direction of the Lodge. He had his gun under his arm and a cartridge bag slung over his shoulder. 'I think I shall shoot some clays,' he announced. Willie, mindful of his chat with the Colonel the day before, bit his lip and moved Edward to one side.

For the next half-hour the Count monopolised the trap. Edward's single tremulous request to have a go was dismissed with a curt 'Be silent, boy'. When the small supply of clays ran out, the Count turned on his heel without a word and strode back towards the Lodge, leaving Willie, Archie and Edward to pick up his ejected cartridges and clear up the meadow.

That evening Willie drew up at the front of the Lodge in his Land Rover. The Colonel winced as the Count glared at the head keeper/stalker, ignored his offered hand, merely pointing wordlessly towards his rucksack to indicate that Willie should put it into the vehicle. The Colonel shot the latter a warning glance – *remember our talk*, it said – without any need for verbal reinforcement. Willie responded with a tight smile and a nod. 'We'll be off after the gaun buck then,' he said tersely.

The 'gaun buck' that Willie had promised the Colonel they'd try for was an especially fine roebuck that had taken over the plantation area as his territory. Good roe were scarce in this part of the Highlands, and this one had long, heavy, six pointer antlers and was built like a prizefighter. He had held the plantation for the last few years and Willie knew that he would soon start to 'go back' as he aged; now was the time to cull him and let a new buck take over. Yes, Willie thought, the Count could have him but it would be on his terms despite the promise he'd made to the Colonel. The strategy would just need a little thought.

Not a word passed between stalker and guest as they drove up to the far edge of the plantation. 'It'll be a longish approach,' Willie explained to his charge. 'With the wind in this direction there's nae option.' The Count merely grunted and watched as Willie loaded the rifle and picked up his stick. He looked enquiringly at the rucksack. Sighing gently, Willie shouldered that as well and wondered again at the weight of it – whit the hell was the man carrying in there, he puzzled?

Three painstaking and cautious miles later, the two of them, Willie leading, came to a high point overlooking a glade in the plantation. They had already passed up the chance of two other bucks at the Count's insistence. 'You promised me ze big one,' he told Willie disdainfully on each occasion, 'and I fully expect you to deliver.'

Quietly, Willie took the rucksack off his back, laid it on the ground as a support and placed the rifle on top of it. The Count settled himself comfortably behind it and gestured with his head for Willie to continue. Lying next to him, Willie raised the call to his lips and blew a few short peeps. 'Now we wait,' he said firmly.

Willie had watched the buck from this point several times in the past fortnight and knew that it would not be far off. He was not disappointed. Only a few minutes had elapsed before a russet brown shape appeared at the far side of the clearing among the trees. He felt the Count stiffen beside him, but laid a hand on the man's arm as a signal not to shoot just yet. The

Count shrugged it off irritably but held his fire. After two more peeps on the call, the buck's head went up, and he started to cross the clearing cautiously towards the waiting stalkers. At a range of about fifty yards he stopped and stood broadside.

The rifle spoke and the buck fell as if poleaxed. In silence, they watched as it lay still for a couple of minutes before Willie stood up, took the rifle, and made his way forward to check the lifeless form before beckoning the Count to join him. 'A braw shot,' he announced, holding out his hand in congratulation. For the second time that day the gesture was ignored.

The Count prodded the carcase with his toe and gazed happily at the antlers. He could already visualise his trophy on the wall and was mentally rearranging the story in his mind as to how he had singlehandedly stalked and brought the beast to account. 'Tomorrow you will clean the head for me,' he told Willie. 'Now you will walk back and fetch the jeep.'

'Shall I no' gralloch the beast first?' Willie asked, knowing in advance what the answer would be.

Willie knew his man and had guessed correctly what the bulging rucksack contained. 'Do not be a fool, I am a *jaeger*,' the Count replied. 'But first you will hang it up for me. You have carried all of the equipment I need for the task.' Smiling inwardly, Willie dragged the carcase to a tree at the top of the clearing. The Count marvelled at the man's stupidity in selecting an awkward uphill route to a clearly impractical small pine tree. Still, it didn't worry him. It would be the work of minutes to gralloch the animal while the keeper made the long trip back to collect the Land Rover in the rapidly diminishing daylight. As the Count extracted an array of knives, bone saws and cameras from his rucksack, Willie took a folding blade from his pocket, hocked the animal and with an effort lifted it up to hang from a convenient branch. He noted that the Count had not offered the hoist contained in his exhaustive stalking kit. 'I'll be awa' then,' announced Willie, and was unsurprised when he did not receive a reply.

In the gathering gloom, the Count briefly admired his prize and then unsheathed his knife, a beautiful handmade tool with silver bolsters and a buffalo horn handle. He knew that it was razor sharp; he expected his staff to keep all of his hunting equipment in first-class condition. He set the point to the animal's belly and made the first cut. Working by the light of a head torch, he was surprised by what he took to be a nettle sting. Ignoring it, and by now with blood covering his forearms, he was surprised to receive a couple more. He looked around for the offending plant, intending to tread it down out of harm's way, but caught sight of two small flying shapes in the torch beam. He flapped at them irritably with a hand and continued with the gralloch.

The red wasp, *Vespula rufa*, is not normally an aggressive species. It constructs its nest just below the ground and is busy by day but, as temperatures fall and the light fails, it becomes torpid and inactive. Now, though, the first few drops of warm blood created a stir throughout the nest and the impact of a rumen falling heavily onto it roused hundreds of small bodies into a buzzing fury.

Another sting and the Count looked down at his arm to see, to his horror, that it was covered in small, crawling forms. Another glance around revealed a cloud of infuriated, buzzing wasps, which his ears had been deadened to due to the temporary deafness following his shot. Starting to panic, the intrepid hunter tried to brush off the dozens that had already settled upon him, incurring many more stings in the process. Dropping his knife, he abandoned the gralloch and fled the scene.

Willie picked him up in the headlights an hour later, sitting disconsolate at the side of the track and rubbing feverishly at his arms and neck. For the first time ever the Count was visibly pleased to see him and actually expressed genuine gratitude, at first for the offer of water to wash his sticky, blood-encrusted and already itching body, and then at the production of antihistamine tablets from the Land Rover first aid kit.

Willie grinned in the darkness. The single sting that he had received in this very place a week ago was still red, inflamed and irritating him. At the moment, though, it didn't annoy him at all. Back at the Lodge he was even able to respond with a guileless shrug to the Colonel's suspicious stare as the Count, scratching and complaining, was led away to a hot bath and a coating of calamine lotion.

Keeper's Tip: Good shooting coats can be expensive but are worth every penny. Nothing spoils a day as much as being cold and wet.

SOME HINTS FOR SAFE SHOOTING

1. ALWAYS TREAT GUNS AS THOUGH THEY ARE LOADED AT ALL TIMES – even when you know that they are not. Most shooting accidents happen with 'unloaded' guns.
2. Ensure that your gun is in proof and good order. Never use a faulty or doubtful gun.
3. Only carry the correct cartridges for the gauge and chamber size of the gun you are using. Don't mix cartridges in your bag or pocket.
4. Be muzzle aware – always know where your gun is pointing, whether in a slip or out of it.
5. Check your barrels frequently for obstructions, and always before loading.
6. Between drives – carry your gun in a slip.
7. Always unload your gun before crossing an obstacle, or undertaking any activity that prevents you having full control of it.
8. Misfires: assume the worst! Keep your gun pointing in a safe direction for at least twenty seconds before breaking it. Check your barrels if you experience a soft or unusual discharge.
9. Identify your target before raising your gun, and be sure of the backstop, or where the shot will fall, before firing.
10. Look for clear sky around a flying target before shooting at it. Only shoot forward or behind the line – never at a target crossing it.
11. Always be aware of the danger of ricochet from water or any solid object.
12. Whether a standing or walking Gun, ensure that you are aware of where neighbouring Guns, beaters and spectators are at all times.
13. NEVER POINT A GUN – LOADED OR UNLOADED – IN AN UNSAFE DIRECTION.
14. NEVER RELY ON A SAFETY CATCH.

THE GLAMORGAN FUSILIERS

THE ADJUTANT'S BIRD TABLE

From the Regimental Records of the Glamorgan Fusiliers

The Glamorgan Fusiliers have long been regarded in the modern Army as a sporting regiment. Others prided themselves on the prowess of their rugby or boxing teams, or had a special reputation for providing a formative training for the generals and field marshals of tomorrow, but the Fusiliers had long held themselves to be different – one of those old-fashioned and highly valued institutions where the only gun that one discussed in the Mess discharged shot rather than high explosive projectiles, and the CO's mount would have been equally at home hunting with hounds as charging into the Valley of Death. Now, alas, times have changed, and the only memories remaining are to be found in the hunt buttons worn on an officer's blazer, or the now faded leopard skin that once belonged to a feline that tried to raid the cookhouse tent once too often at some point during the Zulu wars. Nowadays money is short and attitudes have altered, and the cry is one of professionalism and the ever threatening promotion exam rather than a hulloa.

Perhaps I paint rather too gloomy a picture. There was once, in the Officers' Mess, one who would try to revive the sporting glories of the old days, albeit on a budget as there were strict limitations as to what could be achieved on a subaltern's pay. Second Lieutenant Albert James Teal had always wanted to be a soldier and, rather by luck than judgement, managed to bumble his way through officer training at Sandhurst; there he had quickly come to be recognised as a mild but largely harmless eccentric. Given his childhood love of field sports and therefore the attractions of the Fusiliers' reputation, it was perhaps inevitable that he had ended up commissioned into that Regiment, although he had been a little shocked to find that there was more to soldiering than shooting and fishing. Nevertheless, he was happily welcomed into a Regimental fold where individuals were treasured, and came quickly to be known by his new comrades as Bertie or The Duck, depending on how the inclination took them.

It could never be said, though, that he was the stuff of which generals were made. If he ever carried a baton in his knapsack it was unlikely to have been a field marshal's – more likely to be one of those cunningly constructed sticks containing a nip of two of a suitable life-sustaining antifreeze solution. Alternately admired and tolerated by those around him, he was one of that happy breed who cheerfully muddles along in his own inimitable way, taking whatever disasters that might befall him (and, sadly, there was no shortage of these) in his stride.

Second Lieutenant Teal had tried all manner of field sports, and now felt that it was high time to give falconry a go. (This, we must remember, was back in the days before a licence was necessary to own a hawk.) An occupied buzzard's nest was soon located out in the wilds of a local training area. Assisted by a couple of his more dubious soldiers, he managed not only to secure himself a nearly fledged youngster but also a badly sprained ankle and a ripped set of battledress trousers. As the ankle healed, he set himself to training his newly acquired hawk. Following the advice offered by an old Badminton Library volume borrowed from the rather valuable set owned by the Mess, even he was surprised by his progress and after only a month was thinking about taking his protégé hunting.

The next step, he decided, was to construct a dummy rabbit to introduce his hawk to the proposed quarry. A skin was easily procured from the local butcher and wrapped around an old set of pyjamas (the Mess laundry understandably rebelled when these were eventually submitted for washing) along with a bicycle chain and half a pound of sausages. These, Teal decided, would add the necessary smell factor to add realism to his construction. The buzzard, by now named Diana (Teal fancied himself as a student of the classics) was duly introduced to this apparition. It would be fair to say that the poor bird was not impressed: rather, she was at first stupefied and then terrified as an enthusiastic Teal hurled his rather punch-drunk dummy bunny in all directions at the end of a length of baling twine. It took the rest of the afternoon before Diana was eventually located halfway up the church tower in a neighbouring village. The rabbit lure did not last long in any case. Appropriated by the CO's dog, it did not reappear until it was located, smelling horribly, under a file on the Adjutant's desk. It soon became apparent that the Adjutant, normally a tolerant and fair-minded man, had it in for the unfortunate Teal. His first edict concerned the hawking bag in which Teal carried lure, hawk food, knife, cigarettes and other essential items of equipment. As this was not a military item, the Adjutant very reasonably pointed out, it was improper to wear it as part of a webbing uniform set. As Teal conducted most of his hawk training during the lunch break, a time when it was totally inconvenient to change in and out of civilian clothes as well as snatch a mouthful of food and gulp down a swift pint at the bar, this was something of a setback at first. As it was, Teal solved the problem with a degree of flair that was unusual even for him.

A deep and bitter rivalry existed between the Duke of Rutland's Yeomanry and the Fusiliers, rumoured to have its origins during Napoleonic times, when the two regiments had been billeted in the same town. Apparently no less than two duels had been fought with pistols over the favours of a certain highly regarded young lady. These had resulted, fortunately, in no fatalities (one had been decided by a minor flesh wound, and the other in complete misses, which had so shocked the combatants that they had gravely shaken hands and given the matter up). To add insult to injury, the lady in question had gone on to marry a naval type. Whatever the origins, as unreasonable rivalries do, it had continued to the current day, whether on the sports field or at the annual Bisley shooting competition, even surfacing occasionally in heated letters to the *British Army Review*. Teal's solution was brilliant in its simplicity: he obtained a strap in Yeomanry colours, a noxious blend of pink, cerise and a spectacularly acid green, which he used to sling the hawking bag over his shoulder for his lunchtime sessions. After a week or two of this he reverted to wearing the bag more conventionally on his plain green webbing belt, and was not in the least surprised when nothing more was said about it.

Outside the Officers' Mess dining room, in the middle of an immaculately tended garden, stood a bird table. Crafted with loving care out of seasoned oak by the Regimental Pioneers and complete with a carved image of the Fusiliers' cap badge, it was the pride and joy of the Adjutant, who delighted in putting out food daily for a rich variety of small birds to feast upon. That the Adjutant held his bird table sacred did not go unnoticed by the younger and more irreverent officers. On one occasion three gnomes, with rosy cheeks and brightly painted in reds, blues and yellows, materialised overnight in the garden. One was fishing in the pond, another leaned on a miniature shovel and the third serenely watched life go by from atop a toadstool painted, naturally, in regimental colours. The fact that this latter being sported a flourishing moustache of the type favoured by the Adjutant and also carried a captain's badges of rank on his shoulders did not go unnoticed. The resulting extra duties awarded to the offenders, who included Teal, ensured that many long-planned weekends away did not come off and at least one promising romance failed to flourish from severe neglect.

Young officers can, however, be an irrepressible bunch and as the heat from this escapade cooled down, one bright spark proposed that the bird table should be the next target for their attentions. As the Adjutant appeared on his way to the Mess for lunch, the word was quickly spread. Settling into his usual seat to enjoy the cook's latest offering, the unfortunate man gazed absently out of the window and into the garden beyond. Atop the bird table, instead of a blue tit pecking on a lump of suet, sat a large buzzard, contentedly and untidily plucking a very dead pigeon. Teal's foresight had let him down; the culprit was obvious and the result sadly predictable. Teal was consigned to a month of continuous extra duties and the hawk, banished, was never seen in camp again. Undeterred by this setback to his plans to enjoy a combined military and sporting life, Teal looked elsewhere for a suitable pursuit. Clearly there was insufficient room in the enclosure housing the regimental mascot – an evil-smelling and foul-tempered ram – to house one of his father's hunters as well. No, he had to look to pastimes that demanded less in time and facilities and, he had to face it, money. What, he wondered, would be cheap, take up little space, and still be fun and productive? Suddenly it hit him. Surely even the Adjutant could not object to something small, inoffensive and above all controllable. The next day he would start to look for one. What fun it would be, he thought, to have his very own ferret.

> **Keeper's Tip:** Always carry a priest. Game that is not killed outright needs to be despatched as quickly and cleanly as possible.

New and nobler efforts characterize the aims of mankind in the development of their civilization, and the sports of the field have, to a large extent, been superseded by other exercises, it may be less healthful and invigorating, but certainly more elegant, intellectual, and humanizing. **Mrs Beeton's *Book of Household Management* (1861)**

Driven What?

You can encounter some strange sights during a pheasant drive. Though the colony of wallabies introduced into the Peak District in the 1940s no longer seems to exist, others do in certain places, thanks to escapes and deliberate releases. The sight of Skippy bouncing past must give one pause for thought. There is plenty more out there to surprise the complacent Gun as well. One Hampshire shoot of which I was a member had semi-wild llamas in the woods, and many an unsuspecting new Gun must have wondered about the contents of his hip flask as half a dozen broke cover past the pegs.

Guinea fowl are rather more commonplace. Though it is not legal to release them deliberately, many keepers keep a few around the release pens as feathered guard dogs, for the cackle they can put up when disturbed by an intruder is enough to wake the dead. Occasionally they will take wing during a drive, although they are more inclined towards escaping on foot or making for the high branches to watch the beaters pass by. Once in the air, however, they can be superb flyers and a punitive fine is often attached to shooting one. On one occasion it was the keeper's birthday and, with a present in the form of an increased end-of-day tip in mind, I shot at two such birds during one drive. As is quite usual when you are in full view of the entire beating field, I missed both handsomely.

Another shoot in North Wales boasted a population of feral peafowl in the woods. These were definitely forbidden fruit, and anyway they were quite safe as self-preservation always came first. A beater's cry of 'peacock *forwaard*!' was a warning to take evasive action and duck as a leviathan hurtled at head height through the line. Elsewhere in Gloucestershire a syndicate owner had decided to hatch off some genuine American wild turkey eggs (quite illegally, I might add) and add the results to a couple of his release pens. Of some twenty birds, only one was ever shot and the rest disappeared. Nobody knows for sure what became of them, but suspicion rested firmly on the shoulders of a few local 'characters'. I only wish that I had been present on one very well-known shoot when the main drive of the day produced a half-naked couple bolting past the Guns, clutching pathetically at bundles of their clothing. Presumably they had been trying to recreate a scene from *Lady Chatterley's Lover*; I suspect that the idea lost its allure after that.

Now you know your first big cock pheasant is a sight to see. There maybe ain't nothing as dramatic, whether it's an elephant or a polar bear. A cock pheasant is like a mallard duck. Maybe the pintail or canvasback is better to eat, but there is nothing in the flying department as wonderfully gaudy as a cock pheasant or a he-mallard. Well, maybe a peacock, but we have so few peacocks in our neck of the woods. You take a big cock pheasant and shoot him, you got a real bird in your hand. He'll weigh about four pounds, and he has this lovely long tail, and he has a ring on his neck, and he is colored green and red and brown and white, and he even has ears you can see. He is not so much dinner as trophy, but when he is cooked correctly, he is not so much trophy as dinner, if you see what I mean. **Robert Ruark, *The Old Man and the Boy***

A Ferret in the Mess

From the Regimental Records of the Glamorgan Fusiliers

Life in the First Battalion of the Glamorgan Fusiliers had settled back down to what passed for normal. Second Lieutenant Teal's buzzard had left the barracks under a cloud after the unfortunate, if cherished incident concerning the Adjutant's bird table, a tale which it must be said imprinted itself firmly into regimental lore; it now seemed that falconry was a sport that the Army felt it could live without. In the meantime, Teal's life returned to the daily routine of parades, range work, map reading exercises and of course the inevitable extra duties that came his way as a result of what he viewed as unfortunate misunderstandings. The Adjutant, on the other hand, saw them rather differently.

Teal had to do something, he decided, to break up the monotony of his daily life and rapidly came to the conclusion that a ferret might be just the solution. In any other regiment this might have been considered 'not quite the thing' for an officer, but the Glamorgan Fusiliers were cut from a different cloth. Eccentricity, to them, was a valued quality. For example, there was a long-standing and deep-seated admiration for the battalion second-in-command, the younger son of a peer, who had an impressive private income and was widely considered to be the untidiest officer in the Army. It was rumoured that he had vowed never to let an iron make contact with his battledress trousers, and he was known (though never to his face) by the nickname of Wurzel. Then there was the Operations Officer, a languid old Harrovian, who once offered the Colonel-in-Chief, a senior member of the Royal family, a hand-rolled cigarette. Legend records that the 'tab' was accepted gratefully and indeed relished. Yes, a ferret would fit in well enough with the regimental ethos.

Enquiries in the public bar of The Rat & Drainpipe put Teal in contact with Big Eddie. The latter, a dubious character of indeterminate age, could always be relied upon for supplies of fresh salmon or pheasant, in or out of season, with no questions asked or answered. He was happy to help. Over a quiet pint a deal was struck and Eddie left the bar for an undisclosed destination. Minutes later he was back. Money changed hands and Teal found himself the proud owner of a pretty little jill with bright pink eyes, soft white fur and, he quickly discovered, a set of teeth like a vice.

Accommodation for his new acquisition did not prove to be a problem. It would have been unlike Teal to have planned that far ahead, but luckily the stout cardboard box that normally contained his best parade hat proved an ideal receptacle, once emptied. But by the time he went to check on his charge the next morning, she had already demonstrated her powers as an escapologist and was not discovered until several hours later, curled up and sleeping happily on a pile of rags. The cleaning lady, in whose cupboard she had taken refuge, was unimpressed and fled screaming up the corridor in search of the Mess Manager. Thus it was that the Adjutant learned of Teal's latest acquisition.

The interview in the Adjutant's office was, Teal reflected afterwards, a little terse, but he could not help admiring the man's self-control. He had been frightfully laid back, in fact – his moustache had barely twitched throughout, the vocabulary was less inventive than usual, and although there had been the usual exhortations regarding 'proper control' and 'last chances', he had even forgotten to hand out the customary extra duties. The regular awards of the latter made Teal a particular favourite among his fellow subalterns, as their share of Orderly Officer duties was vastly reduced, freeing up their lives considerably for beer and romance, sometimes both. Thus Teal, under strict instructions not to deviate from his intended path, made for the Regimental Pioneers, who had made such a fine job of constructing the Adjutant's bird table. For the second time in twenty-four hours, money changed hands and by teatime a solidly built hutch, with double thickness chicken wire and stout locks, stood in one of the Mess garages. The Mess Manager had got to the Adjutant first, leaving Teal under no illusions about the possibility of keeping the ferret in his room.

The little jill became tamer by the day and was quickly a Mess favourite as well as Teal's platoon mascot. Her regular treat was to be allowed into the bar every evening after dinner, and Teal's friends rapidly discovered that there was nothing she enjoyed more than a saucer of Old Belcher's Carthorse Bitter. This, regrettably, had to be stopped after the jill became overwrought one night, scampered at full tilt into a wall and staggered off in search of somewhere warm and quiet to recover. The sanctuary turned out to be a tweed jacket left rather unwisely under a chair; the owner only became aware of the fact much later when searching a pocket for his pipe and finding something rather more unpleasant instead.

Unlike Teal's much-maligned buzzard, and to the very great surprise of his friends, the ferret turned out to be a very capable huntress. A variety of warrens at the local rifle range complex produced vast quantities of rabbits and, as Teal's proficiency with purse nets grew under the expert tutelage of two of his soldiers, so did the size of the bag. There was the occasional surprise as well; just what the shelduck was doing down a rabbit hole Teal never managed to fathom, but man, bird and ferret had a considerable shock and the very devil of a time disentangling it from the net. Inevitably, on some occasions the jill refused to come meekly to hand, but soon, in the best military tradition, a contingency plan was established. A runner would be despatched to the company lines, *Operation Weasel* declared, and Teal's platoon would mobilise to recover their by now much-loved mascot. The resulting accumulated excavations eventually made the Channel Tunnel itself appear as if the work of a child in a sandpit.

The Mess Manager was happy, too, as the fruits of Teal's labours came to supplement the messing account which he always complained was too meagre. Recipes took forms including rabbit casserole, *lapin au vin, coniglio alla cacciatora* and a host of others that appeared regularly on the menu, albeit disguised. Subterfuges were, alas, necessary; too many mess members had been raised on tales of *Peter Rabbit* (some, the Adjutant and other more senior officers might have maintained, still read them, lips moving). The occasional strange-looking chicken bone was easily explained away as an especially large fowl, and most diners were blissfully unaware of their supper's provenance. For once, Teal was proving a success.

It couldn't last, of course. The jill hadn't escaped from her hutch once since it was first built, so why, of all times, did she choose to do so on the evening of the Christmas Ladies' Night? (Later examination of the hutch showed it to be locked solidly with no visible holes, so eventually the general consensus was that the hand of a playful subaltern was involved.) The occasion was a special one, one of the few when wives and girlfriends were permitted to join the men to dine in the Mess. In later years, of course, husbands and boyfriends would come to be guests as well, but in those days the Mess was a very male preserve. The affair was always glittering: officers dressed in their mess kit of blues, reds and generous amounts of gold braid, the ladies in finery which seldom saw the outside of the wardrobe and smelt, perhaps, just ever so slightly of mothballs. The regimental band would play in the minstrels' gallery above the dining room, vast amounts of silver (most of which was the booty of long past campaigns from beyond the days of Empire) were laid out in force, and the light was provided by a host of flickering candles. Rabbit, for once, did not feature on the menu.

The main course had just been served when the jill appeared on the top table, peeking coyly at the Colonel's wife from behind a large silver salver. The latter, a slight lady possessed of a nervous disposition, stared incredulously at the ferret for a moment, in total disbelief at what she was seeing. An expensive and supposedly all-encompassing education involving Roedean and Girton College had certainly not prepared her for this. The ferret stared back for a moment and then decided to make friends, scampering forward and putting its front paws on the edge of the lady's dinner plate before sniffing its contents appreciatively.

Teal, alerted to events by sniggering colleagues at the far end of the table, did not help matters. Swiftly leaving his seat in what he deemed an excusable breach of Mess etiquette – it was not really done until the toasts had been drunk – he thought to rectify the situation by scooping up the jill and then thrust it towards the Colonel's lady while inviting her to give it a pat. A short, sharp shriek was followed by a crash of crockery and cutlery, as the poor woman's constitution could stand the ordeal no longer and resolved it by fainting.

It was inevitable that the ferret would follow in the footsteps of the buzzard, and it was duly returned to Eddie at The Rat & Drainpipe. Naturally, no refund was forthcoming. The hutch was commandeered by the Colonel by way of reparation, to provide a home for his children's guinea pigs. As for Teal himself, his place in regimental legend was sealed as he became the only officer ever awarded no less than fifty-six extra duties, completed on a day-on, day-off basis.

Ferreting was clearly no longer an officer sport, even in the Glamorgan Fusiliers. The mainstream beckoned; it was time to find some shooting and get himself a dog instead.

Keeper's Tip: Be aware of where your gun is pointing at all times: be muzzle aware.

Dingbat

From the Regimental Records of the Glamorgan Fusiliers

The Glamorgan Fusiliers, like so many others, was a 'doggy' regiment, and a visitor to the Officers' Mess needed to watch his footing carefully at the morning coffee break if he were not to trip over one of the dozen or so assorted breeds that roamed freely while their owners discussed the affairs of the day. Inevitably, labradors were in the majority: 'Dog, Black, Officer for the Keeping Of' might have run the description in Queen's Regulations.

The Fusiliers, of course, prided themselves on being somewhat different from the rest of the Army. The Quartermaster owned a magnificent Irish wolfhound by the name of Harriet, capable of emptying an entire coffee table of biscuits in a passing sweep of its cavernous mouth, and famed throughout the battalion for spectacularly clearing the CO's desk in one breathtaking act of sheer exuberance. Unfortunately the CO was behind it at the time, in the act of admonishing a defaulter, when roughly nine stone of animated fur suddenly hurtled along the length of his desk.

Harriet was by nature a gentle soul until it came to cats. Only one of the feral animals that lived around the Quartermaster's department had ever stood its ground, arched its back and hissed at her, an act usually guaranteed to cause a normal dog to back down. On this occasion the cat had made a tragic mistake, and the poor creature's fellows quickly learned to seek the safety of a tree whenever Harriet made an appearance.

The Paymaster had a Staffordshire bull terrier. This dog, named Bodger, was widely admired for his party trick: this entailed him biting onto a whippy branch, pulled low enough by his owner for him to latch onto and then, as the branch was released, he would swing several feet into the air. There he would stay suspended for a couple of minutes, growling and worrying at the branch with evident pleasure, until reluctantly persuaded to return to *terra firma*. Meanwhile the Regimental Sergeant Major, a huge bear of a man with a waxed moustache, a chestful of medals and an awesome fighting reputation, would walk between his military quarters and barracks daily with the family pet peeking coyly out of his greatcoat pocket.This animal was a tiny Yorkshire terrier, which his children had named Fluffy.

Even the CO had a dog, Susie the Jack Russell, an endearing and friendly creature who travelled everywhere with her master, sitting cheerfully in a basket on the front of his bicycle as he cycled daily between his married quarter and Battalion Headquarters. She would then occupy her bed in the corner of his office until it was time to visit one of the many areas of her owner's command, trotting happily at his heel unless distracted into a brief, unsuccessful but satisfying chase should a squirrel be spotted. Her only real misdemeanour had been to misappropriate a dummy rabbit belonging to Second Lieutenant Teal during his brief foray into falconry and leave it festering quietly under a file in the Adjutant's office. The Adjutant did not like dogs, but, realising that he stood alone among his fellows in this matter, he had enough sense not to advertise the fact.

It was against this background that Teal, after his disastrous attempts at maintaining first a buzzard and then a ferret in a military environment, decided that a dog was the way forward. A silent sigh of relief went around the Officers' Mess that common sense had finally prevailed. So it was that Dingbat joined the Order of Battle.

Teal had chosen the name for no reason other than that he liked it, but it was uncannily apt. The dog in question, a re-homed springer spaniel that a fellow officer about to be posted abroad had assured him was part-trained, had a trustworthy, butter-wouldn't-melt sort of face, but fitted his name perfectly. For in those pre-computer days, the word dingbat had two meanings. As a gently abusive Army slang term it meant a somewhat empty-headed, scatty or unreliable person, although in this case it might have been an unfair description. It was also the common name for the No 7 Mark 1 anti-personnel mine, a device resembling a miniature clay pigeon dressed in a camouflage jacket, which was designed to turn up unexpectedly and do a surprising amount of damage for something so small.

Whilst unreliable, Dingbat was not stupid. He'd already encountered the Regimental Goat and been put swiftly to flight, so concluded that anything bigger than him needed to be given a wide berth. He and Teal rapidly became inseparable though this did not deter occasional disappearances as Dingbat quickly discovered dustbins, a source of incredible joy and surprising treats. His regular raids left a trail of devastation at the back of the various Messes and canteens, although such were his ghostlike comings and goings that the blame was inevitably pinned on other, less circumspect canines. A besotted Teal would not listen to suggestions that his faultless companion might be capable of such crimes, and blithely visited the Guardroom on a regular basis to collect him from the Regimental Police. Indeed, Dingbat was a favourite of these custodians of military discipline, and would happily jump into the back of their Land Rover in the knowledge that a supply of biscuits awaited him while his master was summoned to pick him up.

Training turned out to be remarkably straightforward; Dingbat's previous owner had indeed laid the foundations well. In what seemed no time at all progress was being made, although Teal might have warned the Guardroom that he would be firing a starting pistol as part of the training routine. It was bad luck that the barracks was on high alert at the time, and the Adjutant was not amused that the Quick Reaction Platoon had been scrambled to surround a bemused spaniel and his rather more alarmed owner on the rugby pitch. Teal might also have familiarised himself more carefully with the dummy launcher before loading it with a .22 blank and firing it accidentally at waist level. Luckily nobody was in the way, and he saw the shattered car window as easily rectified, although a regrettable expense. That it was the Adjutant's new sports car, though, was unfortunate, as was the fact that the Adjutant was watching from his office window at the time. Still, such things have to be put down to experience Teal thought resignedly, polishing his Sam Browne belt to a high gloss before heading off to inspect the Guard for what was to be the first of fourteen successive nights.

As training progressed, to the amazement of his fellows Teal found himself the owner of a biddable, if occasionally quirky dog. Every evening, Dingbat would wait patiently outside the dining room, where all dogs were forbidden to enter, until his master had finished eating, then join him in the bar before an evening walk. If the spaniel had one less than wholesome habit, it was the attraction to him of fox dung. Like Dingbat, the local foxes also appreciated a plentiful supply of poorly secured dustbins and left frequent evidence of their nocturnal visits about the barracks. On one particularly warm summer's day, Teal and the Operations Officer were walking across to a lecture (it was a particularly ambitious talk on temperance, to be delivered by the Padre) with Bodger at heel and Dingbat ranging ahead of them. As a car approached, Teal raised his hand and gave a short whistle; Dingbat, thirty yards away, looked back and promptly sat to await further instructions. The Operations Officer expressed his admiration while Teal preened, not noticing that Dingbat had been distracted by a fox offering and was now on his back in it, doing his best to disguise his own scent in the most efficient way a dog knows. The lecture saw the subaltern and his springer banished to a far corner of the hall, unloved and unwanted. It was with great relief that Teal discovered the scent-neutralising properties of tomato ketchup shortly afterwards, even though ownership of a pink dog quickly attracted some ribald comments.

In his long and distinguished career in the Glamorgan Fusiliers, Dingbat committed but one truly heinous crime, and this in fact went unreported. It was unfortunate that the Second in Command, a patriotic Welshman, had chosen to utilise the term 'drubbing' when gleefully describing that weekend's events at what was then the Four Nations match at the Cardiff Arms Park. The CO, an Englishman, had taken as much offence at the comment as it was intended to give, especially with that year's championship hanging in the balance. Heated words followed on both sides – much to be regretted later, when apologies were exchanged and friendly relations renewed over several glasses of claret.

The 2IC left the CO's office and returned to his own. He entered the already open door, only to be greeted by the sight of Susie the terrier and Dingbat tied at the successful conclusion of a tryst made inevitable by her coming, unnoticed, into season. The 2IC, smiling quietly to himself, quietly closed the door and left them to it.

A little over two months later, five pups were delivered in the kitchen of the CO's married quarter, to the great delight of his daughters. Liver and white markings had somehow crept into the black and tan of their mother, while feathered tails, long legs and rounded ears with a distinct tendency to flop down hinted gently at the identity of the father. Teal, in all innocence, never knew what had happened, whilst the CO could never be sure but frequently looked askance as subaltern and spaniel passed by: however it was generally acknowledged that these were the best hunting, retrieving and ratting dogs ever seen on a shoot day.

The 2IC may have chuckled to himself in private but the local squirrels never saw things the same way again.

> **Keeper's Tip:** Always make sure you know what can and cannot be shot, and don't be afraid to ask if necessary. Many shoots have strict rules regarding ground game.

When you have shot one bird flying you have shot all birds flying. They are all different and they fly in different ways but the sensation is the same and the last one is as good as the first. **Ernest Hemingway, journalist and author**

You Can Tell a Man by His Dog

My father always used to maintain that you can tell a lot about a man by the dog he keeps, and as you look around you on a shoot day it can often seem that there is a lot of truth in this. A professional deerstalking friend, well known for his blunt and uncompromising nature, owns a German wirehaired pointer that nips me every time I visit. It's not a serious bite, mind, but just enough to remind you that he is there and who is in charge. There are exceptions to the rule of course. An Army colleague once owned a standard poodle called Poppy. As the man stood over six feet tall and served in the SAS nobody saw any need to offer comment.

In my own regiment one man and his dog were made for each other. The dog was a red setter, a breed never really noted for its intelligence, bullishness or, let's be frank, trainability (here I must apologise to any owner of a red setter which is a paragon of virtue – I just haven't ever met one). Like its owner (who was also, incidentally, red-haired) the dog was constantly wandering off, never there when you wanted it, and couldn't remember any instructions it had been given for more than a few seconds – if it even had plans to obey them at all.

One day I was chatting with the Commanding Officer in his office. He, in his own sly way, was trying to get me to offer comment on one of many recent disasters created by the owner of the setter. I thought for a moment, unwilling to drop my friend in it, and found the perfect answer by quoting my father's assertion. The Colonel thought for a moment and smiled with an unusual degree of admiration. 'Thank you, that sums things up rather nicely. Well done. Now, tell me what do you think about black labs?'

Too late, the CO's dog came to mind, a young black labrador with the energy and grace of the cartoon Tasmanian Devil,

which had only that morning at coffee break shredded two very expensive Officers' Mess cushions, cocked its leg on the Padre's briefcase, and left an unpleasant reminder of its presence in the cloakroom. Feeling a little uncomfortable, I glanced downwards to see my own springer upside down on the rug in front of the CO's desk, front legs in the air and back ones akimbo, wriggling and grunting with evident pleasure as it eased an itch on its back that no paw could reach.

There was no option but to backtrack clumsily, make my excuses and flee.

Civilized life has altogether grown too tame, and, if it is to be stable, it must provide a harmless outlet for the impulses which our remote ancestors satisfied in hunting. **Bertrand Russell, philosopher**

Keeper's Tip: When practical, keep your gun broken until it needs to be made ready for use.

Tales from Glen Garron

Mixed Tidings

One for sorrow, two for joy
Three for a wedding, four for a boy
Five for silver, six for gold
Seven for a secret ne'er to be told
Eight a wish and nine a kiss
Ten's a bird you ought not miss

The people of Glen Garron are not normally superstitious by nature, but magpies have always held a special place in local folklore. It was unusual to see the birds in any numbers; Willie and Archie Cameron's concerted, continual pest control campaigns with gun and Larsen trap made sure of that, so old Mrs McKenzie, whose son and daughter-in-law ran the Post Office, would always bow and greet a magpie with civility as her grandparents had taught her instead of holding her collar until she had seen four more to forestall bad luck. More than one forefinger would touch a forehead in surreptitious salute if one was noticed, and even the Colonel, that most sensible of men, could be heard to mutter 'Good morning Mr Magpie, please give my regards to Mrs Magpie and all her baby Magpies' if one chanced to fly overhead.

So it was that the black and white shapes busily picking over the old carcase of a sheep in a lower field were greeted in different ways. Lady Mary, driving past on her way to the shops in Inverness, saw only the four perched on top of the woolly mound. She smiled to herself and secretly hoped for another grandson to spoil. Willie, watching from higher up the hill, counted seven and wondered what the secret might be. Another set of eyes saw eight and made a fervent wish.

Archie, travelling behind Lady Mary and rather less prone to superstition, merely stopped his pick-up and reached behind him for the shotgun. At the report the remaining birds scattered in various directions, one passing directly over where Willie and his companion were sitting. Willie, unarmed, simply saluted it carefully. From the passenger seat of the Land Rover Nick Highworth, a relative newcomer to Glen Garron who had already learned to be wary of Willie's sense of humour, laughed at him and ignored the bird. 'Ye'll no' want to anger Dodiag,' he was told, to his snorting amusement. Willie shrugged, and together they drove on up the hill to see how the nesting grouse were getting on and if there were any early broods.

Two hours later, well out onto the moor, Willie almost dismissed the white shape in the distance as a rock. Something made him study it more closely; as he watched, the shape spread broad, white wings and took off, clutching something in its talons. Willie tracked it with his binoculars. As the bird came closer, he was just able to make out that the object was a young mountain hare before the great white owl and its prey dropped into the heather. Momentarily forgetting the incredulous Nick Highworth standing alongside him, Willie whistled softly to himself and scrambled up a nearby boulder to get a better view. From there he saw the female snowy owl, larger and slightly darker than its pure white mate, rise from a depression in the ground to receive the offering of food.

'Isn't that…?' started Nick.

'Aye,' Willie forestalled the rest of the sentence. 'We haven't seen one of those here in twenty years, and ne'er a nesting pair o' snowies.' Clearly this was the 'secret ne'er to be told' that the magpies had warned of, and the keeper now wished that he had not given in to Nick's request to accompany him onto the hill. 'No' a word to anyone,' he admonished, swearing Nick to secrecy with a forbidding glare. The last thing he wanted was the moor invaded by twitchers: they would undoubtedly disturb the grouse and the nesting waders as they drove their four-wheel-drive vehicles recklessly over the delicate heather in the endless quest for a sighting or a photograph. Worse yet, there was one person in the village he didn't trust at all. Sandy Macpherson, a retired teacher, was known to have an extensive egg collection, and what would he do if word reached him of the incredibly rare birds out on the moor? Willie had never heard of snowy owls nesting this far south. It was probably a once in a lifetime event in these parts, and it simply had to succeed.

That evening in The Kelpie, Willie was horrified to overhear Nick starting to tell the landlord of the day's excitement. Fortunately it was early and the bar was virtually empty; Willie detached a complaining Nick from his conversation with Ally and led him to a corner table.

'Will ye no' keep your trap weel shut?' he hissed.

'Oh come on,' Nick replied. 'What's the harm?' It seemed that Willie's concerns about Nick's ability to keep a secret were well founded; the man loved to tell a story and flaunt his knowledge, and it was clear that something desperate would have to be done if word of the snowy owl nest was not to get out.

'Auld Dodiag, that's the harm,' Willie explained. Behind the bar, Ally overheard the name and carefully touched the wooden counter for luck. 'Ye didnae salute her this morning, and she'll curse ye if you dinna keep her secret.' He recounted the tale of the seven magpies he had seen on the dead sheep that morning and the forthcoming secret they had foretold. Dodiag, he explained to Nick, was a witch of Gaelic legend who, it was said, took the form of a magpie – it was she whom you had to salute to avoid bad luck, and ignoring her warning might result in a wicked curse. Generations of Glen Garron parents had used her as a dire threat to misbehaving children.

Nick slapped the table with his hand and laughed out loud. 'Dear Lord, you Highlanders are a raw lot!' he exclaimed. 'Do you really expect me to fall for that one?' He recalled an earlier incident when he had been tricked into believing that a big cat had stashed a sheep carcase high in a tree, and then supposedly attacked Archie Cameron, causing Nick a near heart attack and making him a laughing stock for many weeks to follow. 'You'll not get me that way again!'

Willie sighed as Nick bade him goodnight and left, still chuckling, for home and supper. It was time, the keeper thought, to have a chat with his son Archie.

The next morning Nick awoke to the sound of chattering from

outside his bedroom window. Drawing back the curtains he was confronted by a magpie: it eyed him through the glass with no sign of alarm before flying off to perch on the garage roof, calling once more before departing. Nick was about to turn away when he realised that his brand new Land Rover was no longer where he had parked it on his return the previous evening. Throwing on a dressing gown, he sped downstairs and out of the front door to find that the vehicle had rolled, handbrake off, down the slight slope before gently coming to rest in the privet hedge.

Fortunately there was no damage done. Nick sighed with relief, started the Land Rover and returned it to its proper place on the driveway, carefully applying the handbrake and leaving the vehicle in gear for good measure. He saw that his daily bottle of milk, delivered from the local shop, was on the doorstep. Picking it up, he returned inside and made a cup of tea. Opening the fresh bottle he tipped in a splash, which curdled instantly into white, unappetising lumps. As he resolved to have a stiff word with the shop about supplying him with sour milk, he could have sworn that he heard the chatter of a magpie outside, though on looking out of the window he could not see one.

The rest of the day went ever further downhill. As he left the house an hour later, Nick discovered that one of his tyres was now flat, though after exchanging it for the spare he could find no sign of a puncture. Some bird, however, had perched on the wheel recently and relieved itself messily over both rubber and valve. He drove to the filling station fifteen miles away to reinflate it and fill up the fuel tank for a long-planned visit. A sign proclaimed that there was no fuel, and that the next delivery was not expected for a few days. Nick cursed; now he wouldn't be able to get to the gunsmith to collect his new shotgun in time for the next day's clay shoot. He had been looking forward to the event for some time and had bragged to anyone who would listen about the gun, a bespoke model with high grade walnut stick and personalised engraving depicting his features and a covey of grouse. Having advertised its arrival so publicly he was now going to look rather foolish. In the background a magpie chattered. Nick looked for it unsuccessfully, shook his head, reinflated his tyre using the garage air pump and headed home instead.

On the way back he stopped at the shop for a few supplies and bumped into Willie, to whom he recounted his woes. Willie gazed at him sadly. 'Aye, that would be Dodiag,' he was told. Nick snorted in derision and went home.

No sooner had he got through the door than the telephone rang. It was his daughter Amanda, currently spending a long weekend in London with her mother. To Nick's mounting alarm she told him that she had decided to forsake life in Glen Garron and take a job she had been offered in Australia. Nick was horrified; he doted on his daughter and couldn't bear the thought of being separated from her by six thousand miles, left alone with a wife who complained constantly about life 'in the sticks'. As the conversation ended he put the phone down and gazed distractedly into the middle distance, wondering if his dream of retirement in the Highlands was simply not to be. Outside, a flash of something black and white caught his eye and was gone.

He sat disconsolately on a kitchen chair, lost in thought, when a *tap-tap-tap* on the window disturbed him: he looked up just in time to see a black beak and head disappear. By the time he got to the door there was nothing there.

He called Willie. 'Listen, old boy, I don't believe in your mumbo-jumbo about old Dodie or whatever her name is, but just in case, if there was such a thing as a curse, how do you lift it?'

'Ye're a wise man,' he was told. 'Come over to my place, I know wha' tae do.'

Nick drove up the driveway to the Lodge, turning off towards the keeper's cottage where Willie was waiting for him. He led him into the kitchen. A not entirely pleasant smell was coming from a frying pan where two bird's legs, black feet still attached, lay sizzling. 'What on earth are those?' Nick asked.

'Pyat,' he was told, to his confusion. 'Och, magpie to you,' Willie explained. 'The only way to lift the curse is to eat them while swearing to make right wha' ye have made wrong.'

Nick considered. If there was even the slightest chance of rectifying matters, and his beloved Amanda being persuaded to change her mind about emigrating, it would be worth it. He swore to Dodiag that no further word would he breathe about the snowy owls, and with a grimace devoured both legs. Willie, in a rare moment of weakness, allowed him to leave the feet. Outside, a magpie rattled its call briefly in the distance and then was silent. Nick arrived home to find the light flashing on his answerphone. Pressing the play button, he was overwhelmed to hear Amanda's voice telling him that the Australia job had fallen through and, really, she loved life in Glen Garron far too much to leave. He recalled his vow to the witch and resolved to keep it no matter what.

Archie pulled up outside Willie's cottage. 'All done?' he enquired of his father. 'Aye,' Willie replied, 'that should do it. You can put yon tame birdie back intae the Larsen. The call and decoy can go in the shed, and tell Amanda that I owe her. I think we'll take your Ma for supper and a wee dram at The Kelpie – it's been a braw day which calls for a wee celebration, and I need to stand Angus from the garage a drink. I've a funny feeling that I can persuade one awfu' daft Sassenach to buy us a round or two as well.'

By the time that the grouse season opened, four white owlets had fledged successfully from the nest on the moor, watched over from a safe distance by Willie, Archie and a more than willing Nick. Willie was quite satisfied that they and their parents had moved on before driving that corner of the moor for the Colonel's first shooting day, and hoped fervently that the birds would return again next year.

So did someone else. Sandy Macpherson frequently walked the moors and had spotted the nesting owls long before Willie Cameron had ever set eyes on them. He had watched Willie and Nick from a distance and was happy that they should keep the matter to themselves. Yes, it was true that he had an egg collection but it had been passed down the family from a Victorian ancestor; a keen birdwatcher but certainly no collector, he was vaguely ashamed of it but kept it for old time's sake. As superstitious as any man, he too had seen the magpies gathered on the dead sheep and taken the opportunity to make a wish. Once the owls had fledged and flown it had come to fruition.

To this day, from its accustomed perch in the top boughs of a Caledonian pine on the edge of the moor overlooking both Lodge and village, a single magpie frequently watches unseen and chatters quietly to itself as the people of Glen Garron go about their daily business. Had anyone ever heard it, they might have sworn that it sounded for all the world like laughter.

Keeper's Tip: Carry a simple cleaning kit in the car. This may mean the difference between having to abandon a day or being able to clear a blocked barrel and carry on.

Vegetarianism is harmless enough, though it is apt to fill a man with wind and self-righteousness. **Sir Robert Hutchinson, President of the Royal College of Physicians 1938-1941**

A Cautionary Tale

Not far from Inverness, eight Guns and our partners were walking up grouse on the opening day of the season, the Glorious Twelfth of August. The keeper at the centre controlled proceedings with a mixture of arm signals and radio commands; I was on the right-hand end of the line, equipped with a small hand-held walkie-talkie, as was our party leader far off to the left.

A blur of movement erupted from the feet of my neighbouring Gun, proving to be a blue hare that was fired at twice before crossing my front to drop, clearly lung shot, just beyond the electric fence which marked the limit of the estate's march and with which I had been instructed to keep in line. The fence was low and I felt that I could just reach it by hand. A careful tap with a finger suggested that it was turned off. Unloading my gun and laying it to one side I reached across to retrieve the hare.

The next thing I knew I was picking myself up several feet away from the fence, to the accompaniment of delighted whoops and laughter from the remainder of the shooting party. The radio crackled and a laconic voice sounded from the other side of the moor. 'Nice one, Sparky.'

ON & OFF THE PEG

A FATHER'S ADVICE

If a sportsman true you'd be
Listen carefully to me…

Never, never let your gun
Pointed be at anyone.
That it may unloaded be
Matters not the least to me.

When a hedge or fence you cross
Though of time it cause a loss
From your gun the cartridge take
For the greater safety's sake.

If 'twixt you and neighbouring Gun
Bird shall fly or beast may run
Let this maxim ere be thine:
'Follow not across the line.'

Stops and beaters oft unseen
Lurk behind some leafy screen.
Calm and steady always be:
'Never shoot where you can't see.'

You may kill or you may miss
But at all times think this:
'All the pheasants ever bred
Won't repay for one man dead.'

***Mark Beaufoy*, 1902**

Mark Hanbury Beaufoy (1854-1922) lived a life packed with achievement. Educated at Eton and Trinity Hall, Cambridge, he played football to county standard, supported the radical concept of an eight-hour working day and introduced it to his vinegar firm in Lambeth, and was elected as a Liberal Member of Parliament for Kennington. He was High Sheriff for Wiltshire and also served as a Justice of the Peace. He founded the Beaufoy Institute in Lambeth to succeed the 'ragged school' which his family had established before the Education Act of 1870, and continued a long Beaufoy family tradition as a benefactor of the City of London School. He also served as Chairman of the Kennel Club for the two years before his death.

Yet it is for none of these things that he is remembered, but rather for a short piece of verse he wrote for the eldest of his three sons, Henry, to accompany the gift of a 28 bore shotgun on the boy's fifteenth birthday in 1902. Beaufoy had two shoots, one at Coombe House near Shaftesbury and another at Ashmore in Dorset, and all three boys were enthusiastic Shots. Sadly the youngest, Robert, lost an arm during the 1914-18 war, but became a renowned one-armed Shot. George, the middle son, was killed when a bomb fell on the family vinegar distillery during the Second World War.

A hundred copies of the poem presented to Henry (which came to be known as 'A Father's Advice'), were printed and given away to friends. It quickly became popular among the shooting fraternity and circulated far more extensively than the writer ever intended. Furthermore, Beaufoy did not always receive the credit; a gamekeeper in Sussex sent the poem to a magazine claiming it as his own; others said that it had been found among the effects of a British officer killed in South Africa; and it was also suggested in the *Sporting Times* that the headmaster of a school had written it (the headmaster in question quickly refuted this). It was widely reprinted, usually without permission, and gunmakers included copies in boxes of cartridges. The poem was said to have been popular at Sandringham, and was even posted in the grouse butts at Glenkirk, Inverness-shire.

Eventually Beaufoy himself wrote to the *Sporting Times* to admit authorship in 1910, concluding of the verses: 'Perhaps they have not been wholly useless – if so I am amply rewarded.'

Despite being referred to as 'Commander' Mark Beaufoy on some subsequent copies of his work, serving in the Royal Navy was not one of his many life achievements. Extra verses have been added by other writers from time to time, but Beaufoy never did so. It is said that he did intend a further verse, warning against resting a gun against a wall where it might be knocked over with disastrous consequences, but never wrote it. One unknown hand provided an addition, 'After Mark Beaufoy', to a copy in the Glenkirk butts, which read:

Do not curiously enquire
Your neighbour's bag, how oft he fire;
'I hope you had some sport' you'll say;
At least that is the better way.

The original recipient of the poem, Henry Beaufoy, like his father before him also served as a High Sheriff, this time for Oxfordshire. He was visited by a writer for *The Field* in 1956, at which time he was sixty-nine years old and living at Steeple Aston in Oxfordshire. He still owned, and remained immensely proud of, the gun he had received along with his father's verses when he was fifteen. He also had on display, preserved in a glass case, the first bird that he had ever shot with it – a dabchick. He died in 1958.

Despite its age, the poem has never lost its validity or popularity, and most game Shots are able to quote at least the first verse. Many will admit to having to prove that they could recite it in full to a parent or relative before being allowed to learn to shoot. Purdey, the renowned gunmakers, offer a version printed on a pocket handkerchief and you can buy beautifully produced contemporary prints of it, illustrated by the likes of popular country artists Rodger McPhail and Bryn Parry. Even today, you could do a lot worse than hang a copy on the bedroom wall of a shooting-mad youngster as a gentle reminder of how to behave in the field.

Keeper's Tip: Carry a small first-aid kit in your pocket or game bag. The chances are that you will never need it, but if you do it may be in a hurry.

BASIC SHOOTING ETIQUETTE

Not everyone has benefited from a thorough introduction to shooting by parents, family or friends, and the etiquette of the shooting field can sometimes be a bit daunting to newcomers. There's no need to worry, though, and etiquette is no longer the matter of rigid rules and behaviour that it was in days gone by. Here are a few guidelines which will ensure that you will be accepted anywhere.

SAFETY, SAFETY, SAFETY

A safe Gun is a welcome Gun. Others will be able to relax around you and you will enjoy the day more yourself. From the moment you take the shotgun out of the slip, demonstrate safe handling and be 'muzzle aware'.

WHAT TO WEAR?

You don't need a matching three-piece tweed suit; though it's nice to have one for a very formal day, you might look out of place wearing it on a less formal occasion. You really can't go wrong with a shooting coat (or waistcoat for warmer early season days) over a Tattersall check shirt and an appropriate tie. 'Plus two' breeks in tweed, moleskin or any other appropriate material complete the outfit. By all means go for 'plus fours' (meaning that they end four inches below the knee) or longer if you must – but beware, the Bertie Wooster look has long been out of fashion. You'll want shooting stockings and garters (nobody's going to check if they are elasticated), and this is where you can reasonably display a bit of sartorial elegance with brighter colours if you like. Wellies or boots with gaiters protect your feet; a pair of brogues for dry days are equally acceptable. Having said all that, many people I know turn out for syndicate days in sensible trousers such as moleskins and wearing black gumboots, and nobody is bothered. Just keep the colours subdued. And don't forget a hat; a traditional tweed flat cap suits most people but I've seen some wonderfully eccentric headgear over the years.

YOUR GUN

You're safe with a side-by-side, and these days over-and-unders are increasingly popular. Be prepared for frowns, though, if you opt for a pump or semi-auto on driven shoots, unless you are amongst good friends! Don't forget to take plenty of cartridges, and check if you are going to need non-toxic loads for duck drives and the like.

THE MEET

Plan to be there slightly early and ready for the off, suited and booted, at the appointed time. Most shoots like to start with a briefing on the drives that are planned, safety, quarry species and the like. Time is probably of the essence to fit everything in and it can be frustrating to have to wait for someone. One sporting doctor of my acquaintance was notorious for his lateness, so we ended up telling him that the start was half-an-hour earlier than it really was. He'd still be the last to arrive, though.

PEGS

If the day involves allocating peg numbers (usually a card in a cleft stick which indicates where you'll stand for each drive), usually done by a draw, don't forget your number, and make a note of it if your memory is likely to let you down. You'll probably have to add two or three to the number so that you move up for each successive drive, giving every Gun a chance of being on a prime peg or two as the day progresses. Don't be disappointed if your peg produces less shooting than the others – it is literally the luck of the draw, and your chance will come in due course.

ALCOHOL

The odd nip from a hip flask is fine, but don't forget to offer it round! Most Guns have their preferred tipple, usually based on cherry brandy, sloe gin, whisky or other warming tinctures, but don't be tempted to overdo it. Alcohol and firearms can be a potentially dangerous combination.

BETWEEN DRIVES

Carry your gun in a slip, or at least broken and over your arm where all can see that there are no cartridges in it. Don't load up again until on your peg or placed in position. Keep the noise down, especially when moving into position – the birds are not stupid and will try to move away quietly from any threat.

DURING THE DRIVE

Keep quiet and still on your peg, and don't be tempted to move away from it unless specifically given permission to seek a slightly better position by your host. Don't be tempted to poach your neighbour's birds, and only shoot at those within your legitimate arc of fire. If your neighbour has just missed with both barrels, by all means have a shot if the bird is within range and a safe target. Mark where your birds fall so that you can give pickers-up a reasonable steer when the drive is over.

Don't shoot at birds which are flying poorly or too close. By the same token, avoid unduly long shots where you are more likely to wound rather than kill outright – shoot within the capabilities of yourself and your gun. If you have been asked to walk with the beaters, only shoot at birds breaking back unless told otherwise, and always unload your gun before crossing obstacles such as fences, or ditches that have to be jumped.

Don't shoot ground game such as hares or rabbits unless specifically told to do so. Many shoots prohibit this for reasons of safety. In some places an exception may be made for foxes but remember that you will be loaded with smaller shot than you'd normally use for such a large quarry, so make sure that your target is close enough to be killed effectively. Whatever the case, be very aware of the background before taking any shot, and if your neighbouring Gun is a hunting type you might be better off leaving Charlie well alone – lifelong friendships have been known to end over lesser things!

SHOOT SAFELY

Look for blue sky around your bird, do not shoot at low birds that may have beaters or pickers-up concealed behind them, and above all don't swing your muzzles through the line of Guns. If you're fortunate to be invited to shoot grouse, you will often find vertical sticks either side of the front of your butt to obstruct the swing of your barrels and mark the left and right of your safe shooting arc. On one moor I visited this wasn't considered sufficient, and I had to ask the keeper what the two slotted posts halfway between butts were for. He told me, with a straight face, that these were to accommodate the strengthened Perspex sheets that slotted into them on shoot days to prevent the Guns from peppering each other.

AFTER EACH DRIVE

Unload immediately the end of a drive is signalled; if a late bird gets up, let it go unsaluted. When chatting to your fellow Guns, neither boast about your achievements nor moan about missed chances or a lack of sport. Hopefully you will be complimented on a particularly fine shot – accept modestly! Missed shots should only be mentioned by the person who has done the missing.

FINES

Sometimes there is a fine attached to inadvertently shooting something not on the quarry list for the day, such as a white pheasant or guinea fowl. In my part of the world white pheasants are deliberately put down on some shoots to be taken freely by Guns, with the resulting fines being donated to the funds of the local Air Ambulance. Elsewhere though they may be valuable 'marker' birds that the keeper would rather see left alone. Other offences are taken much more seriously – shooting a greyhen after mistaking it for a grouse can cost you a punitive amount of cash on moors where these birds are preserved. If in doubt, don't raise your barrels.

TIPPING THE KEEPER

This can be a difficult area, and I've come across any number of conventions, which are usually based on the size of the bag.It is much easier to ask your host quietly how much is appropriate, and if you've arrived prepared with a variety of banknotes you will have the right ones to hand. At the end of the day the head keeper will receive the Guns to present them with a brace of birds. Have the tip folded discreetly in your hand, and pass it over as you shake hands with him (or, indeed, her). If you get a chance, a word of thanks to the beaters and pickers-up is always appreciated – not enough people bother, and they have been an essential part of your day.

THANKING THE HOST

Even in this digital age, a text or email is not really sufficient. If you have been a guest, a handwritten note to your host, posted as soon after the shoot day as possible, always goes down well.

If I can offer one golden rule: don't be afraid to ask your host if you are unsure of any aspect of the day to come. You will then turn up properly prepared, enjoy your day more, and nobody will think any the worse of you for doing so.

> **Keeper's Tip:** On a formal day, try to mark fallen birds so that you can give the picker-up a clear indication of where they are. A vague 'over there somewhere' is not helpful!

BEHIND THE SCENES ON A GROUSE MOOR

If you want to see serious numbers of red grouse you will need to travel north, not necessarily as far as Scotland though, as some of the premier grouse moors in this country can be found in the North Pennines of County Durham. The southernmost driven grouse moor in England lies in the Peak District, about halfway between Buxton and Macclesfield and with the urban sprawl of Stockport and Manchester surprisingly only some ten miles off to the north-west.

Wherever the moor might lie, that serious grouse shooters are prepared to make the trip doesn't happen by accident. The season, which starts on the Glorious Twelfth of August and closes on 10 December, is all too often cut short by the weather. Ensuring that the grouse are there in sufficient numbers is entirely dependent on year-round work, often under the most arduous conditions. This is real wild bird shooting – you cannot simply release red grouse as you might do with pheasant or partridge. It's all about managing the environment to create a habitat that every pair of wild grouse can fully utilise.

Providing the best possible breeding conditions is vital. A pair of red grouse can produce an average brood of eight or nine, although more are possible and one hen bird was known to hatch and successfully raise a staggering seventeen. Breeding success provides the harvestable surplus on which the moors depend. The weather is one factor beyond any keeper's control and a cold snap at the wrong time can be disastrous, killing both the grouse chicks and the insects upon which they feed.

Constant trapping campaigns are waged against ground predators such as stoats, weasels and rats using tunnels or 'rails' – logs or planks forming crossing points over obstacles such as drains or streams. All traps have to be carefully protected so that non-target species, such as otters, cannot access them. Trapping is essential to keep these small mustelids in check; daily checks are a legal requirement, and the extreme conditions in the hills can reduce their effectiveness so they must be replaced regularly. The ubiquitous Fenn trap – simple, effective and relatively cheap if you are maintaining a trap line of as many as two hundred or more – is a mainstay but future legality may be in doubt. Grouse keepers are already considering replacements. Foxes are simply not tolerated, and many long nights are spent out on the hill with rifle and lamp.

The result of all this predator control does not just benefit the grouse but other ground-nesting birds as well. Waders such as the curlew flourish, as do short-eared owls, merlins, hen harriers – the list goes on, and the modern keeper is realistic about taking a few inevitable losses from protected raptors. It is no accident that you will find a much higher diversity and density of species on a managed moor.

Grouse need grit to aid their digestion, and you will frequently see gritting trays set out at regular intervals across the moor. The development of medicated grit in recent years has proved to be of huge benefit in reducing the strongyle worm, a parasite which lives in the gut of the grouse and has a negative effect on both breeding success and adult bird survival when heavy infestations persist. It is particularly prevalent where grouse populations are high – precisely what the keepers on the big moors are trying to achieve. Medicated grit has helped to reduce worm burdens by some forty percent. Often the trays containing it have a built-in lid, meaning that the grouse can be denied regular access to avoid over-dependency, and also for the necessary thirty-day withdrawal period before the shooting season starts. Elsewhere, trays are simply gathered in. Some keepers prefer not to rely too heavily on medicated grit, though, believing that the worms can develop a resistance to the medication, so they only use it when they experience high infestations. There is only one type of medication available and if the worms develop immunity there is no alternative at present.

As the strongyle worm has been brought under control, a new threat has come to light. *Cryptosporidium* is an emerging disease: it affects the bird by causing the sinuses to swell and the physical effect of increased pressure within the head has led to the descriptive name of 'bulgy eye'. Preventative treatment seems to be the only option. Smaller gritting trays that have the dual advantages of being easier to move around and too small for the grouse to stand in them and defecate are becoming more popular, hopefully reducing the chance of cross-infection.

Heather is essential for grouse and other moorland species as an important source of food and cover. The various growth stages are created through careful management, whether burning or cutting, and the resulting mosaic has the added benefit of making it easier to bring a wildfire under control. While some argue against controlled burning, there's no doubting the ferocity of a wildfire and the devastation that it leaves behind compared to controlled burns. With increasing public access this is an ever-present risk, and the grouse keeper never has it far from his mind – an unwritten part of the gamekeeper's job is to provide security for the sensitive areas. A heavy public presence brings other concerns as well, and vandalism is an ever-present worry. Far worse is the danger of a malicious person placing a trap on top of a wall and photographing it as later 'evidence' of a gamekeeper illegally attempting to trap birds of prey.

Grouse moor management is a constant and largely unseen effort. There is always something going on, and a new challenge around every corner. The work has been described as a triangle, with habitat management, vermin control and parasite control at each of the three points, drawing together at the centre. The keeper needs to be alert, constantly checking and most important of all, proactive – without his efforts there would be little sport, and more importantly the moors would be emptier places even when the shooting season has long since closed.

Keeper's Tip: If in doubt, don't shoot.

BOOKING SHOOTING

Not all of us are fortunate enough to have a regular source of shooting, or to live somewhere with easy access to it. For some it is an occasional rather than a regular treat, whether it be driven game, a walked-up 'rough' day, goose flighting on the foreshore or pigeons over decoys; the variety of what is available is endless, and the only challenge really is getting access to your desired sport.

You could do much worse than employ the services of a sporting agent. Such people take the hard work out of finding what you want; they work with different providers, be they full-sized formal estates or smaller operations, and can tailor your experiences according to your needs.

It pays, though, to follow a few simple guidelines. Firstly, plan ahead! Agents usually start booking for the next season long before the present one has closed, so give them plenty of notice. By the time shooting has finished and most guns have been put into light preservation for the spring and summer, the agent is working flat out to prepare for the coming autumn. Before making your approach, you need to decide exactly what you want to do and when you want to do it. 'I'm looking for some shooting, please send dates and prices' doesn't really provide a good starting point, nor do extended email conversations or games of telephone tag. A little preliminary thought makes everyone's lives simpler.

Knowing what quarry you are interested in, where you want to go for it and when your time frame lies narrows the field down. For instance, grouse start and finish early (the Glorious Twelfth of August until 10 December), but you'll need to be prepared to travel and probably stay somewhere as it will be necessary to go to the north of the country. There are no grouse to be found within an hour of London! If you want to be home in time for supper then you are probably better off looking at what is available closer to home.

Other questions to be considered: do you care how many times you pull the trigger, how high the birds are, or how far you walk between pegs? If you have a dog, is it just for show or do you want to give it a chance to work? Be honest about your fitness, too. Rugged landscapes may be scenic, but covering them on foot is no picnic if your day-to-day lifestyle is sedentary, so be realistic, and the outcome will be more pleasant and satisfying.

If you are part of a team, and the 'roving syndicate' is becoming increasingly popular these days, make this clear. And be specific about which days of the week you can shoot, from 'anything except the first Tuesday of each month' to 'weekends only'.

What about meals? You can have everything from the full gourmand option with linen tablecloths and fine wines, through casserole and beer in the shoot hut, fish and chips at the pub, or sausage rolls and soup on the tailgate of the Land Rover. Then there is accommodation, which can come in any number of grades. Do you want a Highland sporting lodge with singing laird and piped haggis, a pub which welcomes wellies and dogs, or a sympathetic B&B which caters for sportsmen coming and going at all hours with accompanying mud trails? It is your choice.

Finally, by the way, don't forget non-shooting partners; they may not relish trailing around after you in the rain day after day. Your sporting agent will probably be in a position to arrange alternative activities and venues to keep everyone happy – as long as you ask in good time. Even the very best connected agent probably can't conjure tickets for the latest West End hit out of thin air on the day itself!

The bottom line is that the more information you can provide to your sporting agent, and the more specific you can be, the more likely it is that he can come up with your dream destination and sporting package. Do give plenty of notice, though, and don't forget that there are no guarantees. The weather can't be controlled, and neither can all the other variables. If the members of your party fail to connect with the birds put over your heads, if the river is empty of salmon for lack of water, or you fluff that shot at a stag which the stalker has worked so hard to put you within a sensible range of, you really can't blame the agent.

Keeper's Tip: Never accept a gun from anyone until they have physically shown you that it is unloaded.

CHOOSING YOUR CARTRIDGES

Many of those who shoot fail to give much thought to what they load into the chambers of their guns. At best, however, you may not be getting the results that you might with a little research, and at worst you may be damaging the gun – or even endangering yourself. So, without going into too much detail in an area that could easily fill a book, here are just a few essential considerations.

CARTRIDGE LENGTH

It is vitally important to ensure that you select cartridges that are the right length for your gun. Just because they fit easily into the chamber doesn't necessarily mean that this is the case. Take a look at the underside of the barrel, normally covered by the fore end, and you'll find a number of symbols stamped underneath. These are the proof marks – of which there are a bewildering variety – which will tell those in the know where the gun was proofed (that is, tested to ensure that the gun is fit to cope with the internal pressures that firing will subject it to), and in what year. If you are in any doubt about whether your gun is in proof, simply consult a reputable gunsmith. In the same place you should also find the length of cartridge that the gun is chambered for, normally expressed in inches (2½, 2¾ etc) in an older gun but possibly in millimetres instead (65, 70 etc). This is the length of the cartridge when the crimp, or closure at the end of the case to stop the contents falling out, has opened out after firing and not before; two cartridges manufactured differently may look different lengths before firing, but will both be the same length afterwards. Using a cartridge length longer than that for which the chamber is designed can result in a poor gas seal, or 'obturation', and put excessive pressure on the chamber. This can result in cumulative damage and potential blow-outs. You can, of course, use shorter cartridges than the gun is chambered for.

SHOT SIZE

The shot suitable for most forms of game shooting is designated by numbers, starting at No 10 for the smallest and working up to No 1. These are known as 'numbered' shot. Thereafter, as the shot increases in size, the designation is in letters, working from B and BB to LG – 'lettered' shot. Matters can get a little confusing as there is no agreed international system of measuring shot sizes; for example, No 5 shot under the English system equates to No 6 in the USA. If you are looking for consistency when using loads from overseas manufacturers it is wise to check the actual diameter of the shot, rather than the number stated.

Shot size is important to us for two main reasons. Firstly, the smaller the shot size, the more individual pieces there will be to a set weight of load (you get around 97 pieces of No 6 shot to the ounce as opposed to just 77 of No 5 shot), so the denser the pattern that is created. However, the heavier the shot size, the more terminal energy is delivered to the target, and therefore the increased chances of a clean kill – provided that there is sufficient shot to produce a pattern sufficient to ensure hits. It is, in effect, a compromise.

Most game shooters choose No 6 or No 5 shot as all-round loads suitable for most species you'd expect to encounter on a rough shooting or driven day. If you are deliberately targeting rabbits or hares it would pay to step up to No 4, while wildfowl may well call for larger yet. It's true that you occasionally hear of some astonishing long-range shots being pulled off, but more often than not they are the result of a lucky pellet striking a vital organ. The truth is that long shots with insufficient shot sizes all too often result in birds or animals making off carrying insufficient lead to bring them down.

For general purpose clay pigeon shooting, No 7½ is a good compromise, although clay specialists may move between No 9 for really close range shooting and step down to No 7 or even No 6 for longer ranges. Quite frankly, though, if you are practising on clays in preparation for quarry shooting, why not stick to your normal loads? You'll get a better idea of how they perform.

RECOIL

All sporting firearms are a compromise between the weight of a gun and the recoil it produces. A very heavy gun might reduce recoil to a point where it is negligible, but as a result be well-nigh impossible to carry around all day, or to mount and swing effectively. Conversely, a light gun may be pleasant to carry and mount, but produce punishing recoil. If you are experiencing excessive or uncomfortable recoil levels, you can try switching to lower velocity cartridges, or reducing the weight of the shot load slightly. Alternatively, if a semi-automatic shotgun is an option, these disperse much of the recoil as a result of their action, and indeed they are very useful for introducing young or slightly built people to shooting. Otherwise, there are some very effective butt pads on the market, which absorb recoil and protect your shoulder, or it could simply be that your gun doesn't fit you properly. Once again, your gunsmith should be able to offer good advice. If he can't, maybe it's time to try another one!

NON-LEAD ALTERNATIVES

You may need to use non-toxic, or lead-free, shot for a variety of reasons. Shooting wildfowl, or over Sites of Special Scientific Interest, are two of the main ones in Britain, but in some countries lead is banned completely. Alternatives are freely available. Bismuth and tungsten shot are the best in ballistic terms, though expensive. Steel shot (actually soft iron) is far cheaper, but does not have the same density, and importantly can cause considerable damage to the sleeves of the barrels of older guns because it is such a hard material. Some authorities suggest that tungsten is also inadvisable in older guns for the same reason. A modern gun should indicate that it is suitable for steel shot among the proof marks but, if in doubt, a gunsmith will be able to advise you. If you are using non-lead shot, it is usual to change to a shot size larger than you would normally (some suggest two sizes larger in the case of steel), and perhaps you might reconsider whether your effective killing range has reduced slightly.

WAD AND CASE

The wad, which keeps powder and shot in place within the cartridge and drives the shot charge up the barrel on firing, may be constructed of plastic, felt or fibre. Plastic is probably the most common, and there are claims that it shoots more consistently and comfortably, though of course felt and fibre biodegrade quickly and are more environmentally friendly. It is very much a case of personal preference. Plastic cases are without doubt more waterproof than old-fashioned waxed paper cases, and certainly more common, although once again personal preference comes into play. Whatever you choose, don't forget to pick them up at the end of the drive!

PATTERNING

A session at the pattern plate at your local shooting ground (or you can create your own using sheets of paper) can be a revelation. By shooting at ranges between twenty and forty yards with your normal cartridges, you'll discover what patterns of shot you can expect to produce in the field. Why not try a different make of cartridge while you are at it? It is quite possible that you will get even better results.

A FINAL WORD OF CAUTION

It is worth finishing this section with a warning – never mix cartridge sizes in bag or pocket. A 20 bore cartridge can be inserted by mistake into the chamber of a 12 bore, something easily done in the excitement of a busy drive, and then a 12 bore cartridge might be loaded behind it. The resulting detonation would be potentially catastrophic, not simply to the gun but to the person holding it, and anyone close by as well. The same result is possible with a 28 bore cartridge in a 16 bore chamber.

> **Keeper's Tip:** Don't give food to somebody else's dog without their permission. Friendships have ended over less!

THE BLACK POWDER GUN

Sometimes we tend to forget just how easy we have things these days. Imagine that you have drawn a hot peg for this particular drive; somewhere in the wood to your front you hear a faint tapping of sticks as the beaters approach, then birds start to break over you. The gun comes up in a practised swing. You fire once, then again, and feel the satisfaction of a neat left and right. Gun down, thumb pushes lever to one side, the gun breaks open and two spent cartridges eject past your shoulder. A quick reach into the bag and fresh ones come to hand. You drop them swiftly into the chambers and close the gun, looking up for the next bird as you do so ... The whole procedure takes no more than a few seconds.

Now let us step back in time about a hundred and sixty-five years or so, to the England of 1850, the year before Monsieur Lefaucheux was to display his revolutionary breech-loading shotgun for ready-made pinfire cartridges at the Great Exhibition. Instead you are armed with a double-barrelled percussion muzzle-loader. You won't be standing on a peg, though, but walking up some rough ground with a setting dog ranging ahead of you, gun held crossways in front of your body. A covey of partridge flush and you raise the gun, thumbing back the hammers as you do so. Two shots, two birds fall – good shooting indeed.

But now comes the reload. Your entire shooting party halts and the dogs are called in to give you time to create, in effect, two new cartridges from the raw materials you carry with you. Grounding the butt of your gun with barrels uppermost, you reach for the powder flask and carefully measure two-and-a-half drams of black powder into each barrel, pouring it carefully lest any gets spilled or is blown away by the breeze. Next comes the wadding, carefully pre-cut from felt, which is placed in the top of each barrel. You remove the ramrod from its securing hoops below the barrels and push each wad in turn firmly home. Removing the ramrod and holding it carefully to one side, you now take the shot flask and pour an ounce or so of lead shot into each barrel, topping it up with a thinner cardboard wad, stamped out precisely to fit the bore of your gun as the felt wad was. Once again you ram each side down carefully before replacing the ramrod into its hoops.

You lift the gun and turn it over, thumbing each hammer back to the half-cock position, away from the nipple but not fully back as that would permit it to fire. Now you flick the fired percussion caps off each nipple. (These are little copper cups containing a fulminate mixture, which, once ignited by the force of the hammer falling, explode and send a jet of fire through the nipple into the gun where they will detonate the main charge.) One fired cap flicks off easily, but the other is not so willing to move so you have to fumble for a blade to prise it away. Once the nipples have been cleared you replace the caps with fresh ones. These may have to be taken from their small tub, a fiddly business, or you may hold them in a special capping tool, which makes the operation much easier provided that they have stayed upright and feed properly. You check that all is secure, then signal your companions that you are ready to move on.

Even with practice, this process takes rather more than just a few seconds and it is easy to see that it was only the invention of the breech-loading shotgun that permitted driven game shooting to develop to the extent that we know it today. I suppose, though, that the 1850 percussion shooter might have considered himself to be lucky compared to the flintlock user of less than fifty years before. Instead of a modern ignition system based on an easily ignited chemical, the latter relied on the spark from a flint setting off the pan full of priming powder to ignite the main charge in its turn, prey to wind, rain and a very long 'flash to bang' time indeed – if it went off at all. Hooray indeed for all the developments since!

> **Keeper's Tip:** Always unload before crossing an obstacle, or at any other time when you are not in full control of your gun.

IMPROVE YOUR SHOOTING

Maybe you are new to shooting and want to improve, or perhaps you are an established Shot going through a bad patch and wondering why you are not connecting as often as you might. Here are a few suggestions that may be helpful.

MASTER EYE

You would be surprised how many people have never bothered to check their eye dominance, yet knowing this is vital to accurate shooting. Being able to shoot with both eyes open is an advantage but if your eyes won't allow you to naturally align the gun barrel with your target this may not be an option. There are many methods to check your eye dominance. Here are three:

Method 1: Point a finger at a distant object with both eyes open. Close, or cover, each eye one at a time. The eye which is open when the finger remains pointing at the object is the dominant one. When you close it and look through the other, you'll notice that the finger 'jumps' way to one side of the object being pointed at (which, by the way, is an indication of how badly you might be missing a target if your gun mount does not match the master eye!).

Method 2: Make a circle with the tips of your forefinger and thumb and, with both eyes open, place it to encircle a distant object. You might instead use the hole in a CD disc, or one punched in a small piece of card, for this. Keeping both eyes open, bring the circle/hole back towards your face keeping the object in the centre. It will come back to your master eye.

Method 3: Stand square on to the distant object and, with both eyes open, point at it with your finger with the tip uppermost. Keeping both eyes open and your finger still pointing at the object, slowly bring the finger back towards your face. Once again, it should come to the dominant eye.

If your right eye is dominant and you shoot from the right shoulder all should be well, likewise for a left eye/left shoulder combination. If the 'wrong' eye takes over, or you have central vision where neither eye is in overall charge, there may be a need for a correction. This might take the form of a crossover stock, which realigns the natural position of the barrels, or the wearing of shooting glasses with a dot, small piece of gauze tape or smear of Vaseline on the lens to interrupt the vision from the dominant eye, thus allowing the less dominant but correct one to take control. There are plenty of solutions, so don't despair. The simplest way is probably the best – just learn to close the over-dominant eye when you shoot.

Even if you think you know which is your master eye, checking it using one of the methods above is quick and easy if you find that your shooting drops off. Eye dominance can change from time to time for reasons such as stress, tiredness, or simply because you are getting older. A visit to a shooting coach is well worthwhile under such circumstances; they will always be able to suggest practical corrections to any issues.

MOUNT

A major cause of bad shooting, mount is important. The gun should at least fit you; if the stock is too long or too short you will instinctively feel uncomfortable using it. Most people mount the gun into the pocket of the shoulder between collar-bone and joint; too high up, and your barrels will point downwards and vice versa. As a rough guide, the heel (top edge) of the stock should be just below the line of the shoulder. Your trigger hand grasps the gun firmly and pulls it, steadily but not too tightly, into the shoulder; the forward hand rests comfortably supporting the fore end and controls the movement of the muzzle. With your cheek resting on the stock you should be looking naturally down the line of the top of the barrel.

Once again, a qualified coach or an experienced friend will be able to look at your mount and offer good advice. Sometimes, if the stock is too short for you, a slip over butt pad can extend it slightly, whilst a comb raiser will lift up the natural height of your face against the stock if it is too low.

Practise your gun mount (with a gun that has been proven unloaded first) regularly so that it comes naturally to the right position every time. Sometimes try this with your eyes closed; hopefully it will be a pleasant surprise to find everything in proper alignment when you open them.

FOOTWORK

Imagine that your body is a spring. When you are shooting at a static target with a rifle you need to take all of the tension out of the spring so that the rifle points naturally where you want it to. Using a shotgun demands the exact opposite. Putting tension onto the spring enables you, once this is released in the form of the swing, to keep the gun moving naturally. Shooting with rifle and shotgun at static and moving targets respectively require techniques, in fact, as different as those required when playing cricket and rugby – in both these cases there is a ball involved, but there the similarity abruptly ends.

Stand relaxed, with the foot on the opposite side to your shooting shoulder placed forward. Bend the forward knee slightly, and position your rear foot just far enough back to allow you to lift it off the ground without unbalancing yourself. Lean slightly forward into the gun and – here's the important bit – *point the forward foot towards where you intend to shoot at the target.* This will allow your body to work to best effect and produce a swing that keeps on going once the shot is released. Stand square on to the target, and your body will act against this.

Watching very good Shots on a game shoot is an education. Their feet are constantly shifting as they select a target and adjust position to achieve the exact position I have just described. The not-so-good Shots won't move at all. Neither, to be fair, will some of the very, very good Shots – but they have developed their shooting technique to a higher plane anyway.

SWING

It is easy to spot a regular rifleman when he is using a shotgun. The swing starts beautifully, catches up with the moving target – and then stops as the trigger is pulled. Naturally by the time the charge of shot reaches the target it is several feet further on and missed well behind. Thanks to a lifetime of air rifles as a child, rifle shooting in the Army and deerstalking, I'm as guilty as the next person of this. You *must* keep that gun moving!

SHOOTING TECHNIQUE: SWING THROUGH OR MAINTAINED LEAD?

There are two predominant methods of shooting moving targets. The *swing through* method starts behind the target. Imagine that it is leaving a vapour trail behind it; follow along the trail with your muzzles until you reach the target itself, pull the trigger as you pass it and *keep the barrels moving on forward.*

Some people however prefer to shoot a *maintained lead.* This method involves calculating how far ahead of the target you need to aim to allow for the charge of shot to coincide with it, then deliberately keeping your muzzle that far ahead, firing, *and keeping the swing going.*

Both methods work, but for the inexperienced Shot the swing through version is probably the more useful and instinctive one.

There is one excellent method used by the Clay Pigeon Shooting Association to introduce newcomers to shooting. It involves following the target with the muzzles, locking on to it briefly, then deliberately pushing slightly forward of it before shooting while keeping the barrels moving on. It's certainly a great way to get someone to hit a simple crossing target.

Some things only work if you are very lucky. Holding your muzzles still and shooting at where you hope your target will be when the shot pattern gets there – the 'ambush' – very seldom works. Otherwise, in the excitement of the moment when faced with a number of targets, such as a large flush of pheasant or a covey of grouse, it is easy to 'brown' into the centre of them in the hope of hitting something. Trust me, you won't! You have to pick your target and focus on it. Finally, and worst of all, you occasionally see someone shooting wildly into the air in the hope of connecting with something by luck rather than judgement. They very seldom do.

Once again, I can't recommend the services of a professional instructor highly enough. An hour of one-to-one tuition will fully cover all of the above points as well as many more and is worth every penny.

> **Keeper's Tip:** Please remember to pick up your empty cartridge cases, especially if you are a walking gun or out rough shooting.

Some animals are cunning and evil-disposed, as the fox; others, as the dog, are fierce, friendly, and fawning. Some are gentle and easily tamed, as the elephant; some are susceptible of shame, and watchful, as the goose. Some are jealous and fond of ornament, as the peacock. **Aristotle, philosopher**

LOOKING AFTER YOUR GUN

A rigid, foam-lined case is best for transporting your gun, offering it the best protection. Some guns come with a shorter motor case, with specific compartments for the broken-down barrels and stock as well as sundries such as cleaning materials. For when you are in the field, a good quality sleeve is a sound investment. It should be lined with suitable padding to shield the gun against accidental knocks; thin materials are better avoided as they obviously afford less protection. Buckle fittings are much better than full-length zips as these can fail at awkward moments; I have seen a gun fall out of a slip thanks to a failed zip on more than one occasion. Don't forget to check the carrying strap from time to time, particularly where it joins the slip body.

Rainwater is not too harmful to metalwork in the short term as long as you dry the gun off as soon as you get home, but avoid putting it into its slip wet if you can. Beware the effects of sea water on metal if you are shooting on the foreshore, and wipe any blood off immediately – the salts within this are extremely corrosive.

A gun should never go into the cabinet at the end of the day without at least a basic clean; it is, after all, a delicate mechanism that deserves to be looked after carefully. Modern propellants are much cleaner and less corrosive than the old-fashioned black powder, and modern metals much more resistant to rust, but that doesn't mean that you can neglect a gun completely. A simple cleaning regime doesn't take long. All you require are a few simple tools – a rod, phosphor bronze wire brush and wool mop to fit it, some rags, tissue paper and a proprietary gun cleaning oil are all you really need to do a good job. For stocks and fore ends, a separate bottle of a suitable oil for use on wood is a necessary addition. Everyone has their own approach to the job, but the following works for me:

Step 1: *Make sure that your gun is unloaded!*

Step 2: If the gun has got wet, and let's face it, a lot of winter shooting outings involve rain from time to time, break it down to the main component parts (barrels, stock and fore end) and wipe them down with a dry cloth as thoroughly as you can. Don't be tempted to strip the gun further unless you are competent to do so – this is usually gunsmith territory! If possible, leave them to air dry further for half-an-hour or so at room temperature. Avoid direct heat, which can cause warping and damage. The barrels might benefit from sitting on a lukewarm radiator, but beware overheating them on a very hot Aga!

Step 3: If your gun has detachable chokes, remove them and clean and oil them separately. Brush out the barrels using the bronze brush (this metal is softer than the steel lining of the barrels so will not scratch them) to loosen powder residue and other fouling. You can follow through with some crumpled tissue paper to further clean them out. Finally, use the wool mop to spread a very thin layer of gun oil inside the barrels.There is no need to use too much – a little goes a very long way. Pay special attention to the chambers: you can get special short chamber brushes and mops for this, but to be honest I've never found them necessary myself. Check the barrels for cleanliness by holding them up to the light. They should look shiny and bright. Keep an eye open for any pitting that may have formed (if there is pitting, it's time to visit the gunsmith). In cases of extreme fouling, specialist gun cleaning agents are available to dissolve powder and metal deposits – just follow the instructions on the tin or bottle.

Step 4: Use an oily rag to clean the outside of the barrels. Don't forget the recesses formed by the rib on top of them, which are easily overlooked and a classic place for rust to form; a drop of oil on either side can be forced down them along the length of the barrels with a piece of tissue paper.

Step 5: Clean the metal parts of the stock and fore end with the oily rag. Tissue paper, cotton buds or an old toothbrush are very useful for reaching the fiddly parts. Take care not to get oil onto the wood, and avoid applying copious amounts of oil to any working parts or recesses. It will eventually attract and hold dirt and cause problems later.

Step 6: If your gun has a sealed wooden stock, a wipe over with a clean rag should be sufficient. If the wood is 'open', rub a small amount of walnut oil or similar onto it. Bare hands are best, as the friction created warms the oil and helps it to penetrate the wood for better protection. *Do not use normal gun oil for this purpose* – it will eventually weaken the wood and cause it to swell and split.

Step 7: Reassemble the gun and store it, ideally barrels downwards, so that any excess oil runs away from the action and the wood. Once it is in the cabinet, the last thing to do is to wipe any metal you have touched with your bare hands with the oily rag. The oils on one's hands contain salts and these are potentially corrosive.

Watch out for condensation inside the gun cabinet, a particular problem in modern heated houses. A small dehumidifier filled with 'rechargeable' water-absorbing crystals (desiccants) is one solution, another is a corrosion inhibitor such as Napier VP70.

At the end of the shooting season, consider getting your gun serviced by a competent gunsmith. This will not only keep it in peak working order, but highlight any weaknesses that may have developed, or working parts that may be worn or broken, so it is great for your peace of mind as well. Furthermore, you will extend the working life of your gun as well as maintain its value.

Keeper's Tip: If you are invited to join the beaters as a walking Gun, take special care over safe handling and only shoot at birds going back unless told otherwise.

PHEASANTS UNDER BROODIES

Most of the pheasants released into the countryside are bred and reared commercially, but there are still some gamekeepers who keep to more traditional methods. Before the advent of modern incubators, using broody hens to hatch and rear pheasant chicks was very much the norm. This method is more labour intensive, of course, and you need the hens. In Edwardian times everyone kept a few chickens, and it was simply a case of buying them in. Today's keeper has to keep his own supply to make sure that they are ready when needed.

Although any chicken breed can be used, a popular option is a Light Sussex/Silky cross. The pure Silky has downy feathers that can stick to the pheasant chicks, but crossing with the Light Sussex ensures a more solid plumage. Size is also important, as a full-size Light Sussex is too big a bird and might easily crush a newly hatched pheasant. Food quality is the key to encouraging hens to lay, but plenty of nesting boxes must also be available to them, containing false nests with dummy eggs. The birds will even sit on golf balls or stones once the mood comes upon them.

A wise keeper identifies the hens that he wants to use at night when they are settled, only transferring them to the chicken boxes where they will incubate their new charges the next day. Red mites are the reason for this; these blood-sucking parasites are only active at night, and moving the hens during the day avoids taking the mites with them. The mites are a real threat. They cause agitation in the sitting box, resulting in cold clutches of eggs, and can seriously debilitate a bird through blood loss. Cleanliness and biosecurity are important watchwords here.

Meanwhile, the eggs are being produced on the laying field, each pen containing about fifteen pheasant hens to one cock bird. Once laid, the eggs are collected and removed to incubators where they remain for three days before being introduced to the broodies, now fully settled in their sitting boxes, for the final stage of incubation.

The broody hens live in the sitting boxes apart from when they are taken out every morning to feed on a damp mash, although after a few minutes it is usually obvious that they are anxious to get back to their eggs. Before they are allowed to do so they are sprayed gently with water, not only to encourage them to defecate but also to ensure that moisture returns with them to the nest. All of their droppings are carefully removed to avoid any build-up of bacteria. A quick inspection of the eggs is also made at this point to look for any signs of the dreaded red mite – small spots of blood are a telltale, and a prompt for immediate treatment with spray and powder. Only then are the hens allowed to return to their precious charges in the boxes, each containing a base of clean sand and a hay nest. It is important, too, that the boxes are raised off the ground, which allows not only ventilation but protection from predators. Even moles have been known to emerge underneath ground nests and push off a sitting hen.

Once hatched, the pheasant chicks and their surrogate mothers are transferred to the rearing field where each 'family' is housed in its own enclosed pen. The hen is enclosed in a dry box, but the chicks are free to come and go through the bars into a small area initially enclosed by a hardboard hoop. After three days, when all have bonded fully, the chicks are allowed to roam the entire pen and learn to forage for themselves. Chick crumb is available to them all the time and very often they also get a daily feed of mealworms; it is quite comical to watch a chick grab a worm and make off with it before another might steal it. Separate drinkers mean that the height of the chicks' water supply can be raised as they grow. After a few weeks the pen area is doubled to give the chicks more room and during all of this time they are learning rapidly, hunting for natural food from a few days old, while mortality rates are incredibly low.

The hen calls the chicks in to her at night, and is quick to raise the alarm if a predatory bird passes overhead. The advantage of this system is that the hens are doing all the rearing for the gamekeeper: there is no feather-pecking, so no bitting or wing clipping is necessary. The birds are in their pens for six weeks before they go straight to the wood, where they are as prepared as they can be for life in the wild. The whole system is as natural as it is possible to get on a rearing field.

Not only do the chicks get the best possible start in life, but they are also living outdoors rather than in sheds from the moment they hatch. The result is a hardy young pheasant that is not only ready for the woods, but just as importantly more likely to establish and breed naturally next year. Admittedly, rearing with broodies is not an option for large, intensive shoots, but where quality rather than quantity is treasured it is a hard system to beat.

The pheasant is an enigma, the answer to which is revealed only to the initiate; they alone can savour it in all its excellence. **Jean Anthelme Brillat-Savarin, *The Philosopher in the Kitchen***

SOME ASPECTS OF SHOOTING LAW

On the first of September, one Sunday morn
I shot a hen pheasant in standing corn
Without a licence, contrive who can
A greater collection of crimes 'gainst God and Man

Anon

Out of season, and on a Sunday into the bargain! At least nowadays you are unlikely to come across any standing corn in September (the crime in the poem was the bad manners involved in trampling standing crops in search of game), nor do you need a Game Licence any more (they were abolished in England and Wales in 2007, and in Scotland and Northern Ireland in 2011). The shooter does need to know his law, though. As is so often pointed out, ignorance of any law is no excuse for flouting it: but it is especially important to observe shooting laws these days, when the average member of the public seems to look on anyone with a firearm as a potential criminal. Be in no doubt that your Shotgun Certificate is at stake should you be caught out. One caveat: the law relating to firearms and shooting is constantly changing, so you need to be vigilant. The selection of regulations below is included as a guideline only; although correct at the time of writing (2016), it may be liable to change.

OPEN SEASONS FOR GAMEBIRDS AND WATERFOWL (ALL DATES ARE INCLUSIVE)

SPECIES	ENGLAND, WALES AND SCOTLAND	NORTHERN IRELAND
Pheasant	1 October - 1 February	1 October - 31 January
Grey Partridge	1 September – 1 February	1 September – 31 January
Red-legged Partridge	1 September – 1 February	1 September – 31 January
Red Grouse	12 August – 10 December	12 August – 30 November
Black Grouse: Somerset, Devon & New Forest	1 September – 10 December	N/A
Black Grouse: elsewhere	20 August – 10 December	N/A
Ptarmigan (Scotland only)	12 August – 10 December	N/A
Duck & Goose* (Inland)	1 September – 31 January	1 September – 31 January
Duck & Goose* (below High Water Mark†)	1 September – 20 February	1 September – 31 January
Common Snipe	12 August – 31 January	1 September – 31 January
Jack Snipe	Protected	1 September – 31 January
Woodcock	1 October – 31 January	1 October – 31 January
Golden Plover	1 September – 31 January	1 September – 31 January
Coot & Moorhen	1 September – 31 January	Protected

Guernsey, Jersey and the Isle of Man have separate shooting seasons and quarry species.

*Duck & Goose

Under the Wildlife and Countryside Act 1981, the following species of wildfowl can be shot in **England, Wales and Scotland** during their open season:

Duck – Gadwall, Goldeneye, Mallard, Pintail, Pochard, Shoveler, Teal, Tufted Duck, Wigeon

Geese – Canada, Greylag, Pink-footed, White-fronted (*Note: in England, Wales and Scotland only, Canada Geese may be shot all year round under general licences. There are two races of the White-fronted Geese; the European race is abundant but the Greenland race, which overwinters mainly on the west coast of Wales, is in decline. At the time of writing statutory protection is awaited but in the meantime there is a voluntary moratorium on shooting the latter.*)

Under the Wildlife (Northern Ireland) Order 1985, the following species of wildfowl can be shot in **Northern Ireland** during their open season:

Duck – Gadwall, Goldeneye, Mallard, Pintail, Pochard, Scaup,
Ruddy Duck, Shoveler, Teal, Tufted Duck, Wigeon,
Geese – Canada, Greylag, Pink-footed

† The **High Water Mark** is defined variously as:

England and Wales – 'the area of sea shore which is more often than not covered by the flux and reflux of the four ordinary tides occurring midway between springs and neaps'.
Scotland – 'the area between high and low water marks of ordinary spring tides'.
Ireland – 'the limit of where the living seaweed is attached to the stones of the foreshore'.

SUNDAY AND CHRISTMAS DAY SHOOTING

England and Wales – no game (pheasant, partridge, grouse or hare) may be killed or taken in any county on Sunday or Christmas Day.

Wildfowl may not be shot in the following counties on Sunday: Anglesey, Brecknock, Caernarvon, Cardigan, Carmarthen, Cornwall, Denbigh, Devon, Doncaster, Glamorgan, Great Yarmouth County Borough, Isle of Ely, Leeds County Borough, Merioneth, Norfolk, Pembroke, Somerset, North and West Ridings of Yorkshire.

Scotland – although there are no restrictions on shooting game on a Sunday or Christmas Day, it is customary not to do so. However, the wildfowl species listed for Scotland may not be shot on a Sunday or Christmas Day.

Northern Ireland – no wild bird, game bird or hare may be shot on a Sunday. While there is no prohibition on shooting on Christmas Day (unless it falls on a Sunday) it is customary not to do so.

OPEN SEASONS FOR DEER (ALL DATES ARE INCLUSIVE)

SPECIES AND SEX	ENGLAND AND WALES	SCOTLAND	NORTHERN IRELAND
RED, SIKA & THEIR HYBRIDS			
Stags	1 August – 30 April	1 July – 20 August	1 August – 30 April
Hinds	1 November – 31 March	21 October – 15 February	1 November – 31 March
FALLOW			
Bucks	1 August – 30 April	1 August – 30 April	1 August – 30 April
Does	1 November – 31 March	21 October – 15 February	1 November – 31 March
ROE			
Bucks	1 April – 31 October	1 April – 20 October	N/A
Does	1 November – 31 March	21 October – 31 March	N/A
CHINESE WATER DEER			
Both sexes	1 November – 31 March	N/A	N/A
MUNTJAC – there is no statutory closed season, although it is recommended that only immature and heavily pregnant does are shot to avoid orphaning dependent young			

NON-LEAD SHOT

In England, Wales and Northern Ireland non-lead shot must be used for all shooting over Sites of Special Scientific Interest, and for all shooting of waterfowl wherever they may be. Regardless of the quarry species, non-lead shot must be used on any wetland, irrespective of the quarry. Some definitions can be complicated and it is worth checking specific rules for your part of the country.

MAMMALIAN PESTS

The following can be controlled by any legal means at any time in England, Wales, Scotland and Northern Ireland: brown rat, feral cat, fox, grey squirrel, mice (except common/hazel dormouse), mink, rabbit, stoat, weasel (except Northern Ireland).

GENERAL LICENCES

General licences enable, among other things, the control of certain species such as magpies, woodpigeons and carrion crows, which are deemed to be pests. You don't need to apply for a general licence as long as you act within its terms and conditions. They are frequently reviewed, and are renewed every year, so it is important to keep track of what is and what isn't permitted.

WHAT CALIBRE?

Choosing a calibre of shotgun is not very difficult, and most people settle for a 12 bore without too much thought. Its worldwide popularity has evolved alongside the progression of the shotgun from muzzle-loader to breech-loader, and reflects a compromise of weight versus recoil. The 12 bore offers perhaps the optimum balance of what can be comfortably carried, yet still deliver a charge of shot that produces the terminal energy required to bring down the chosen quarry. While in Britain shooting large game with a shotgun is not *de rigueur*, users abroad have found the gun manageable and accurate at shorter ranges when firing a solid slug for tough quarry such as deer or boar, and even that it packs sufficient punch for the job when loaded with the aptly named buckshot. The 12 bore truly is the great all-rounder. In the United States it makes up some fifty percent of the overall shotgun market; in the UK the percentage is probably considerably higher.

The 12 bore user also enjoys a greater availability of shot sizes, propellant loads, and wadding and case materials, as well as cartridge lengths, than the owner of any other gauge; try walking into your local gunsmith and asking for a box of cartridges in a specific mixture of these variants for a less popular calibre of gun, and see where that gets you! In any well-stocked shop you will probably find exactly what you are looking for in 12 bore without too much trouble. In other words, this gun offers you versatility.

Mind you, the 20 bore comes close. It is popular with those who are a little uncomfortable with the weight of a 12 bore, particularly if they need something that is portable over long distances and in rough terrain, and a well made '20' is a delight to handle. Bear in mind, however, that a lightweight gun will not swing itself when following through a moving target in the way that a heavier one builds up its own momentum. An expectation of lower recoil can also be deceptive, and a lightly built gun might be bruising if used with normal game loads for sustained shooting. If that is the case, it is time to switch to a lighter load. In many ways it's a shame that a semi-automatic shotgun is still frowned upon by some formal shoots; the mechanism, relying on recoil to cycle the action, i.e. to eject the fired cartridge and feed a fresh one into the chamber, disperses much of it, with the result that the gun is much easier on the shoulder. So while a 20 bore side-by-side or over-and-under gun might be a bit 'kicky' for a young or slightly built person, a semi-automatic can be the perfect solution and is the first choice of many shooting coaches when introducing a newcomer to the sport.

Personally I am very fond of my inherited 16 bores, a gauge that sadly seems to be in something of a decline. Coming somewhere between the 12 and the 20, they are light enough to be portable yet throw a load that will cope with most game shooting requirements. In the past mine have accounted for quarry as large as Canada geese and full-grown foxes, although you have to be very careful that the range is right. I have to admit that the guns do have a bit of a kick. They are great for walked-up work and on my own small pheasant syndicate, when it is unusual to fire more than a pocketful of cartridges in a day's shooting: but on more than one summer simulated game day, shooting in shirtsleeves at fast and furious 'driven' clay pigeons I have found myself praying for the action to stop by lunchtime! A thick butt pad or similar arrangement makes sense under such circumstances. Sadly fewer and fewer manufacturers are producing new guns in 16 bore, but where the calibre really falls down is in the availability of ammunition. When you can find it (and, in fairness, most suppliers will have something in stock) you have to take what you are offered; sometimes you have to search very hard indeed for non-toxic loads. And of course smaller demand means smaller production runs of ammunition, meaning that the economies of scale fall off and your cartridges will be noticeably more expensive than those for a 12 or a 20. I dread having to buy in a new supply of bismuth loads: it may be necessary to remortgage the house.

Most children are introduced to shooting with a .410, a mistake in my opinion. Although the gun offers very low recoil, which is a huge advantage, it can be discouraging to the novice shooter who struggles to hit anything with a very small charge of shot (on average only some 14 grams compared to the 28 grams/1 ounce or more contained in the cartridges of larger calibres). That doesn't meant that the .410 has no place in the gun cabinet though; it is ideal for shooting rats and other vermin, and although you occasionally see people shooting game with them they are, frankly, not really a gun for anyone but the real specialist. It can be remarkably satisfying to shoot clays with a .410 though, and as a close-range tool for the humane despatch of road casualty deer, the calibre is ideal. If I were introducing a young person to shooting today, I would recommend the increasingly popular 28 bore. It is light, manageable, and low recoil. I know a number of game shooters who use them with great effect in the field.

These, then, are the mainstream calibres available, though they are not the only ones. You occasionally come across the 'big boys' in 10, 8 or even 4 bore, so beloved of wildfowlers. Heavy guns with heavy recoils, they can fire large shot charges with devastating effect on the foreshore, but I think that eyebrows might be raised if you turned up with one for a pheasant day! Your cartridge bills would be high, too, assuming you could actually find commercially produced ones in the first place. Most users revert to reloading their own, using black powder and paper or recyclable brass cases rather than the commoner plastic ones. These are definitely guns for the dedicated specialist.

JIM CORBETT

THE LIFE AND WRITING OF INDIA'S MOST FAMOUS HUNTER AND CONSERVATIONIST

Of all the great sporting writers, Jim Corbett has to rank among the best loved and even now, almost sixty years after his death, one of the most widely read. Between the years of 1907 and 1938 he personally accounted for a total of 33 man-eating tigers and leopards, which between them had claimed some 1,200 human lives. His tales of how he accomplished this, often with the odds stacked against him and faced by an extremely dangerous and challenging quarry, are just as exciting and fresh today as they have ever been.

Edward James Corbett was born in 1875 in Nainital, India. His mother and father, both of whom had been widowed before remarrying, already had seven children between them before adding another nine, including Jim, to a very full household. Nevertheless he had a comfortable upbringing and was well educated. Leaving school at seventeen, he went on to work with the railway as a fuel inspector, but fought in the Third Afghan War and, at the age of sixty-eight, was commissioned with the rank of Lieutenant Colonel to teach jungle survival skills to the Army. His life was certainly full and varied, but it is for his skills as a hunter and naturalist that he is chiefly remembered.

The first man-eater shot by Corbett was the Champawat tiger, a female that had already killed around 430 people in the Kumaon district of India and across the border in Nepal. Despite the efforts of numerous hunters and the Nepalese Army, the tigress continued her reign of terror and became increasingly bold. The entire area of her activities was paralysed, with men refusing to travel beyond their villages even in daylight. Finally, after the tigress had killed a teenage girl, Corbett was able to track and account for it after following a grisly trail of the poor girl's remains. The details of the hunt can be read in Corbett's first book, *Man-Eaters of Kumaon*, which was first published in 1944 and is still in print today. The book was an immediate and massive success; for the American Book of the Month Club alone, the first printing was a quarter-of-a-million copies.

It was no accident that Corbett was so skilled as a *shikari*, an Indian word for a big-game hunter. His childhood had been spent in the jungle where he learnt to identify the calls of the native birds and animals, the 'jungle folk' as he liked to refer to them, becoming a skilled tracker and an acute observer of nature. He was certainly not a recreational hunter, although he was always prepared to kill an animal for food or if it was dangerous. He later described a major turning-point in his life as the moment when he learnt to control his fear, at the age of about eight. Having run, terrified, from a tiger a few weeks previously, he had fled again from what he thought was a banshee screaming. 'I did not know,' he later wrote, 'that the terror of the unknown could lend wings to one's feet.' The next time that he heard the same noise he forced himself, heart beating, to investigate. The screaming turned out to be the sound of two branches sawing against each other in the wind. Thereafter he spent more and more time alone in the jungle, relying on his knowledge and jungle lore, in complete confidence and safety.

Reading between the lines in his matter of fact descriptions of some truly hair-raising encounters, there is no doubting Corbett's personal bravery. He was described by those who knew him as a modest and unassuming man, a far cry from the popular image of a colonial British *sahib*. Standing over six feet tall, with blue eyes and dark hair, he cared little for stuffy convention and dressed casually, usually in bush clothing. He never married, and his sister Maggie was his constant companion until his death. A quiet man, he was somewhat shy and seemed at his most comfortable among his Indian friends. He certainly had a profound understanding of and affection for the people of India, and these feelings were reciprocated, with heartfelt thanks from those he had risked his life to protect. He was also deeply respected by his workforce on the Indian railway. Many revered him as a *sadhu*, or saint.

It is said that Corbett never considered killing a tiger or leopard until there was no doubt that it was a man-eater, and then he would often put himself into some extraordinarily dangerous situations to bring the animal to account. He frequently hunted alone and on foot, often with a small dog of indeterminate breed called Robin. In his story *The Panar Leopard*, he recounts the experience of sitting in an oak tree whilst the leopard, which had already claimed 400 lives, growled continually as it pulled determinedly at the blackthorn shoots bound around the lower part of the trunk to prevent it from climbing up. In pitch darkness, armed only with a shotgun loaded with slugs and no source of artificial light, Corbett could only sit and listen from his precarious perch as the animal tried to reach him. 'I felt sure,' he wrote, 'that if he sprang up he would only need to touch me to send me crashing to the ground.'

A postscript to this episode underlines Corbett's humanity. During his final encounter with the Panar leopard, still in the dark, his men panic and run, taking with them the burning pine torches providing the only available light. Corbett manages to despatch the charging leopard. Instead of being angry, he recognises from his own experience that 'the fear of a man-eater robs a man of courage' and pretends to examine the leopard to save his men their embarrassment for having deserted him. He also comments, rather offhandedly, that by this point he was suffering from an attack of malaria and had difficulty remaining on his feet.

With the coming of independence, Corbett and his sister Maggie reluctantly decided that it was time to leave their beloved India. They settled in Kenya where Corbett continued his work, as a writer and a committed conservationist. In February 1952 he was present at the Treetops Hotel escorting a young Princess Elizabeth when she learned that she had succeeded the throne. He wrote in the hotel register at the time: 'For the first time in the history of the world, a young girl climbed into a tree one day a Princess, and after having what she described as her most thrilling experience, she climbed down from the tree the next day a Queen—God bless her.' He had only just finished writing his final book, *Tree Tops*, when he died of a heart attack aged seventy-nine in April 1955. Both he and his sister are buried in Nyeri, Kenya.

Corbett's name lives on in India. Two years after his death the Ramganga game sanctuary in Kumaon, which he had helped to establish, was renamed the Corbett National Park and remains so today, and in 1968 a newly recognised subspecies of tiger was named *Panthera tigris corbetti*. In an India that has proudly celebrated its independence from Britain since 1947, these are accolades indeed.

Bibliography

- *Jungle Stories* – Privately published in 1935; only 100 copies printed
- *Man-Eaters of Kumaon* (Oxford University Press, Bombay 1944)
- *The Man-Eating Leopard of Rudraprayag* (Oxford University Press 1947)
- *My India* (Oxford University Press 1952)
- *Jungle Lore* (Oxford University Press 1953)
- *The Temple Tiger and More Man-Eaters of Kumaon* (Oxford University Press 1954)
- *Tree Tops* (Oxford University Press 1955)
- *Jim Corbett's India* –An anthology selected by R E Hawkins, Corbett's publisher and editor (Oxford University Press 1978)
- *My Kumaon: Uncollected Writings* – Previously unpublished work and personal material (Oxford University Press 2012)

> **Keeper's Tip:** If you have a dog with you, it is a good idea to make sure that helping to collect fallen birds after a drive will be welcome; pickers-up may find a strange dog unhelpful to their own efforts!

MEA CULPA...

ENTERING THE CONFESSIONAL BOX

Admit it: we have all made a mistake or two over the years. Nobody's perfect, after all, and the occasional slip-up is almost inevitable.

I could tell you about turning up to shoot without the right kit. As a shooting mad teenager, every outing was precious to me, and the evening before would be spent meticulously checking, and rechecking, that everything was laid out and ready to go in the morning. As we get a bit older, though, we tend to get a bit more laid back about such things (after all, we have done it so many times before, right?). I distinctly recall, shortly after joining the Army, one early morning rush to get to Pirbright ranges when I managed to leave the working parts to my rifle in the strongbox in the platoon lines. My Colour Sergeant, an imposing gentleman from the Grenadier Guards with a fluent and inventive turn of phrase, took great amusement (at least I like to think that he was amused) at my expense. I learned many new words that morning, but was somewhat shocked to discover how many animals actually lived in my family tree.

Did I learn from the experience? Decide for yourself. Many years later I was involved in a park deer cull. It was a simple matter of getting up early, grabbing the kit – as I'd done so many times over the years – and driving over for first light. By now I had got into the habit of carrying the rifle bolt in a sheath on my belt, on the basis that it was easy to see if the sheath was empty, so there was no chance of forgetting it. I duly arrived on time, complete with rifle, ammunition and bolt. It was a pity that the bolt I had with me was for my .308, and the rifle and ammunition were .243 calibre. Several years down the line I am still mercilessly reminded of the occasion by anyone who was there.

I could go on to relate the whole story of turning up for a big shoot day with a 16 bore shotgun and a bag full of 12 bore cartridges, or the time I found myself in the middle of Salisbury Plain with three dead roe and no knife – but you get the gist.

Also to be considered is the important business of always identifying the target before going anywhere near the trigger. One episode that took place on a large estate in North Wales, where I was very occasionally allowed to shoot in my father's place, stands out. As a sixteen-year-old whose main sport revolved around the pursuit of pigeons and rabbits on a local farm, this was a special occasion to be savoured and I was always careful to obey the rules in the hope of being allowed back. It was particularly important not to shoot foxes. The estate's owner was a passionate hunting man, known for once having 'cut' a long-standing friend for giving Charlie both barrels during a drive when they had shared neighbouring pegs. Normal speaking terms had not been restored for some five years. Another rule was not to shoot white pheasants; not only was there a fine of ten pounds, a lot of money to a callow teenager in the 1970s, but the owner was rather fond of them and, as the fox story suggests, not particularly forgiving.

So it was that on the second drive of the day I was standing with the sun in my eyes, when a hen pheasant appeared from behind a large oak and directly into the blinding light. As the bird emerged from the sun I was dazzled but still swinging through it perfectly. Its head went back as it collided with the shot pattern and crashed to earth. Triumph – until, as the red spots cleared from my eyes, I realised with dawning horror that the hen was, in fact, pure white.

Fortunately the owner was nowhere in sight, and the keeper was, for once, unusually diplomatic. When he presented me with my hen at the end of the day he did it discreetly, a good job as he had found a second white bird (no one had owned up to that one) to make up the brace. He seemed to find the whole business of a deeply embarrassed teenager very funny. It still cost me a tenner on top of the tip, though.

Then there was a wild-goose chase with no cartridges left, a yearling roebuck which turned into a medal head, or the only pheasant of a rough shooting outing flushing (perhaps an unfortunate choice of word) at a most embarrassing moment. I could also tell you the reason that the local keeper stopped speaking to me, something I'd prefer to gloss over to be honest, but it involved three delightful fox cubs and a choice between the camera or the rifle. The list goes on but perhaps these confessions can wait for another time. I have made plenty of simple mistakes that I look back on now with a laugh or perhaps a wry smile. There is one more, though, that I cannot laugh off. It was a very, very stupid mistake. I broke a simple rule, a rule that I fully understood and had always observed diligently up to that point. As it was, one momentary omission and the result was disastrous.

It was a warm evening in June, about an hour before last light, and I was sitting out for a roe buck on a friend's patch. A very shootable four-pointer appeared in the meadow in front of the high seat and I took the straightforward chest shot with confidence. The buck collapsed instantly and lay, unmoving, in full view. I watched it briefly and stupidly decided that it wasn't going to get up. Keeping my eyes on the buck I unloaded and started to climb down. When I was halfway down the ladder with the rifle over my shoulder and magazine safely in my pocket, the buck stirred, struggled to his feet, stood for a moment, and then trotted into cover and out of my sight.

To cut a very long story short, we searched long and hard. Jo joined me with his dog, a first-class labrador with a proven record of success, and we started from the point where the buck had dropped. There was a little blood sign, which quickly disappeared, but thankfully no signs of bone; the departing buck had certainly shown no sign of a leg injury. The labrador started to track positively and led us well into the woods before both the trail and the light gave out.

We were back first thing next morning with two dogs, both of which agreed on the original trail but lost it at about the same point where we had finished the previous evening. By mid-morning the heat of the sun was baking, the dogs were tired and almost as dispirited as their owners, and we reluctantly gave up.

Most stalkers experience a misplaced shot at some point in their careers, but for me this is the one that was never explained nor, more seriously, rectified. What probably happened was that my bullet had gone high and just missed the vertebrae, stunning the buck without causing any serious damage. I like to think that it made a quick recovery but of course have no way of knowing for sure. If I had waited and watched as I should have done, I would have been ready to shoot again when it stood up unexpectedly. As it is, this will forever remain a story of the one that got away.

You may well wonder why I have decided to share this story. It is quite simple: maybe, just maybe, someone will find themselves in a similar situation one day but remember to be patient and so save themselves a great deal of anguish and self-recrimination. Sometimes no real harm is done when things go wrong, but there are other times when we really do need to cater for the unexpected and avoid unwelcome consequences.

Keeper's Tip: If your shooting has deteriorated for no apparent reason, an hour with a qualified instructor can be worth every penny and will quickly pick up any faults that may have developed with your technique.

HYPERION

This is no more than a piece of fun originally designed to be read on the first day of April. Interestingly, though, a few of the facts are actually correct.

During the First World War, both sides in the conflict were heavily dependent on carrier pigeons in the absence of the sophisticated communication systems that modern armies enjoy today. A fast and dependable pigeon was highly valued and had the potential to help win battles through the timely passage of vital information. One which failed to find its bearings quickly and subsequently crossed enemy lines before becoming properly oriented to its route home was exposed to counter measures which included shotgunning (every British rifle platoon in the trenches had a nominated gunner, usually a gamekeeper in civilian life, specifically detailed for this purpose) and even specially formed falconry units. Accordingly, casualties were high.

Hatched during the summer of 1914 in the lofts of champion racing-pigeon breeder Barrington 'Bee' Lougher of Barnsley and named after the Greek sun god, a bird called Hyperion was one of the most celebrated animal heroes of the war. He quickly came to official notice during his initial training when, flying between the military camps of Aldershot and Catterick, he set navigational and flight records that remain unbeaten to this day. His first operational deployment was to the Headquarters of the General Staff at Amiens in May 1916, where he was regularly entrusted with reports and messages vital to the war effort. His deliveries were frequently made to the most senior officials in the War Office.

Being of lighter than average colour, Hyperion was instantly recognisable and quickly built upon his reputation for speed and reliability. One message flight, a delivery from the Western Front to Horse Guards in London, was timed at an hour and twenty-seven minutes – a remarkable feat by any standards. Perhaps the most historic message that the pigeon ever carried (an earlier assignment, whilst on detachment to the Fleet at Scapa Flow) concerned the loss of Lord Kitchener. An arduous flight in truly appalling weather conditions brought the message to London in a mere seven hours. On receiving the news the Prime Minister, Herbert Asquith, is reported to have remarked 'What dolorous chores we load upon innocent wings'. Such was the condition of Hyperion after the gruelling flight that he was unable to return to active service for a full two months, during which time he recuperated from the stress and trauma of delivering this particular post.

Hyperion had grudging admirers in the German camp. The acclaimed Prussian falconer *Oberstleutnant* Rikard von Dastard of the elite Erste Geierstaffel falconry unit (whose highly decorated peregrine tiercel, Muteli, is credited with capturing more than sixty Allied carrier pigeons during the course of the war), commented ruefully on the speed and agility of a bird that far outmatched his hawk on a number of occasions. 'The desire to catch that pigeon' he wrote later in his memoirs 'eventually became an obsession that ruled my life for over two years'. A broken man, he retired from professional falconry after the war, vowing never to train another bird again. Others took a different view; the Commander of the French Army, Marshal Vraihonette, is quoted after witnessing one of these aerial duels as exclaiming *'Quelle oiseau! Quelle vitesse! Quelle élan!'*

And who knows what other dramas were enacted *en route*, high above the battlefields of western France or the English Channel? Certainly it seems that Hyperion led a charmed life. Despite a number of witnessed near misses, he suffered no injuries of note beyond the occasional broken feather.

By the end of the war Hyperion had flown ninety-two successful missions, at a time when the average life expectancy of an operational pigeon was considered to be twenty at best. King George V personally presented him with the Avian Gallantry Medal at the Aldershot Military Review of 1918. Only one other wartime carrier pigeon ever received this accolade, but this award was made posthumously after the recipient, Speckled Jim, was tragically killed by friendly fire in Flanders in 1917.

Hyperion was retired with honour to the Royal Lofts at Sandringham, where he died of old age on 1 April 1921. It is unlikely that his like will ever be seen again. A statue and memorial can still be viewed there by visitors today. Erected at private expense by a grateful monarch, it bears the inscription:

A Pigeon Redoubtable In Life, His Flight Outranged Ordinary Limits

Keeper's Tip: Avoid white shirts and brightly coloured clothing in the field: you will just make yourself obvious to driven birds and they will then steer well clear of your position.

HANGING AROUND

STORING SHOT GAME AT HOME

When you return home from a successful shooting or stalking expedition bearing your quarry, be it furred or feathered, what do you do with it? In far too many cases somewhere unsuitable is pressed into service. I've seen braces of pheasant and partridge hung on door handles, washing lines and trees in the garden, and, in one horrible example, a roe carcase suspended from a drain pipe (over an open drain) next to a couple of dustbins. As if this wasn't dreadful enough, a foreleg removed from the animal had been used as a chest spreader.

There are specific regulations covering the storage and preparation of game going into the wider human food chain, but these do not apply to anything intended for your own personal use. This doesn't mean, though, that you should neglect a few basic principles to ensure that your prize is kept at its best and properly fit for human consumption. Besides, the better you store the meat until the time comes to prepare it for the table or freezer, the better its quality will be.

At the very least, game needs to hang in a cool, dry place with good ventilation. Hanging, rather than stacking, allows air to circulate and cool the carcase as well as to protect it against four-legged pests and domestic animals. Insects, though, are probably your biggest concern, and a badly fly-blown carcase is fit for nothing but disposal. Muslin bags or tubes are often recommended for keeping game in, and you can buy purpose-made hanging bags, but be aware that flies can often lay their eggs through these. For the best result, you really need some form of fine mesh enclosure, big enough that the game can hang within it without touching the sides, and don't forget to add some form of drip tray to collect any blood.

One excellent product on the market is called a GameSafe. Intended for occasional use, it is a purpose-made, nylon mesh and fabric container in the shape of a rugby ball, which can easily accommodate a brace of pheasant. With a hanging hook, zipped entry and an integral drip tray, the whole thing folds flat for storage when not in use. A larger version, the RoeSafe, will hold up to three roe, or even a fallow or small red deer.

Commercial premises are required to store large game such as deer at a temperature below 7°C, and small game below 4°C. (The reason for the difference is that small game is usually left with the body contents intact, whereas a deer is gralloched before going to larder.) Sadly, if you come back with a summer roebuck or some early season partridge or pheasant it can be difficult to find a suitably cool place at home when outside temperatures are high. Sheds, garages or outbuildings can become hot, and you may want to consider obtaining some form of chiller unit.

Although several purpose-made game chilling units are available on the market, these can be expensive and are probably beyond the means of someone who only has the occasional need of one at home. An alternative is a drinks chiller, of the sort that you see in shops or filling stations displaying cans or sandwiches. My own chiller lives in the corner of the garage (by the door, for easy transfer direct from the car carcase tray). It is very economical to run and is only switched on when needed, reaching fully adjustable operating temperatures in minutes. It was obtained from a local shop refitting its display areas and, despite being in perfect running order, was destined for the tip. The shop owner was delighted to be spared the expense and trouble of having it taken away.

Standing about 180cm (6 feet) high, the chiller's internal dimensions are 150x50x50cm, with solid sides and a glass door. It accommodates any amount of feathered game or a couple of smaller deer with ease, and has even been pressed into taking a fallow pricket on the odd occasion. The internal surfaces are of easily cleaned plastic, and a trip to the garden centre with a tape measure produced a plastic seed tray that fits the floor area perfectly to catch drips. After carefully checking that the roof area concealed no vital wiring, holes were drilled for two eye bolts which support a hanging bar; the bolts are not fixed on the roof of the chiller itself, but continue through a plank sitting on top of the unit to distribute the weight of whatever is hanging inside.

A selection of S-hooks and gambrels make up the basic kit needed for hanging. Chest spreaders are also very useful for encouraging a deer carcase to chill quickly; you can buy these made of stainless steel, but blue plastic water-piping cut to length and with a 'v' cut in either end is a cheap and dishwasher-friendly alternative. A thermometer is another handy addition. You can buy cheap models intended for use with domestic fridges, some of which come with a suction cup attachment which secures to the inside of a glass door. The great advantage of a chiller is that, apart from being insect-proof, it holds the game at a stable temperature far lower than would normally be possible. In high summer, even in a cool room, game needs to be dealt with quickly if there were to be no danger of it going off. Chilled, it can be left with complete confidence for much longer.

If you think that other members of your household may begrudge you the space for a chiller cabinet, think again. Mine has turned out to be very welcome at Christmas and other party times when I have to accept that I lose the exclusive rights to it. With the shelves refitted, it holds turkeys, bottles of wine, beer – in fact everything that the kitchen fridge can't cope with when catering for a house full of people.

Keeper's Tip: Lined wellington boots can develop an annoying squeak with each step as your feet warm up inside them. A very thin pair of socks against the skin, with normal socks over them, will eliminate this problem.

THE OLD MAN'S BOY

ROBERT RUARK, OFTEN UNFAIRLY DESCRIBED AS 'THE POOR MAN'S HEMINGWAY'

The dog changes the position of his head and creeps forward another six yards, and you come up behind him when he freezes again. This time he's looking right down at his forefeet, and when you walk past him he jumps and the world blows up.

The world explodes, and a billion bits of it fly out in front of you, tiny brown bits with the thunder of Jove in each wing. They go in all directions – right, left, behind you, over your head, sometimes straight at you, sometimes straight up before they level. Then a miracle happens.

Out of those billion bits you choose one bit and fire, and if the bit explodes in a cloud of feathers you choose another bit and fire again, and if this bit explodes you break your gun swiftly and load, figuring there's a lay bird and you can turn to the Old Man with a grin and when he says, 'How many?' you can answer 'Three'. More likely you'll answer, 'One' or 'None'.

(on shooting quail, from *The Old Man and the Boy*)

It must have been back in the early 1980s that a shooting friend lent me a book, suggesting that I might enjoy it. At first I wasn't so sure; it seemed to be a collection of short stories about a boy growing up in the Deep South of the USA, far removed from my usual choice of reading material. Nevertheless I dipped into it at random, and was immediately lost in an exhilarating description of hunting quail over pointers. From then on every episode gripped me, whether it covered the misery of setting out for a duck blind on a freezing winter day, the hunting of white-tailed deer with a shotgun and an ill-assorted gang of woodsmen, or the description of one ridiculous yet sublime attempt to harness a bad-tempered goat and train it to pull a cart. The stories, though so far removed from my own sporting upbringing, somehow struck a chord. The book was *The Old Man and the Boy*, written by an American called Robert Ruark, who quickly became a favourite author.

The Old Man and the Boy was a collection of stories taken from Ruark's regular columns in American shooting and fishing magazine *Field and Stream*, and was first published as an anthology in 1957. It was followed by another book, *The Old Man's Boy Grows Older*, in 1961. In addition to these, Ruark also wrote a number of novels and a best-selling account of an African safari, *Horn of the Hunter*. It is for his African works and the *Old Man* books that he is mainly remembered today, attracting something of a cult following worldwide, but particularly in his native United States.

Robert Chester Ruark was born on 29 January 1915 in the small town of Wilmington, North Carolina, where he spent his childhood. Wilmington lies close to the Cape Fear River and the east coast beaches of the Atlantic Ocean. By his own account, he was something of a loner, though considered a child prodigy among his fellow pupils, and it is telling that his writing says little about friends of his own age. His home life also appears to have been difficult. Growing up during the Depression, his parents struggled to make ends meet; in his novels, which use much autobiographical detail, Ruark portrays his father as ineffectual and his mother as domineering and intrusive. It seems that Ruark did his best to avoid home life and spent most of his time with his grandfathers. The Old Man character is an amalgamation of these, but seems mostly based on Captain 'Ned' Atkins on his maternal side. The Old Man is by turns a teacher and an equal, and a source of wisdom, philosophy and inspiration. Above all he has a wicked and sometimes juvenile sense of humour – just the right sort of mentor, in fact, for a boy learning how to use rod and gun and discovering his way in the world. Ruark's description of the effect of the Old Man's death on the Boy, in a piece entitled 'All He Left Me Was The World', is genuinely moving.

At just fifteen years old Ruark went to college, where he decided to pursue a career in journalism. After a couple of false starts, including going to sea in a tramp steamer and a disastrous spell as an accountant, he eventually found employment and his star was just beginning to rise when the war intervened. Serving in the US Navy, Ruark saw action in the Atlantic and the Mediterranean before eventually returning to Washington, where he quickly picked up a reputation for writing witty and provocative newspaper columns. Adding fiction, in the form of magazine articles and two light-hearted novels, to his writing success, for the first time in his life he was making enough money to pursue a childhood dream put into his head by the Old Man: to go on safari.

In 1951 Ruark, accompanied by his wife Virginia, landed in Nairobi and began what was to be, for him, a lifelong love affair with Africa. Two years later his account of the safari, *Horn of the Hunter*, was published. It is a snapshot of a world about to be swept away by the emergence of African nationalism, and is widely considered to be the finest book written on African hunting in the twentieth century. Simply but beautifully and sincerely written, it is not just a thrilling series of hunting adventures, but also a truthful and affectionate depiction of a world that was about to disappear forever. It is also a self-effacing account of one man's voyage of self-discovery; he freely admits his fallibility, and his reaction to a string of misses, or his disgust with himself for using a totally inadequate rifle for large quarry, are typical of the honesty of his writing.

The two-month safari also introduced Ruark to professional hunter Harry Selby, who despite his relative youth was to take on the mentor role originally provided by the Old Man. The two men were to hunt together for the next twelve years. Selby, thanks to *Horn of the Hunter*, quickly achieved something akin to superstar status, which he regretted. Although professionally it ensured advance bookings for years ahead, personally it alienated him from his fellow professional hunters.

Ruark was back in Kenya in 1953 when he witnessed first-hand some of the worst excesses of the Mau Mau uprising. Ostensibly a safari, Ruark's visit quickly turned journalistic and also furnished him with the material and characters for his first serious novel, *Something of Value*. It was an immediate bestseller but was not universally well received. The book pulled no punches regarding the brutality of both sides of the conflict, and still has the power to shock today. In many ways it was too accurate for comfort and Ruark's even-handed treatment of the protagonists won him few friends in Kenya. (Sixty-odd years on, the book remains fresh and well worth reading, by the way.)

Ruark's attitude towards Ernest Hemingway, with whom he found himself constantly being compared, was complex although there is no evidence that the two ever met. Hemingway was a literary giant of the day and Ruark seems consciously to have followed in his footsteps – his first safari booking with Harry Selby was partially driven by a desire to hunt with one of Selby's team, a tracker called Kidogo, who had also hunted with Hemingway many years earlier. Ruark confessed that the description 'the poor man's Hemingway' irritated him, but after Hemingway committed suicide in 1961 there is no doubting the sincerity of his written tributes. In his final novel, *The Honey Badger*, Ruark uses the killing of an ancient elephant as a metaphor for the passing of the 'old' Africa that he so loved. 'I did for the old elephant what Hemingway did for himself,' the central character remarks. The latter is unashamedly based on Ruark himself, and the novel characterises his attitude towards a vanishing era.

Ruark did not live by halves; he worked, played and drank hard. Selby noted how he would arrive for a hunting trip looking grey and tired, to improve visibly as Africa worked its magic upon him. However, his physical health continued to decline and he did himself no favours, drinking heavily and pushing himself to the limit, though he clearly knew that he was killing himself. His death in London on the 1 July 1965 from cirrhosis of the liver robbed the sporting world of an outstanding writer at his peak.

If you have not come across Robert Ruark before, why not give him a try? For sporting stories written simply and well, with a wealth of excitement, charm and a genuine love for hunting and the people involved in it, I don't think that he can be beaten. I hope that you will agree with me.

> Robert Ruark on sport hunting: *Death is not a terrible thing ... not if you respect the thing you kill, not if you kill to feed your people or your memory.* (***Horn of the Hunter***)
>
> *You might as well learn that a man who catches fish or shoots game has got to make it fit to eat before he sleeps. Otherwise it's all a waste and a sin to take it if you can't use it.* (***The Old Man and the Boy***)
>
> Robert Ruark on dogs: *The trouble with people is dogs, and the trouble with dogs is people. But somehow, one breed can't seem to get along without the other and still call it a life.* (***The Old Man's Boy Grows Older***)

Never underestimate a dog. If he's got sense enough to be bred from a family with a nose and a sense of decency, any mistake you let him make is your fault. (***The Old Man and the Boy***)

Robert Ruark on young Shots: *Any time a boy is ready to learn about guns is the time he's ready, no matter how young he is, and you can't start too young to learn how to be careful.* (***The Old Man and the Boy***)

Robert Ruark on leisure: *Today there's a lot of people who don't understand, when they see me sitting out in the yard, that I'm not really loafing. I'm recovering from the past and storing up for the future.* (***The Old Man and the Boy***)

Bibliography

- *Grenadine Etching* (1947) and *Grenadine's Spawn* (1952) – historical romps
- *I Didn't Know It Was Loaded* (1949), *One for the Road* (1949), and *Women* (1967) – anthologies of Ruark's early newspaper columns
- *Horn of the Hunter* (1953)**
- *Something of Value* (1955)††
- *The Old Man and the Boy* (1957)**
- *Poor No More* (1959)†
- *The Old Man's Boy Grows Older* (1961)*
- *Uhuru* (1962)†
- *The Honey Badger* (1965)†† Ruark's final novel, published posthumously
- *Use Enough Gun: On Hunting Big Game* (1966)*
- *Robert Ruark's Africa* (1991)* A collection of Ruark's magazine articles
- *The Lost Classics* (1996)* A further collection of hunting adventures

* Sporting reading (** recommended)
† Novels (†† recommended)

Tales from Glen Garron

Of Meissen Men

People may not always be what they seem – but perhaps first impressions are preferable

'Well, they're rather different to our Americans, aren't they?' the Colonel mused to himself, frowning slightly as one of the house guests lit up a small, acrid cheroot. He was very glad that Lady Mary was not here to see someone smoking in her drawing room where the group had gathered for drinks before dinner, and frankly not to hear some of the language. Mary was especially proud of this room; he couldn't see it from where he was standing by the door, but the heavy, glass-fronted display cabinet in the far corner contained her inherited collection of fine porcelain. Fortunately his wife had left for London the previous day to visit her daughter and their new grandchild, a brother for young Edward, while the Colonel had reluctantly stayed behind at Glen Garron to host the visitors. Still, Shuna the cook's blinis topped with haggis were a surprising success, and the chilled Cava was holding out until the imminent call came to move to the table.

'... and of course the man's a complete cock!' the speaker concluded, with a loud, braying laugh, looking around for somewhere to dispose of his ash. The Colonel found a small dish in a drawer and took it over to him.

'Thanks, old man,' the smoker said without turning, and carried on talking to the other two men who, it must be said, were looking rather uncomfortable.

The Colonel moved back to the party organiser, a man he had already decided that he liked. 'Who is that?' he asked in a low voice.

His companion shrugged. 'Not one of the regular syndicate, I'm afraid. His name's Ron Everleigh-Grainger, and apparently he's a commodity broker. We had to advertise a vacancy when one of the regular Guns dropped out at the last minute – it seems that a pearl wedding anniversary takes precedence over the Glorious Twelfth and the options were either shooting or divorce. Anyway, Harry suspected that his wife might have decided to combine the two, so he had to cancel.' Both men laughed sympathetically. 'The agent had this chap on his books, so it solved a last-minute problem though I don't think that he'll be joining us again.' He flinched as another loud burst of raucous laughter cut across the room.

It was with some regret that the Colonel had decided to sell a second day of grouse shooting this year: there were bills to be paid and maintaining a moor is not a cheap undertaking. His regular party of Americans were due the following week, but this roving syndicate, an all-male gathering, was something of an unknown quantity. The Lodge could easily accommodate them and the revenue would be very welcome after two poor breeding years with only the smallest surplus of birds to sell, mainly as walked-up sport. This year had been much better, with big broods of grouse seen across the moor and the season promised to be excellent. Tomorrow would be a driven day.

After a hearty breakfast, the shooting party gathered with their vehicles on the gravel driveway at the front of the Lodge. Ron Everleigh-Grainger was dressed in a checked tweed suit that was just a shade too loud and equally slightly too large for him, the inevitable cheroot hanging out of the corner of his mouth. He leaned on the bonnet of his new yellow BMW, registration RON 1, looking rather jaded. The Colonel knew why, having found the empty bottle of his best malt under the armchair from which the visitor had held court into the small hours the previous evening. He offered the man a civil greeting, only to receive a hearty slap on the shoulder and a 'Mornin' General' in return. He sighed, forced a smile in response and told himself that the Lodge would be his again that evening, and that anyway Mary would be back by the end of the week.

Guns were introduced to their loaders for the day. All were local men and women, chosen both for their reliability and discreet ability to gently control the less experienced guest in matters concerning safety. They would also quietly offer advice to those who were having difficulty coming to terms with the day's testing targets. Led by the Colonel in his elderly Land Rover, the small convoy made its way up to the moor where they were shown to their butts and Willie Cameron, waiting with Archie and the beating team, was radioed to commence the day's proceedings.

The day was a considerable success. Most of the Guns shot well, and a bag exceeding expectations was achieved. Shuna's lunchtime hampers, brought up in her pick-up, were eaten at the butts between morning and afternoon drives and loudly praised to her beaming delight as she tidied plates, glasses and debris away before loading up to return to the Lodge.

The day ended, Guns delighted with their sport, as they gathered with the beaters to admire the bag while Willie and Archie sorted young birds from old to assemble braces for the guests to take away. Each in turn shook hands with Willie as they received their birds, thanking him for the team's efforts while discreetly passing a note folded in their palm into his hand. When Ron's turn came he tucked a single ten-pound note into the breast pocket of Willie's jacket, patting him on the shoulder with his other hand and muttering 'Cheers, Jock'. Willie, more outraged by the size of the tip than the greeting, merely nodded his head in thanks. He watched Ron carry his guns over to the BMW. There was something familiar about the slips, and a curiously clean oblong of glass on the rear window of the car made him wonder. So did the pristine state of the personalised number plates against the rather travel-stained bodywork of the car.

The Guns departed, anxious to be clear of the small winding roads of the glen in daylight before joining the A9 trunk road for their onward journeys. Meanwhile the hosts headed back to the Lodge, where Shuna would have beer and a bracing stew laid out ready for all the loaders, beaters and pickers-up, as was the custom at Glen Garron.

Waiting for them on the Lodge driveway was a red and white police car. The occupant, who the Colonel recognised as the local constable, was standing with Shuna on the steps. 'I noticed that when I got back from lunch,' she said to the Colonel, pointing at a broken window on the ground floor. 'While I was out wi' your lunch someone's been in and had awa' the mistress's best china.'

'Sorry, sir,' the policeman added. 'I'm afraid that they've made a bit of a mess.'

The drawing room had been ransacked and the locked glass doors of the display cabinet forced open. The Colonel groaned; his wife's treasured collection was gone. Much was insured and replaceable, but her three favourite pieces certainly never could be. The figurine of Beltrame, a traditional Italian comic character, along with the two dancing Harlequins had been made in about 1740 in the German town of Meissen, famed for the manufacture of porcelain that was second only to the very best that the Orient could produce. All three pieces were immensely rare and had been in Lady Mary's family since beyond memory, and of all her possessions these meant the most. Their actual value, high enough in itself, was certainly secondary to their sentimental value. It was unlikely that any similar figurines existed in the world. The thieves had done well, the Colonel thought, though it surprised him that little else appeared to have been taken. It was as though the porcelain had been deliberately targeted by someone in the know.

Willie and Archie had been talking quietly outside and now came into the drawing room to join the Colonel, Archie pocketing his mobile phone. 'We need to have a chat with yon constable,' Willie announced. 'I think I know who's responsible for a' this.'

A few minutes later a message was being sent over the police radio network, giving descriptions of a vehicle and the two men who would be in it. The police car drove off, to return not long afterwards, a beaming constable in the driving seat.

'We got them, but only after a wee chase – which ended up with our two friends' car upside down in a ditch! The occupants are okay but I'm afraid that your crockery has had it,' he continued apologetically. 'It was all piled into a box in the boot and didn't survive the crash. Never mind, none of it was that new, was it?'

Uncharacteristically, the Colonel swore softly to himself. What the devil was he going to tell Mary? The poor girl would be heartbroken. Almost absent-mindedly he listened to the policeman's explanation of how the culprits had been tracked down.

'We had a run of these robberies last year, well spaced out across the Highlands and North Yorkshire moors, all taking place during the shooting season, then they suddenly stopped. Thanks to your gamekeeper I don't think we'll be experiencing them again this year.'

It was something that Archie had said which had got Willie thinking. The previous evening in The Kelpie there had been an incident when a visitor, booked in for one night only and somewhat the worse for wear, had made an unwelcome grab at Amanda the barmaid. 'He didnae persist, mind,' Archie had reported, smiling happily, 'though he won't be seeing through one eye for a week or two.'

Subsequently Willie had realised why Ron Everleigh-Grainger's gun slips were so familiar: they had originally belonged to the owner of an estate over on the west coast where he had accompanied the Colonel for a pheasant day the previous winter. Willie, asked to load for the owner's son, had himself accidentally scratched the deep parallel lines in the fine Spanish leather of the new double slip while crossing a barbed wired fence. The mistake had mortified him at the time but been taken well by the host and forgotten until now. That estate had itself been robbed while the household was involved in a guest pheasant day only a few weeks later, this time of the contents of the gun room after the thieves had mysteriously discovered a hidden key.

A quick call to Amanda had confirmed that the Englishman staying at The Kelpie had been picked up in a flashy yellow car shortly after the shooting party had dispersed. Later enquiries would show that it had been hired from a well-known firm – whose sticker had been removed from the rear window – just the day before. It was pure good fortune that the alert occupants of a patrol car had noticed the distinctive registration number before Ron Everleigh-Grainger (who turned out to be a confidence trickster called Lennie George, long sought by the police), and his accomplice had had a chance to change it back to the hire car's original plate. Mr George, it turned out, had a long list of alter egos, and false personalised plates to go with each one. 'Ron', of course, was never under suspicion, as he had always been out with a shooting party whenever thefts had occurred. All he had done was reconnoitre and pass details back to his accomplice, who had later been able to burgle an empty house knowing full details of staff, security arrangements and the location of any especially valuable items.

All of this was of no reassurance to the Colonel, who looked forward to the return of his wife with no little trepidation. Lady Mary duly arrived in her little red hatchback, left at Inverness Airport while she had flown south. As he tried to find the words to break the news of the destruction of her family heirlooms, Lady Mary forestalled him.

'It's lovely to be back darling, and I can't wait to hear all your news, but could you get my bags in first? Do be careful with the small one though; I took the Meissens with me to get them valued properly whilst I was in London, and it seems that we need to increase the insurance by rather a lot. It really would be awful if something happened to them, wouldn't it?'

That hunting has in many instances been carried out to an excess is well known, and the match given by the Prince Esterhazy, Regent of Hungary, on the signing of the treaty of peace with France, is not the least extraordinary upon record. On that occasion, there were killed 160 deer, 100 wild boars, 300 hares, and 80 foxes: this was the achievement of one day. Enormous, however, as this slaughter may appear, it is greatly inferior to that made by the contemporary king of Naples on a hunting expedition. That sovereign had a larger extent of ground at his command, and a longer period for the exercise of his talents; consequently, his sport, if it can so be called, was proportionally greater. It was pursued during his journey to Vienna, in Austria, Bohemia, and Moravia; when he killed 5 bears, 1,820 boars, 1,950 deer, 1,145 does, 1,625 roebucks, 11,121 rabbits, 13 wolves, 17 badgers, 16,354 hares, and 354 foxes. In birds, during the same expedition, he killed 15,350 pheasants and 12,335 partridges. Such an amount of destruction can hardly be called sport; it resembles more the indiscriminate slaughter of a battle-field, where the scientific engines of civilized warfare are brought to bear upon defenceless savages. **Mrs Beeton's *Book of Household Management* (1861)**

Keeper's Tip: Don't tie your dog to your belt, game bag or shooting stick – a sudden lunge can tip you off-balance with dangerous consequences. Carry a suitable tether for when standing at your peg (the ones that screw into the ground are excellent). If you can't control your dog, it really should not be out with you.

A SHOOTER'S GALLIMAUFRY

Although the invention of gunpowder has been credited to a wide variety of cultures, including the Chinese, Arab, Greek and Muslim, there is no hard evidence to confirm any of these as the originators. It is true that the Chinese did create various pyrotechnic substances but these were probably not true gunpowder. The first written evidence of its existence does not appear until the twelfth century, when a Franciscan friar, Roger Bacon, described 'the powder, known in divers places, composed of saltpetre, sulphur and charcoal'. What this 'powder' was used for is not certain, and it is possible that the flash and bang it created was little more than a novelty at the time.

The earliest known formula for gunpowder, as recorded by Roger Bacon, consisted of a mixture of 7 parts saltpetre, 5 parts sulphur and 5 parts charcoal. By the late eighteenth century it had developed to the more sophisticated and efficient 15 parts (75%) saltpetre, 2 parts (10%) sulphur and 3 parts (15%) charcoal.

Saltpetre, or potassium nitrate, is an essential component of gunpowder. This substance does occur naturally but only in hot, dry climates (India was a major source at one time) so in medieval Europe it had to be manufactured. This was done in several ways, one of which was to set up 'niter beds' of straw, through which human as well as animal urine and dung were filtered so that the nitrates could be extracted. It is said that the by-products of members of the nobility were thought to produce the best saltpetre, presumably because they enjoyed a richer diet.

One early problem with gunpowder was its tendency to separate into its constituent parts. During the fifteenth century the French overcame this problem by inventing 'corned' powder, which entailed mixing the ingredients whilst wet, then drying the resulting paste to create granules. Not only was this safer than dry mixing, but it created a powder that ignited faster and with greater regularity.

Early firearms relied on a system based initially upon a smouldering fuse, and then later on the sparks from a flint, to ignite a small amount of priming powder in an external pan, which in turn set off the main charge within the gun. Inevitably there was a delay between the two separate ignitions, from which we get the term 'flash to bang' time. Sometimes the priming powder would ignite but fail to set off the main charge – hence a 'flash in the pan'.

It wasn't until the early 1800s that an alternative ignition system to the unreliable external pan of priming powder was invented. It followed on from the discovery of fulminate of mercury, a highly volatile substance which only needed a sharp blow to detonate it. The Reverend Alexander James Forsyth of Belhelvie, Aberdeenshire, used this principle to replace the flint of the gun with a straightforward hammer; this ignited 'detonating powder' directly into a vent, which led to the main powder charge. This revolutionary system was patented in 1807 and the percussion principle was born.

Forsyth's detonating powder was quickly improved upon by other inventors. One early system involved pills of powder, coated in varnish and placed into the vent to be struck by the hammer. Another sealed small pinches of detonator between two pieces of paper, much like the modern day caps or *amorces* used in children's toy guns. Ultimately, however, the powder was put into a short copper tube with a closed end: the open end was placed directly into the vent and crushed by the falling of the hammer to fire the powder. The final logical progression was a small copper 'hat' with a small coating of detonating powder inside it, which was placed onto a nipple over the vent and fired by a hammer in much the same way. Who was actually first to invent this, the percussion cap, is much disputed; a number of people, including gunmakers Joseph Manton and Joseph Egg and noted sportsman Colonel Peter Hawker, all laid claim to the idea. Whatever the case, the percussion cap was firmly established by the early 1820s and it is generally agreed that, without it, firearms development could never have progressed as it subsequently did, and the breech loading gun with an 'all in one' cartridge would not exist as we know it today.

Although gunpowder was available much earlier, it is believed that guns were not used for the hunting of birds in Europe until at least the fifteenth century. Even then, they were so clumsy and unreliable that it was not until the eighteenth century that their efficiency had improved sufficiently for the sport of hunting with a shotgun to become popular.

Early live-quarry shooting with shotguns was of necessity more of an exercise in fieldcraft, i.e. getting as close as possible to the target and then shooting at it on the ground or on water. Only as ignition systems became more reliable did 'shooting flying' start to come into vogue. The first English book to consider the shooting of flying birds seriously was Richard Blome's *The Gentleman's Recreation* published in 1686, though it was not until the early eighteenth century that the practice seems to have become more widespread.

The principle of applying 'lead' to a moving target clearly took some time to catch on; Blome wrote in The Gentleman's Recreation*: 'Some are of the Opinion that must Shoot something before the Fowl, otherwise it will be past before the Shot can come to it: but that is a vulgar Error, for no Game can fly so quick, but that the Shot will meet it.'*

As long as sportsmen were confined to muzzle loading shotguns, which took time to reload once discharged, game shooting was usually conducted 'walked up', over pointing or setting dogs. Once a shot had been taken a party would halt to allow the firer to reload and the order given to 'hup your firearms'. The modern dog handler's command to 'hup', telling his dog to sit, has its origins in this instruction. It was not until the advent of rapidly-reloaded breech loaders that driven shooting as we know it became truly practicable.

The measurement of the bore of a gun has its origins in how cannon were categorised – for instance, a four-pounder would fire a four-pound lead ball. The bore, or gauge, of a gun follows the same system, but using fractions of a pound. Thus a 12 bore would be barrelled for a single round lead ball weighing 1/12th of a pound, a 20 bore a ball weighing 1/20th of a pound, and so on. The only exception is the .410, which is only referred to as a 'bore' by convention; in reality the measurement is the actual diameter of the bore in decimal inches, a curious combination in itself of Imperial and decimal measurements. Americans tend to refer to 'gauge' while the British talk in terms of 'bore', but they are in fact the same thing. Nineteenth century large bore black powder rifles are described in the same terms, and it was only later that calibres based on bore diameters, in inches or millimetres, came into being.

When black powder was the commonly used propellant for firearms, it could vary considerably from batch to batch, so a standardised test was necessary to measure its quality and power. This was done using an *eprouvette* (the word today means 'test tube'), a simple fixed mortar tube usually cast of iron or brass and angled at an exact 45 degrees. Into it would be loaded a standard quantity of powder along with a standard weight of shot, typically 24 pounds. The distance the latter fired would be compared to a definitive normal range to determine the powder quality.

Early firearms, both rifles and shotguns, had much longer barrels than we are used to today. This was necessary because of the slower-burning nature of black powder: it needed more barrel length to develop the necessary gas pressures to eventually expel the projectiles with the desired velocity than modern, faster-burning propellants.

Choke, in the simplest possible terms, refers to a constriction at the end of the shotgun barrel designed to concentrate the pattern of shot and hold it together more tightly over a longer distance, thus extending the effective range of the gun. The best way to understand choke is to consider how much of a charge of shot you might expect to see contained within a 30-inch diameter target at a range of 40 yards. Improved cylinder should place about 50% of the shot pattern within the target, with ¼ choke it should be about 55%, ½ choke (also known as modified cylinder) producing 60% and ¾ choke (improved modified) 65%. Full choke would increase the hits to about 70%. A trip to the pattern plate is a good idea. By shooting with the cartridges you plan to use at ranges varying between 20 and 40 yards you will be able to see what your individual gun actually achieves. By all means experiment with different cartridges to find what works best.

Most game guns come with fixed chokes, though more and more manufacturers are offering 'multichoke' guns with interchangeable inserts. This makes a gun much more versatile under a wider variety of circumstances – for instance, for normal game shooting you need rather less choke than you might for the longer ranges and tougher quarry involved in wildfowling. Skeet shooters use very little choke at all, as they are shooting clay pigeons at relatively short ranges. A good combination for normal game shooting might be that provided by improved cylinder or ¼ choke for closer shots, and ½ or ¾ choke for slightly further targets, in a double barrelled shotgun. It is easy to become confused, however, and the best advice of all to the occasional shooter is to find what works best for you in the field and leave it at that, rather than constantly changing your set-up in a frustrating search for perfection.

The mid-nineteenth century was a time of great innovation in firearms design. Portsmouth gunsmith John Aubrey offered the ingenious *Polychrest* choke, a wedge-shaped insert which, when fitted to the end of the muzzle, caused a charge of shot to split into two distinct patterns as it left the gun. Half of the shot would be directed to where the gun was pointing, while the other half would shoot to a point some two feet to the left or right of this depending on how the choke was set up. The name 'polychrest' was taken from a medical term, still used today, meaning a single remedy for several different ailments. Another design, registered under the name *Surprize*, extended the concept to the swivel guns mounted on naval vessels to counter enemy boarding parties, although the Admiralty did not take it up, to Aubrey's great disappointment.

Aubrey's advertisement explained the reasoning behind his invention: 'By this engine,' it read, 'the Gun may slay two birds of a covey with but the one charge, or shoot boldly into a flock with the expectation of an astonishingly increased success.' The 'splitting choke' did not catch on; shooters, unsurprisingly, preferred to rely on a more accurate second barrel. A regular sporting correspondent of *The Times*, one Captain Harte, scathingly described it as 'the gunsmith's mistake', a name by which it came to be more commonly known. Only a few examples have survived. One can be seen in the Maturin Collection maintained by the Royal Armouries in Leeds along with the original *Polychrest* design, prototype and proving pattern plate which were submitted to the Patents Office by Aubrey in 1841.

Traditional side-by-side sporting shotguns are usually designed so that the first pull of a single trigger, or the front trigger of a pair, discharges the right-hand barrel first. Game guns usually have fixed chokes, with the right-hand barrel choked looser than the left-hand one. This convention is a throwback to walked-up shooting; the first shot at a flushed bird would be at relatively close range, where the shot did not have much of a chance to spread out, whilst the second would be at a target that was further away. Keeping the shot pattern tighter for the second was therefore more advantageous at the greater range.

To be able to hit a moving target consistently demands that the shooter understands deflection shooting, meaning in simple terms aiming where the target is going to be rather than where it is now. Many of the fighter aces on both sides in the First and Second World Wars understood this concept implicitly, thanks to an upbringing involving shooting sports.

It is a common impression that the pheasant is slow-moving in flight, while the partridge moves much faster. This, however, is a misconception caused by the pheasant's larger size in comparison to the partridge's smallness and rapidly whirring wing beats. In fact the pheasant is moving more quickly and needs considerably more lead if you are not to miss it behind. By comparison, experienced shotgun coaches will suggest that you decrease the lead by at least one third for a partridge if you are not to miss in front. Mixed drives containing both species can be a real challenge as you have to adjust your technique to deal with the different targets, and accomplishing a 'right and left' at pheasant and partridge can be an extremely satisfying feat.

'Proof' is simply the process of test-firing a gun, using a much larger load and thus much higher pressures than would be normal, to ensure that the gun is safe for use. The gun is then marked with proof stamps, usually below the barrels in the area covered by the fore end. This process is required by law, and is conducted at one of the two proof houses in London and Birmingham. All new guns sold in this country must bear marks of proof, either from these houses or overseas establishments recognised by the International Proof Commission. The Proof Act requires that 'no small arm may be sold, exchanged or exported, exposed or kept for sale unless and until it has been fully proved and duly marked'. Britain recognises, among other countries, proof marks from Austria, Belgium, France, Germany, Italy and Russia, though not from the USA or Japan – guns imported from these countries must be proofed here before being offered for sale.

If you have an older gun it is worth examining the proof marks, which may show that it has been proofed for black powder only rather than the more modern propellants that create higher pressures on firing. Some manufacturers of 'best' quality guns submit them for proof before the expensive and time-consuming processes of engraving and the other finer aspects of finish are applied, just in case many months of work are rejected by the proof house.

The shotgun is certainly versatile, and can be used to discharge projectiles wildly different from the usual charge of lead shot. Flexible baton rounds, a sort of bean bag filled with a dense material, rubber slugs or shot, and even tear gas shells have been developed for crowd control, and the military have experimented with grenade rounds containing exploding projectiles as well as 'flechettes', a dense cloud of small darts discharged in a single shot.

In days gone by, cartridges would sometimes be loaded with rock salt, which would undoubtedly sting while being unlikely to cause fatal injuries at longer ranges. They were used by dog trainers to discipline unruly dogs, or by gamekeepers confronted by poachers. Thankfully such practices belong in the past. Today, 'bird bombs' are used to scare away birds on airfields and the like; these discharge an exploding projectile designed to make a lot of noise, rather like a firework, and a similar principle is used to create 'screechers' for a similar purpose. On the sporting end of the spectrum, hunters abroad often carry flare rounds for use in emergencies; apparently they come in low and high altitude versions. Solid slug is often used overseas for larger game, and a more accurate version of this is the Brenneke round. Designed in 1898, the Brenneke remains very popular. It has what appears to be rifling incorporated into the lead projectile, which doesn't, as is often believed, impart spin, but actually allows it to pass through the choked end of the barrel, and the wad remains attached to the slug to create drag to further enhance stability and increase accuracy. Another popular variant is the Foster slug, with a hollowed recess at the base of the projectile to improve stability. Both are surprisingly accurate at shorter ranges.

You occasionally come across some very bizarre loads in shotgun cartridges. A recent development in the USA has made it possible to discharge an arrow broadhead from a 12 bore. The example I saw was fired surrounded by a sabot, a plastic filler which creates a seal whilst inside the barrel and detaches from the projectile as it exits the muzzle. It certainly wasn't very accurate, and nobody seemed able to explain exactly what the point of it was in the first place.

A revolutionary new shotgun design was exhibited at the 1851 Great Exhibition. Built by a Parisian gunsmith called Lefaucheux, it featured barrels which hinged to allow the introduction of cartridges containing shot, powder and a fulminate mixture to ignite it, all in one package. A pin protruded from the cartridge and out of the breech end of the gun where it could be struck by an external hammer and fired. Though some critics decried the gun for its weight, increased recoil and poorer performance compared to the muzzle loaders in use at the time, the pinfire cartridge was born and provided a building block for what quickly became a new fashion for breech loaders.

The main problem with the pinfire cartridge was the fragility of the pins protruding from the cartridges themselves. The first centrefire cartridges such as we know them today appeared in 1861, introduced to Britain by Mr George H Daw. In these, the percussion cap that had previously sat on a nipple on the exterior of a muzzle loader was relocated and sunk into the base of the cartridge itself, where it could be struck by a pin contained within the internal mechanism of the gun. It was safer and quicker to load than the older pinfire type, and the 1860s shooter would find little obvious difference between his early firearm and a more recent side-by-side hammer gun. By 1871 the first really successful hammerless gun had been developed and, barring a few simple innovations, the shotgun has evolved very little since that time.

Many attempts have been made by gunmakers to improve on the basic design of the shotgun since the achievement of the hammerless, centrefire gun, but very few have really caught on. Two successes were Remington's first pump action shotgun of 1907, and John Moses Browning's automatically-loading shotgun of a few years earlier. The design of the latter, which used the recoil to eject and reload a fresh cartridge, has changed little in over a century.

In 2004 Remington introduced their EtronX electronic ignition system. This replaced the percussive detonation provided by a spring-loaded firing pin with a cartridge ignited by a 150-volt electrical pulse. Whilst the system had a few minor advantages over the more familiar type, the cost of a new gun was almost double that of a more conventional model and the idea fell out of favour.

Another innovation, this time from the 1960s, was the Gyrojet family of firearms. These fired what resembled bullets but were in fact small rockets containing their own fuel source; one featured in the James Bond film *You Only Live Twice*. They included pistols, rifles, and even an experimental 'pepperbox' design with twelve barrels. Although light, thanks to the minimal internal pressures generated by the rocket system, accuracy was poor and the ammunition expensive. A few were sold commercially and the design was trialled by the US military (some even saw service in Vietnam), but production soon ceased.

These guns occasionally appear for sale, usually in the United States, but even the most common version will cost around $1,000. If that sounds cheap, you'll need to take the cost and availability of ammunition into account as well. If you can find it, it costs over $100 a round.

The largest shotgun calibre still seen in the shooting field is the 2 bore, a monster of a gun which demands a powerful physique to control it, and they are very rarely encountered. There are probably only a few dozen still in use in Britain. The 4 bore is slightly more common, and used primarily for goose shooting. Owners have to reload their own ammunition and save their brass cases carefully once fired. With 4-inch cartridge cases containing up to 3½ ounces of shot, these can produce efficient patterns as far out as 80 yards away. The 8 bore is the largest shotgun calibre for which you can hope to find commercially produced ammunition, but you will probably have to search hard and be prepared to pay a hefty price. A recently viewed advertisement asked £100 for 25 cartridges loaded with No 3 shot.

Some think that a sound moderator or suppressor can only be fitted to a rifle or pistol that fires a solid projectile, but moderators are available for shotguns as well. Most popular is probably the Hushpower system, which sleeves along the length of a single or over-and-under barrel. Available to fit a number of gun models, they are surprisingly effective and very popular among vermin controllers. However, the added weight radically affects the balance and 'swing' of a gun, so they are considered a specialist tool rather than a general game shooting gun.

A sound moderator is considered by law to be a firearm in its own right, and takes on the characteristics of the gun to which it is fitted. Thus to acquire one for use on your stalking rifle you will need permission to do so on your Firearms Certificate, though it is possible to buy a shotgun moderator over the counter on production of a Shotgun Certificate. For use on an 'off ticket' air rifle generating less than 12 foot-pounds of muzzle energy, you won't need a licence for a moderator at all – but woe betide you if you then fit it to a .22 rimfire!

Some interesting cartridge loads appear from time to time. If you find yourself troubled by the undead, look no further than ammunition manufacturer Hornady, who offer a range of munitions in a variety of calibres for rifle, pistol and shotgun under the name of Zombie Max. I showed the advertising video to a group of students during a firearms theory lesson one Hallowe'en; one earnest individual, to the great amusement of his fellows, asked what was special about the loads and how they actually worked to despatch zombies. Having never needed to use them, I'm afraid that I had to admit ignorance, but suspect that they are little more than standard loads in lurid packaging.

The 'Defence' gun, designed by James Puckle in 1718 to fire both round and square shot (the patent claimed that the latter would 'convince the Turks of the benefits of Christian civilisation'), is echoed by a newer, but much more practical shotgun load from Winchester ammunition. Instead of traditional round pellets, the Blindside cartridge features cubic shot with rounded corners which stacks more efficiently, allowing 15% more shot to be contained in the available space within the cartridge. The manufacturers claim an increase in the kill zone of the pattern of some 25%. Intended mainly for use by wildfowlers, the shot is steel and the cubic shape is specifically designed to hit harder than conventional rounded pellets.

Another interesting development in shotgun loads has been driven by the proliferation of 'drones' – remotely piloted helicopters, many of which carry cameras – that are now readily available to the general public. A backlash was inevitable as people started to object to their privacy being invaded, and a number of companies in the United States now offer anti-drone shotgun ammunition. Most of it is little more than standard cartridges loaded with heavy shot, but one manufacturer claims that their 'ferromagnetic' shot disrupts the electronic controls of the drone even if it doesn't manage to smash it beyond repair. Most worrying is Tacnition's Drone load; advertisements offer a 3-inch cartridge firing 9 pellets, claimed to be depleted uranium buckshot, with a range of up to a kilometre. Given the apparent massive toxicity of the payload, the description ought to be taken with a large pinch of salt. I suspect that such a thing would be unlikely to catch on on this side of the pond anyway.

You might want to think twice before taking a pot-shot at a drone in any case. Even in the States there are warnings that taking such direct action might put you on the wrong side of the law. The US Federal Aviation Authority is of the opinion that drones are classified as aircraft, and shooting one down unlawfully is punishable by up to 20 years in prison and up to a $250,000 fine.

The late 17th Viscount Mountgarret would have approved of developments in anti-drone ammunition but his story provides a timely warning to British shooters. In 1982, outraged by a hot-air balloon flying low over his grouse moor in Yorkshire just as a drive was about to start, he took two shots at it. The pilot was hit in the neck while the two passengers (an aircraft technician and a fish fryer) very sensibly ducked. Mountgarret claimed that he had fired 'deliberate and calculated' warning shots because the balloon occupants were in 'extreme danger' from the guns below. The magistrates thought otherwise and fined him £1,000 and a further £600 costs. Later he also had his Shotgun Certificate withdrawn.

Mountgarret was nothing if not eccentric. At the end of a shooting day he sometimes invited guests back to his house to take part in 'indoor golf'. A feature such as his double bed would be appointed as the 'hole', and participants would chip their way to it with club and ball, including a trip up the stairs if necessary. Considerable damage was often done to household contents in the course of the game.

Gunsmiths, deciding that two barrels on a shotgun might not be sufficient for some people, have occasionally produced triple or even quadruple barrelled versions. It is even possible to buy them 'off the shelf' from Turkish company Akkar. Marketed under the name of Mammut (Mammoth), their family of triple barrelled guns are arranged in a triangular stacking configuration and chambered for 12, 20 and 28 bore cartridges. They cost from around £1500. One respected UK reviewer was pleasantly surprised by the weight and good handling of an example under test.

A more traditional 'side-by-side-by-side', made by renowned Edinburgh gunmakers John Dickson & Son for the 1st Marquess of Linlithgow in 1891, was sold at auction in 2010 for £43,000. Weighing just 7 pounds and nicknamed The Holy Grail, it is believed to be the only 16-bore, round action side-by-side-by-side ejector ever built and was still in perfect working order.

Joseph Manton (1766 – 1835) is considered by many to have been the finest gunmaker of all time. His standards were high, turning the gun from a mere working tool into a thing of beauty. His innovative approach and constant drive for perfection had a profound influence on the early nineteenth century gunmaking industry, and spawned the era of the 'best' London gun. Among his workforce were such names as Thomas Boss, William Greener, Charles Lancaster and James Purdey, all of whom went on to create their own dynasties. The latter is reported to have said that 'but for him we should all have been a parcel of blacksmiths'.

Geoffrey Boothroyd (1925 – 2001) was a prolific writer with a regular column in Shooting Times, *an acknowledged authority on the subject of firearms in general and considered the world's leading expert on shotguns in particular. He was most famously responsible for arming James Bond with his trademark Walther PPK pistol. After the first of Ian Fleming's novels,* Casino Royale, *was published, Boothroyd wrote to him praising the novel but decrying Bond's .25 Beretta as 'a lady's gun – and not a very nice lady at that!'. Further correspondence between the two not only saw Bond re-equipped, but Boothroyd named in future stories as the armourer 'Q'.*

When in France

When our children were small, we had great fun camping with them during the summer holidays. One year we stayed on a campsite in the Champagne region, a fully equipped ground complete with two carp lakes and a family-friendly bistro and bar set alongside the river that ran through the site. Looking down into the river from a bridge, it was clear that there was no shortage of wild brown trout.

On our first evening there I wandered down to see if there was any activity; the river was alive with rising fish.

The next evening, I put together a little six-piece travelling fly rod that I had managed to hide among the holiday luggage, and made my way to the river for the last half-hour of daylight. There were rising fish everywhere, but no sign of any specific fly life so I tied on a general pattern, which was totally ignored. Puzzled, I changed fly with the same result. Around me were other campers equipped with bubble floats and whatever baits they could rustle up, all having a similar lack of success.

Over the next few nights the results were frustratingly similar, though the locals were clearly amused by the strange *Anglais avec la mouche*. I collected a regular audience at the bar on the far side of the river, who clearly enjoyed shouting what I hoped were helpful comments across the water. By now I had virtually thrown everything in my fly box at the trout and provoked absolutely no interest. This was getting embarrassing. I needed to catch something, if only for reasons of national pride.

Eventually, as the daylight was fading, I turned in desperation to the appropriately named Last Hope, a pale moth imitation that I had never really had that much faith in. No sooner had it hit the water than a large mouth engulfed it. The rod bent, and shortly afterwards a beautiful wild brown trout of about a pound and a half lay on the bank. I looked up to a raucous round of applause from my audience and couldn't resist a polite bow in return.

Intrigued at what the fish had actually been taking off the surface of the water, I spooned out the contents of its stomach. I should have guessed – this was a French trout after all. It was crammed full of small, floating snails.

Tales from Glen Garron

2040 – A Keeper's Lament

When did it all go so wrong? Archie Cameron asked himself wearily as he surveyed the Glen Garron moors from the viewing point on the tourist trail. For as far as the eye could see a forest of rank, old heather stretched, barren and unwelcoming. How different to his Da's day when it was carefully managed into a patchwork of various growth stages to provide food, cover and refuge to all manner of birds and animals.

It's a good job that auld Willie never lived tae see this, he thought. The Fenn trap ban had been just the start of the decline. The trap lines had been taken in, and predation had gone through the roof as suddenly the population of stoats and weasels spiralled out of control. Soon afterwards, a blanket ban on heather burning caused grouse numbers to fall so rapidly that the Colonel had reluctantly decided that there just weren't enough to justify shooting any more. A punitive new tax regime aimed at landowners had forced the sale of ground that had been family-owned and cherished for generations: suddenly there was no way left to make ends meet.

The Colonel had died shortly afterwards, some said of a broken heart, and Lady Mary had had no option but to sell the Lodge to the Charity, who had turned it into a visitor centre and designated the wild places of Glen Garron a nature reserve. Legions of scientists, '*phuds*' as Willie had dismissed them disparagingly, earnest young things with strings of qualifications, had descended on the Glen with their ambitious 'action plans' and decided that 'regeneration' was the way forward. The advice of anyone without letters after their name, irrespective of age and experience, went completely unheeded.

Willie was cruelly dismissed as an old-school anachronism; he hadn't lasted long after that and they had buried him alongside the rows of ancestors in the village churchyard. Archie had been kept on with the glorified title of 'Ranger', in reality a sort of odd-job man to maintain the visitor access, provide a bit of local 'flavour' and do the dirty jobs that the new management found distasteful. He'd had to move out of the keeper's cottage, now an expensive holiday home, and into a featureless modern bungalow on a newly built estate. There were few familiar faces left to have a drink with in what he still liked to think of as The Kelpie, now owned by a pub chain and renamed 'The Whisky Galore!'; most of his childhood friends had moved away to seek work elsewhere as there was little left for them here. There was no Amanda behind the bar any more either – what on earth had she ever seen in that ecologist?

Now, twenty years on, there seemed to be barely a red grouse left on the moor. There had been a heather burn recently, but of entirely the wrong kind. A disposable barbecue left smouldering by picnickers not far from a merlin's nest had started a wildfire, terrifyingly fast and totally uncontrollable as it raced through the tinder dry old heather. It had only burned itself out when the wind had backed in a stroke of pure good luck. Hundreds of acres of moor had been devastated, left scarred, blackened and lifeless. *Well,* Archie thought, *at least there'll be some food for the grouse when the ling comes through again – aye, if there are any grouse left by then to eat it, that is.*

The two remaining blackcock had lekked for the last time on their traditional site only a couple of years ago, but there had been no attendant audience of greyhens and he hadn't seen one since. *Some wildlife ranger I am,* Archie snorted to himself angrily. *There's nae bliddy wildlife any more.* As if to contradict him, a pair of hooded crows flew overhead, cawing mockingly. At least the corbies were doing well, and no wonder; the last of the ladder traps had been broken up long ago, and Archie was no longer allowed to carry a gun as he went about his daily business. Apparently it sent the wrong message to the visitors, and didn't the crows know it. The Charity had long since deemed pest control by shooting too expensive in any case as the ban on lead shot was total now. *Hell, Da', whit would ye say?*

The Garron no longer held salmon; a combination of uncontrolled poaching, netting in the estuary and a hydro-electric project downstream had seen to that. The only life on the river now was fleets of canoes from 'Bonnie Wee Highland Adventures' based in what used to be Inverpockle House. There were still trout in some of the hill lochs, but these were only ragged-tailed farmed rainbows, stocked weekly for the put-and-take fishermen to trawl for with their spinners and brightly coloured lures.

Archie set his face into a fixed smile as a file of cagoule-clad walkers trudged past him, eyes fixed on the path ahead. Loud music came from one of several cars parked next to him, the occupants eating sandwiches and looking bored, while a couple of scramble bikes sped past, gunning their engines and scattering gravel. Two more black and grey corbies strutted, unabashed and unafraid, next to the overflowing rubbish bin and as Archie watched, a car window wound down long enough for one of the occupants to toss them an unwanted piece of bread crust. None of the visitors paid any attention to their surroundings or the stationary figure dressed in a plain black anorak with the blue Charity badge on his sleeve. How Archie missed the practical estate tweeds which now hung, unused, in a wardrobe, kept for old times' sake but now the uniform of a bygone era.

Archie glanced at the information board at the front of the viewing point, illustrating the various forms of wildlife you might aspire to see from here. *Ach*, there might still be the odd grouse if you were lucky, but the golden eagles and hen harriers were long gone. The unchecked fox population had done for the last of the latter, and as there were no gamekeepers left to blame, the Charity had no option but to grudgingly accept that fox predation was responsible. Only the occasional wader nested here any more, and Archie smiled wryly at a very old memory of snowy owls. The much vaunted wolves still turned up once in a while to take a sheep or two, but there were no deer left here in any numbers for them to prey upon and the locals locked their livestock away carefully every night. The picture of a lynx was fanciful; nobody he knew had ever actually seen one, but Archie knew that between them and the pine martens nothing lasted for long on the ground these days. The wild cat had gone the way of the capercaillie, and he doubted that he would ever see either again. The once beloved moor was now a mere shadow of its old self, a refuge for little more than minor predators and scavengers.

Eight white giants stood on the far hillside, the sails of all but one stationary, despite the light breeze. It was underneath one of them that Archie had picked up the last eagle left in Glen Garron, a pathetic bundle of feathers lying immobile below the great turbines. At one time he had kept records of the legion of birds that had fallen prey to the huge windmilling blades but long since ceased to bother. Nobody was interested in his records – he'd been told in no uncertain terms they might threaten the attractive subsidies the Charity received for having them on their land.

He sighed and climbed into the brightly coloured pickup, still spattered with peat from the effort of towing yet another off-roading driver out of a hag. Nobody seemed interested in controlling the weekenders in their four-by-four vehicles, fitted with the inevitable snorkels and seemingly useless winches, driving about wherever they wished. The poor fragile habitat hadn't a chance.

Now it was time to eat some supper before a night spent in the regeneration areas, driving the newly created tracks with rifle and spotlight to shoot any remaining roe or red deer, irrespective of sex or age, that might dare to show up and threaten the precious new trees. Close seasons were a thing of the past; deer no longer had such protection and were now treated as just another threat to forestry and agriculture. *If it's broon it's doon*, Archie thought with a grimace, hating himself for what he now had to do. He needed to get a move on; it was an hour's round trip to sign out rifle and ammunition from where they now had to be lodged in the police station armoury, and that new sergeant was a stickler for paperwork.

A quick check of his wallet confirmed that he was carrying proof of passing the twice-yearly marksmanship test now demanded by the law, and Archie hoped that the police would have the right ammunition in stock at a sensible price. Picking it up from a gun shop was a thing of the past, even if there had been a gun shop still left open in the area; thanks to Health and Safety laws, alongside a burgeoning compensation culture, home loading was out of the question now. Every single round fired had to be justified and accounted for these days, with empty cases returned and tallied monthly against the national police computer. The following morning any carcases would have to be weighed, tagged, recorded and then checked into the council yard for incineration. The TB explosion down south had put paid to the once-thriving venison industry for good and anyway, people didn't want to eat meat that came in fur or feathers rather than a vacuum pouch.

Archie woke with a start, sweating heavily, as a hammering on his bedroom door brought him rudely back to the present. 'Will ye no' get a bliddy move on, ye damn'd idle layabout!' A voice that he recognised with deep relief echoed round the corridor. 'It's a braw day and the ling will nae burn itself. Get yer breeks on, man!'

Archie smiled. The sun was streaming through the curtains and it was indeed rare braw outside. An inviting smell of bacon wafted up from downstairs and he suddenly remembered that it was Amanda's night off tonight. He thrust the nightmare behind him, swung his legs out of the bed and sat up to face the day. Could that really be the future, he wondered?

No' on my watch, he resolved, *nivver, nivver on my watch.*

Long before firearms were available as a means of providing wild game for the table, and certainly records go back to the thirteenth century, it was a common practice to trap duck in tunnels made of nets, into which the birds were driven. The net would have a large, hooped entrance but steadily decrease in diameter as the duck swam into it, and a number of these 'pipes' would lead up different inlets from the main pond in a star configuration. White decoy mallard, specifically bred for their colour, would be used to lure in wild birds, which were then funnelled steadily into the nets.

By the sixteenth century another technique had been developed in the Netherlands using dogs, which would appear from behind a series of screens. Usually the size and colour of a fox, these dogs would attract the attention of the duck and then lead them into the nets. The word 'decoy' itself comes from the Dutch *de kooi*, literally 'the cage', or possibly *eendenkooi*, meaning 'duck-cage'.

Some of these old decoy ponds still exist and the remains of many others are recognisable across the UK. A working example is operated by the National Trust at Boarstall in Buckinghamshire where, if you plan your visit to coincide with them, demonstrations can sometimes be seen. Other working decoys exist in the Netherlands, though trapped wildfowl tend to be ringed for scientific study rather than ending up on the dinner plate.

Dog breeds specifically created to lure wildfowl are known as Tollers ('toll' is an old English word meaning 'to lure'). The Kooikerhondje is one such breed, while the Nova Scotia Duck Tolling Retriever is another. The Kooikerhondje is a small, red and white dog the size of a spaniel, which was originally bred in Holland as a duck decoy dog; the Nova Scotia Retriever was specifically bred on the eastern coast of Canada as more of a hunting dog, trained first to lure the duck to within gunshot range and then to retrieve them afterwards. Some purists suggest that the tail of this retriever should always have a white tip which, when wagged, helps to attract the wildfowl.

Punt gunning originated as a means of taking wildfowl for the commercial market and has been practised for around 200 years, although the professional wildfowler had all but disappeared by the early 1900s. The method is now undertaken by only a handful of people on the coasts of Britain, and then purely for sport. It involves pursuing wildfowl in estuaries and on the open sea in a purpose-built low craft resembling a canoe (the punt), which has been constructed to enable it to contain a larger than usual gun. The punt has only a few inches of freeboard and is initially propelled by paddles. Then the gunner lies prone and manoeuvres into position with poles as he stalks to within a suitable shooting range, around 60 yards, of large flocks of birds on sand and mud banks at the water's edge. Both gun and punt are usually painted grey as camouflage against the sea's surface.

The punt gun itself is a fearsome thing, usually purpose made and measuring in the region of 8 feet long, the long barrel being essential to ensure an effective burn of the propelling powder. As they were individually made, bores could vary considerably but muzzle diameters might be anything between 1 and 2 inches (today the maximum permissible size is 1.75 inches), firing up to a pound of shot propelled by black powder. Large shot, such as BB, AAA or No 1 is normally used, ensuring that there are very few wounded birds left to be despatched, although the gunner almost invariably carries a lighter gun as well, such as a 12 bore, for this purpose.

Operating a punt demands a great deal of skill, fitness and seamanship; it is not for the person for whom shooting alone is the main attraction of his sport. The punt gunner is lucky to get one shot in an outing, and often has to abandon a stalk because there are non-target species among the pack of duck. Mallard, wigeon, teal and pintail are the main quarry; it is rare to get a shot at geese as these are usually feeding inland during the day.

Sir Ralph Payne-Gallwey, the founding President of the Wildfowlers' Association of Britain and Ireland (later BASC) was a keen practitioner, as were actor James Robertson Justice and a young Sir Peter Scott. Research carried out by BASC in 1995 found only 45 dedicated punt gunners still operating. They averaged between them about 7 outings every season, resulting in 4 shots; on the occasions when they managed to get into position for a shot, the average bag was 16 birds although bags far exceeding that number are possible.

Game books vary enormously in style and content. Some people are content to record only the date, location and what was shot, while others catalogue the weather, the names of fellow Guns, and anything else that they feel a need to retain for posterity. You can buy game books that are leatherbound and beautifully illustrated or more modest versions, that just provide a place to record the basics; it is really up to you what information you want to keep for future reference and pleasure. Most shoots these days ensure that Guns are given a card with the tally for the day and the names of those present so that they can transfer the information to the game book when they get home.

It is usual for the pages of game books to offer pre-printed columns, so that the bag can be sorted by species: pheasant, partridge, woodcock, duck etc, with a final column headed 'Various' for the odds and ends that turn up in the bag. Keeping meticulous records can become an obsession. It is said that one titled gentleman, tired of life, carefully wrote 'One Baronet' under the Various column before reaching for the family Purdey.

The necessity to hold a gun licence was not introduced into English law until 1870 – they cost 10 shillings (50 pence) a year, and were widely regarded as no more than a cynical move by the Exchequer to raise revenue. It was not until 1903 that the Pistols Act restricted the sale of pistols to those over 18, and there was no further notable firearms legislation until the Firearms Act of 1920, which restricted ownership of rifled firearms, a response to fears raised by the recent Revolution in Russia and a rise in terrorism. The requirement to hold a Shotgun Certificate did not arise until the advent of the 1968 Firearms Act.

Standing over a metre high and weighing up to 16 kilograms, the great bustard dwarfs even the mute swan (a mere 11 kilograms) and was once the largest bird to be found in Britain. At one time it had an open season from 1 September to 1 March, and was pursued by sportsmen concealed by stalking horses or mounted in farm carts; it was also popularly coursed with running dogs.

Sadly, changes to agricultural methods, egg collectors and unrestricted shooting reduced numbers to the point when the last pair to breed successfully (until recently) was in 1832. After a female was shot in Cornwall in 1843, the bustard disappeared until abortive attempts to reintroduce the species in Suffolk around 1900 and at Porton Down, Wiltshire, during the 1970s and 1980s. Another attempt commenced in 2004 with the release of 22 birds at a site on Salisbury Plain in Wiltshire, and more following every year thereafter. The first breeding success was in 2009 and there have been many more since, making the future for this magnificent bird look promising. It is possible to view the birds in the release area by contacting the Great Bustard Group through their website (greatbustard.org). It is an inspiring experience and highly recommended, and the re-establishment of the bustard as a UK resident is now looking increasingly likely.

Did you know that it is illegal to carry a knife with a locking blade in public unless you have good reason to do so? This might include travelling between your home and the workplace where you need the knife, so a stalker or shooter who needs one in the field is safe under this exemption. If you forget to take it out of your pocket afterwards, though, you could end up in trouble. Otherwise only non-locking knives with folding blades under 3 inches (7.62cm) long, such as the ubiquitous Swiss Army knife, may be kept in your pocket.

On the Glorious Twelfth of August every year there is a highly publicised 'race' between fashionable restaurants to get the first grouse of the season down from the northern moors and onto London dinner plates that evening. The logistical effort to get a handful of birds to the chefs in time to be prepared and cooked can be ridiculously expensive, perhaps as much as £50 a bird. Most people agree that even a young grouse benefits from hanging for at least a day or two anyway, and preferably more, to improve the flavour. Diehards will argue against this, of course, and anyway the whole event is great fun, if something of a public relations stunt. For those who want to eat hung grouse on the Twelfth at a more sensible price, there is now a cheaper alternative if you live far from the moors – frozen grouse can be purchased from some supermarkets for less than £10 a brace.

Although trophies of the chase are most associated with larger game, or perhaps the odd woodcock pin feather in a hatband, you occasionally find smaller game mounted and displayed to commemorate a special occasion. In our house, tucked away among the deer antlers, are two of the family's most treasured trophies. They are the single pads of two rabbits, carefully dried in the airing cupboard and mounted on oak plaques along with a brass plate bearing initials, place and date, marking each of my son's first rabbits shot with the little family .410.

The flight speeds of some of our game birds and wildfowl might surprise you, as size frequently catches people out by giving an impression of slowness, while fast, flickering wingbeats and unpredictable flight can make a bird seem to be going faster than it actually is. The following list of level flight speeds, gathered from a number of sources, may persuade you to apply more lead, or perhaps a little less, at times:

Red grouse	*– 63 mph*	*Mallard*	*– 55 mph*
Black grouse	*– 62 mph*	*Grey partridge*	*– 45 mph*
Snipe	*– 60 mph*	*Capercaillie*	*– 45 mph*
Ptarmigan	*– 60 mph*	*Red-legged partridge*	*– 40 mph*
Golden plover	*– 60 mph*	*Shoveler*	*– 40 mph*
Canada goose	*– 60 mph*	*Wood pigeon*	*– 37 mph*
Pheasant	*– 56 mph*	*Teal*	*– 35 mph*
Pintail	*– 56 mph*	*Woodcock*	*– 30 mph*

As for the top avian predators, the peregrine averages up to 65 mph in level flight and stoops at as much as 200 mph when hunting. The golden eagle, although looking deceptively slow because of its size, has been measured doing 80 mph in level flight (although the average is somewhat slower); the stoop, however, can be an awe-inspiring 150 mph, which explains why red grouse can be such a regular prey item.

For the record, the fastest recorded average bird speed is for the grey-headed albatross, one of which maintained a constant 78.9 mph for over eight hours, according to a study by the British Antarctic Survey.

There is a much-repeated urban (or could it be rural?) myth that says if you hit a pheasant with your car, you are breaking the law if you stop and pick up the carcase, although the driver of the car behind you is allowed to do so. This is completely untrue; all wild animals and birds (including released game, which reverts to wild status the moment it leaves the pheasant or partridge pen) are *rex nullius* or the property of nobody in the eyes of the law. Once dead, they belong to the person on whose land they die. Thus the road casualty pheasant belongs to the road authority or local council depending on the circumstances. Mind you, I have never heard of anyone being charged with theft for picking up roadkill. More care needs to be taken when shooting near land boundaries, though. A bird that is shot on your side but falls on your neighbour's land technically belongs to him, though most shoots have agreements in place which allow them to gather in shot game.

There are considerable variations in the level of formality that you will encounter on a shoot. On my own 'walk one, stand one' syndicate we have a mix ranging from local farmers to retired Army Generals, and preferential treatment is neither expected nor given. It is often very different elsewhere though. Early in my shooting career I was on a similar format of shoot in very hilly ground where, for one drive, the 'youngsters' were told to climb a steep slope to work a flanking movement and hopefully push a few partridges over the more senior Guns below. I was surprised to find a couple of grey-haired gentlemen who had easily reached their half century toiling up the hill alongside me. Why hadn't they taken up their positions at the bottom, I asked? The answer came with a wry smile: 'On this shoot you're not considered old until you hit sixty-five and have had at least one hip replacement!'

Consciousness of rank can be taken to extremes. Towards the end of the season on a major military shoot we were told very firmly that it was 'cocks only', and that any hen birds in the bag would be viewed with considerable displeasure. On the very first drive, a hen pheasant accordingly flew down the line of Guns to a refrain of 'Hen!' ... 'Hen!' ... 'Hen!' ... BANG.

'Good shot, General!'

We have come a long way from the rigidly formal world of organised hunting in centuries gone by. Formal shooting then had its own rules, and woe betide anyone who was caught committing the slightest breach of etiquette. At one time a transgressor might be ritually beaten with the flat of a sword, or more recently 'fined' a case of vintage port or champagne for errors of behaviour in the field. Today, organised shoots tend to be far less formal, and the only time bad behaviour is really frowned upon is where it concerns safety.

The largest number of grouse shot walked-up by one Gun was achieved by Maharaja Duleep Singh in 1871, when no less than 440 fell to his gun in a single day on the Grandtully Castle moor in Perthshire. After his Indian estates were taken over by the British East India Company along with the Koh-i-Noor diamond (which was later set into Queen Victoria's crown) he proceeded to transform himself, with great success, into a sporting English country gentleman. He never forgave the Queen for the loss of the Koh-i-Noor, referring to her as 'Mrs Fagin' (after the thief in Dickens's Oliver Twist*) for the rest of his life.*

The most driven grouse killed by an individual was a total of 1,070, a record set in 1888 on Blubberhouse Moor in Yorkshire by Lord Walsingham. The drives started at 5.12 a.m. and finished at 6.45 p.m. with two teams of beaters pushing the birds backwards and forwards over his head across a narrow neck in the moor during a total of twenty drives. He went on to add a further 14 birds to his total during the walk home. It has been suggested that a large number of the bag were picked up exhausted having been harried to and fro all day and, although the feat was applauded at the time, it is very doubtful that it would attract the same approval today.

In 2015, the shoot-finding service GunsOnPegs advertised driven grouse shooting in Essex. The Low Moor shoot, situated between Basildon and Southend-on-Sea, boasted released grouse supposedly bred and reared from an enclosed flock originally sourced from the Yorkshire Dales. A typical day was described thus:

> *We ask Guns to meet at 8.30 a.m. for breakfast which will be followed by a quick safety brief from the head Game Keeper Charlie Raynard in the Lidl car park opposite the shoot lodge. After the safety brief we will draw our pegs for the day and head down London Road to the first drive. We will do two drives then stop for elevenses (bramble brandy, Ribena and rook pie) before we fit in another two drives before lunch. A three-course lunch will be served in our custom built shoot lodge just behind Lidl and after lunch we will have one more drive to finish the day off. Once the last drive is finished the Guns will meet the keeper back at the lodge and be given a brace of grouse to take home.*

It may be worth noting that the advert was uploaded to their website on 1 April; despite this, GunsOnPegs report that they received a number of genuine enquiries about bookings from some ultimately rather embarrassed prospective clients.

It is difficult to resist mentioning a few of the more obscure and sometimes archaic local laws found in some of the states and cities of the USA that affect the shooter. Firearms owners often receive mixed messages; for example, in Maine, Massachusetts and South Carolina, citizens are required to take their guns to church with them on Sundays in case of a surprise attack by Native Americans. Some rules are pretty confusing: in Pocatello, Idaho, a law was passed in 1912 stating that 'the carrying of concealed weapons is forbidden, unless some are exhibited to public view' whereas in Seattle you cannot carry a concealed weapon that is more than six feet in length. Other rules are rather more reassuring. In Pennsylvania it is against the law to discharge a gun, cannon, revolver or other explosive weapon at a wedding and, better yet, in Utah it is illegal to detonate any nuclear device.

Of course the hunter has to be very careful not to breach local regulations. Kansas laws forbid both the shooting of rabbits from motorboats and the use of mules to hunt ducks, and in Cleveland, Ohio, it is illegal to catch mice without a hunting licence. You cannot even take a picture of a rabbit from January to April in Wyoming without an official permit. In both California and Tennessee (a landlocked state) the only thing you may shoot from a moving vehicle is a whale.

Animal welfare is clearly important in some places. Neither Excelsior Springs, Montana, nor La Crosse, Wyoming, will tolerate the worrying of squirrels, and it is illegal to mistreat rats in Denver, Colorado. Nobody is allowed to cross state lines in Minnesota with 'a duck atop his head'. To thwart the real extremist, in Los Angeles it has been ruled that nobody can lick a toad and, most worrying of all, if you live in Florida you may not have sexual relations with a porcupine. It is an offence to feed alcoholic beverages to a moose in Fairbanks, Alaska, whilst bear-wrestling matches are forbidden in Alabama. If you harass Bigfoot, Sasquatch or other undiscovered subspecies in Washington, you risk a fine and/or imprisonment. (Although nothing to do with sporting shooting, I particularly like the fact that New Orleans forbids the practising of voodoo within the city limits; you may not paint sparrows in Harper Woods, Michigan, and sell them as parakeets; and the penalty for jumping off a building in New York is death).

As ever, one has to wonder why the enactment of some of these laws was ever found necessary in the first place.

Although only HM The Queen, her invited guests and members of St John's College, Cambridge, are permitted to eat mute swans in England, where they are the monarch's property, killing them is of course forbidden under the terms of the 1981 Wildlife and Countryside Act. Just how they reach the table is, fortunately, a quandary never likely to be faced by any reader of this book.

The 1985 film *The Shooting Party*, set in pre-First World War England, features a number of labrador retrievers. In fact the labrador had only recently been introduced to the UK at that time, and Kennel Club records show that less than 300 had been registered in the country by 1912.

You might encounter any number of spaniel breeds in the field, most of which have as their main purpose the finding and flushing of game. The word 'spaniel' comes from the Old French espaigneul *or* espaignol, *meaning Spanish, as the dog is thought to have originated in Spain. These dogs were used in the English hunting field as early as 1576. In the early 1800s there were still considered to be just two main types: the springing, hawking or starter spaniel, used for the general purpose of flushing game, and the smaller cocker (or 'cocking') spaniel, which was more specifically intended for hunting woodcock. Both might have been born in the same litter, but were selected for their function purely according to size and weight. It was not until 1895, when the Spaniel Club was formed, that breed standards for the springer and cocker were formally devised, and the Kennel Club separated the two types in 1902.*

Since the fifteenth century, collections of group terms that could be applied to animals, birds and people have been compiled. One of the earliest was laid down by Dame Juliana Berners in *The Book of St Albans* (1486), where she asserted that 'every man claiming to be gentle' should be familiar with them. This was but the first collection and the list has grown since; many of these words have fallen into disuse over the years, but here are a few:

A *cete* of badgers
A *wake* of buzzards
A *murder* of crows or magpies
A *brace* (shot), *team, flock, raft* or *paddling* of ducks
A *business* of ferrets
A *leash* or *skulk* of foxes
A *raft* (on the water), *gaggle or flock* (on the land), *skein* (in the air) or *plump* (flying close) of geese
A *drove, husk* or *down* of hares
A *blast* of hunters
A *sorde* or *suit* of mallard
A *tidings, congregation* or *gulp* of magpies
A *plump* of moorhens
A *covey* of partridge or quail
A *muster, ostentation* or *pride* of peacocks
A *bouquet, nest* or *nide* of pheasants
A *flight* or *kit* of pigeons
A *congregation* or *wing* of plovers
A *bevy* of quail or swans
A *nest* of rabbits
An *unkindness* or *crowd* of ravens
A *boiling* or *parliament* of rooks
A *dopping* of sheldrakes
A *walk* or *wisp* of snipe
A *pack* or *trip* of stoats
A *sounder* of boar or (wild) swans
A *spring* of teal
A *colony* or *pack* of stoats
A *company* or *trip* of wigeon
A *fall* of woodcock

The origins of the bowler hat, once an important uniform item of a City gentleman, lie in gamekeeping. In the mid-nineteenth century the top hats usually worn by keepers were not very robust and were easily knocked off. It is generally accepted that the younger brother of the 2nd Earl of Leicester, Edward Coke, commissioned the design of a close-fitting hat with a strong, low crown and narrow brim to protect his gamekeepers' heads when out riding and dealing with poachers. The order was placed with London hatters Lock and Company, who in turn tasked Thomas and William Bowler with producing the headgear. When Coke collected the first hat in 1849, it is said that he tested it by placing it on the floor and stamping hard upon it. The hat passed the test and was worn thereafter by Coke's gamekeepers at Holkham Hall in Norfolk.

At the time it was Lock and Company's practice to name a new hat design after the customer: accordingly it became the 'Coke' hat. As it was believed then that the actual design was the idea of another Coke, William, a nephew of the 1st Earl of Leicester, the hat also became known as the 'Billy Coke' and ultimately the 'billycock', before the more popular epithet of bowler was applied. Whichever Coke was actually responsible for the design, the hat is still worn with pride even today as a badge of office by keepers at Holkham, but this privilege is only earned after a year of service.

Instances of Lyme disease in England have quadrupled in just the last twelve years. First noted in the United States, the bacteria that cause it are passed on to humans by ticks and can result in long-term heart and joint problems. The classic sign is a bullseye-shaped rash spreading from the site of the tick bite: this might take anything between two and thirty days to appear. Other symptoms can include tiredness, muscle pain, headache and a high temperature. The disease is easily diagnosed from a blood test, and if dealt with promptly is not difficult to treat effectively. There have been recent suggestions that the disease is infectious, although there has yet to be any scientific proof of this.

After consulting obedience trial judges from both the American and Canadian Kennel Clubs, Stanley Coren, professor of canine psychology at the University of British Columbia, published a book entitled The Intelligence of Dogs *in 1994. Ranking different breeds against their working and obedience intelligence, he concluded (perhaps unsurprisingly) that the border collie was the brightest of the dog breeds. Among the gundogs, the golden and labrador retrievers came 4th and 7th respectively, followed by the English springer spaniel (13th), German shorthaired pointer (17th), cocker spaniel (20th), Weimaraner (21st) and German wirehaired pointer (44th). At the very bottom of the list, in 80th position, was the poor Afghan hound. It may come as some surprise that the Irish setter, never really noted for a high IQ amongst shooting types, was well up the list at 35th, whilst the poodle was placed 2nd.*

The opening of the 2015 wildfowl season did not go well for a 25-year-old woman in the US state of Indiana. She had laid her shotgun on the ground, safety catch off, when her chocolate labrador stepped on it and accidentally shot her. She was hit in the left foot but was fortunately able to be released from hospital soon after receiving treatment. An environment official later noted that the woman had not attended a hunter education course and urged all shooters to do so.

To add insult to injury, the dog's name was Trigger.

Staying with the Duke of Portland at Welbeck Abbey in November 1913, Archduke Franz Ferdinand was almost the victim of an accident when shooting pheasants. The Duke records the event in his memoir, Men, Women and Things*:*

> *'One of the loaders fell down. This caused both barrels of the gun he was carrying to be discharged, the shot passing within a few feet of the Archduke and myself. I have often wondered whether the Great War might not have been averted, or at least postponed, had the Archduke met his death then and not at Sarajevo the following year.'*

Franz Ferdinand and his Duchess were both assassinated in the Bosnian capital some seven months later, on 28 June 1914. Their deaths were considered to be part of a series of events which ultimately led to the start of the First World War.

Keeper's Tip: Make sure that you carry ample ammunition, and take at least twice as much as you think you'll need if you have a slightly unusual calibre such as a 16 or 28 bore. Your fellow Guns are unlikely to be able to resupply you if you run out.

Max

After a false start with a German shorthaired pointer which proved to be entirely the wrong dog for me, my life has been marked by a succession of springer spaniels. All have been fantastic in their own ways, but Max was by far the best in pure gundog terms. Enthusiastic and tireless, he would work all day and still have the energy to go on when the rest of the field was exhausted. He'd find and flush birds which two or three other dogs had gone past, and he was utterly fearless in thick cover. He was also an exceptional retriever who'd frequently wipe the eyes of the steadier labradors present by finding the unfindable bird that everyone else had given up on, and he was independent enough to be cast loose after a strong runner which he'd often turn up with as much as half an hour later. Yet it was in a field entirely unrelated to shooting that he really distinguished himself and won a special affection within the family.

We were living in an Army married quarter not far from the main gate of the camp that I worked in. Our sons were still small and James, the youngest at three years old, was going through a phase of waking during the night to be found pottering around the house in the small hours. At about four o'clock one morning my wife woke me with a dig in the ribs to tell me that she could hear the dog barking outside. 'Rubbish' I replied. 'He's locked in the kitchen.'

He wasn't of course. James had woken up, managed to open the front door (I started taking the key out of the lock and hiding it after this) and let both himself and Max out to go for a walk together in the dark, following the line of street lamps. Eventually they had made it as far as the camp guardroom where the Guard Commander had been surprised to find a small boy in his pyjamas, accompanied by a spaniel, standing at the barrier demanding a drink of squash.

The duty corporal didn't recognise the child, but as Max spent every day at work with me and was a familiar feature on the battalion Friday afternoon run he easily put two and two together and knew where the pair came from. He went to pick up James to deliver him home but here his problems began. Max, normally the most sociable and friendly of dogs, was having none of it. Placing himself protectively in front of James he raised his hackles, bared his teeth and dared anyone to get past him to the boy under his protection.

Thinking fast, the corporal took the best course open to him. As we looked out of the bedroom window wondering what was going on, we beheld an unusual sight under the street lights. The battalion Quick Reaction Force, a dozen soldiers strong, was advancing up the road towards our house in a wide 'horns of the buffalo' formation, ushering ahead of them a delighted three year old who'd never known so much excitement in his life, accompanied by a dancing, barking spaniel who was determined to defend his friend at all costs.

From that day on Max could do little wrong in our eyes although it did cost me a couple of cases of beer to the camp guard – as well as champagne in the Mess when the Commanding Officer found out.

Keeper's Tip: If you are in doubt about any aspect of the day or the etiquette involved, don't hesitate to ask your host or the keeper. Both will be happy to clear up any uncertainty you may have, especially if they know that you are new to shooting.

Tales from Glen Garron

A Bird in the Hand

Some secrets are made for keeping

It had been a long day's march and the men were tired. There were almost five thousand of them, trained and disciplined soldiers, yet they were becoming worried. They had travelled too far, the troublemakers were starting to suggest, to expect any support and it was already rumoured that they were lost. The ancient forest stretched dark and uninviting around them, and the usual rough banter had tailed off. The only sounds now were the tired tramp of sandalled feet and the clink of armour.

The first shower of arrows arrived without warning, and the empty woods were suddenly filled with screaming, running, blue-faced figures, crudely armed and dressed in animal skins. It was impossible to count them; they came from all sides in a deafening wall of sound. There was no opportunity to adopt the well-practised defensive formations, only time for the soldiers to link shields as well as they could and brace themselves against the onslaught of a horde without number. Armoured professionals though they were, there was no hope. The native enemy, in vastly overwhelming numbers, enraged by the presence of foreign invaders and careless of their own lives, howled as they threw their bodies against the shield wall. For the weakened defenders the end was inevitable, as section after section of shields crumbled under the sheer weight of numbers and their elated adversaries poured through to commence the slaughter. None escaped.

'Bury them,' said the leaders of the blue-painted men. 'Erase them from memory. Hide all signs that they were ever here.' And so it was done. Five thousand men disappeared off the face of the earth, leaving no trace of their existence bar a few inevitable spoils of battle and the single gilded symbol of their victory that was borne away.

'Bliddy rubbish!' Willie Cameron exclaimed, as the film credits rolled on the television screen. 'Whit the hell do they know…' His voice tailed off as Archie looked across the room at him and raised an eyebrow.

'What do you mean, Da'?' he asked his father.

'Nothing, nothing,' Willie replied rather lamely. Archie, rather puzzled, shrugged and let the matter go.

It was Lady Mary who responded to the front door bell, an old fashioned brass bowl and clapper connected to a chain at the front entrance to the Lodge. Standing outside was an attractive if hard-faced blonde woman in her mid-thirties, dressed in a severely cut business suit and clutching a handbag. 'I am here to see your master,' the woman announced, in a distinct American East Coast accent, with neither smile nor preamble.

Lady Mary sighed inwardly. Dressed for gardening and with her hair in a mess, she knew that she didn't look like the laird's wife, but there was something about the visitor's manner that grated distinctly. On a whim she decided to play along. 'Certainly, Miss,' she replied in a convincing Highland lilt. 'Do you have an appointment, and who shall I say is calling?'

'Lara Benelli of the *Washington Enquirer,*' was the response. 'No, my good woman, I don't have an appointment but I expect he'll want to see me. I'm told that he has some information I need. And it's Ms, not Miss, if you don't mind.'

Lady Mary smiled at her, bobbed a curtsey and waved a hand towards the hall in invitation. 'Very well, Ms Benelli. If you'll just wait here I'll go and find him.' Five minutes later Lady Mary showed the reporter into the study where the Colonel, brought in from the kitchen garden where he and his wife had been planting potatoes together and hastily washed, combed and jacketed, now waited. 'Thank you Mary, that will be all,' he told his wife, with a slight smirk.

Ms Benelli sat down uninvited and removed a notebook from her vast handbag. 'Now,' she said, 'tell me about your golden bird.' Searching in the depths of the bag for a pen, she missed the slight start of surprise before the Colonel settled his features into an expression of bland enquiry. 'Would that be the eagle,' he asked politely, noting the beginnings of a triumphant smile on his visitor's face '... or the plover? We have grouse here as well, but they tend to be red or black. Sometimes we get goldfinches on the bird feeders, though?' he concluded inquiringly, with a hopeful look.

Ms Benelli didn't bother to hide her annoyance. 'Look mister, I've been looking into this story for a while now.' The Colonel chose to ignore the bluntness. 'There's a whole trail of artefacts that led me here, and I want you to tell me what you know...'

Not long afterwards the reporter left the Lodge frustrated. It was clear that the old fool didn't know anything and that she'd been wasting her time, and she had been careful not to go into too much detail about what she was looking for. It wouldn't do for a rival to beat her to the scoop on this one. Never mind, there was still that gamekeeper down in the village. Maybe she'd get something out of him. These rustic types were pretty slow-witted, she thought, and a few free drinks usually opened them up quickly enough. She got into her hired car, revved it unnecessarily and drove off down the drive, wheels spinning and gravel scattering in all directions.

The Colonel watched her leave from the study window. Lady Mary entered the room and raised a quizzical eyebrow. 'Strange woman,' he replied to the unspoken question. 'Rather rude and obtuse. She seemed interested in our birdlife, but I don't think she got what she was after and frankly I didn't feel much inclined to offer more. A shame, very ungrateful and not a bit like those rather nice American types who come here every year for the shooting on the Twelfth.' He lifted the telephone. 'I just need to make a quick call. See you back in the garden in a couple of minutes?'

That evening in The Kelpie, Willie Cameron found himself being questioned relentlessly by the overly direct American woman as she plied him with whisky. This he enjoyed enormously; his capacity for vintage malt was legendary though normally beyond his means (Mrs Cameron kept a strict check on the household accounts) so he took full advantage of the situation. Ms Benelli, however, he did not warm to. As the evening went on, her charming approach slipped and she did not bother to hide her irritation as she came to realise that this dim-witted savage of a gamekeeper was going to be of no help. Still, her interest was piqued by something else that Willie mentioned in passing, and she saw the glimmerings of a consolation story. It might not be the stuff of Pulitzers, but was just the sort of thing that her Editor, no friend of a people they both viewed as 'the idle English rich' (everyone on this pitiful little island was English to them), liked to publish in the *Enquirer*. Reaching for the ever-present notebook, she started to scribble furiously as a now slightly slurring Willie expanded on his chosen theme.

The next morning Willie parked his battered old Land Rover by the stables at the back of the Lodge and opened a low oak door with an ancient, huge key. Stooping to enter, he descended a series of granite steps into the Lodge cellars and made his way by torchlight to a far corner. He turned at a slight sound behind him.

'I was thinking,' said the Colonel, as he stepped out of the shadows where he had been waiting for his old friend the keeper, 'it's about time that we let your Archie in on our little secret. After all, we're neither of us getting any younger. Sadly the rules don't allow for daughters and young Edward won't be ready for a few years yet. Shall we have a look at Herself?' Between them, the Prize was always referred to as Herself.

Archie went to a dust-covered sideboard by the cellar wall and depressed a hidden catch. Silently, the sideboard slid to one side to reveal a recess in the ancient granite covered by a heavy curtain. This the Colonel solemnly pulled to one side to reveal what was within. On a stone plinth stood a golden metal bird just over two feet high, wings outstretched, its talons gripping a ball on which was inscribed a simple 'IX'. Both men knew that below the ball was a slot designed to receive the long pole on which the bird was once carried.

In AD 117 the Ninth Legion of the Roman Empire had been dispatched north from their garrison in York to subdue the rebellious tribes in Caledonia before disappearing without trace, the cause of which has been a source of debate and conjecture to the present day. Willie and the Colonel knew better. Far from help and unsupported, the Ninth was wiped out by a savage and fatally underestimated enemy; this was their standard, the Prize borne away from the battlefield and kept in secret by a series of guardians, a duty passed from father to son throughout the centuries.

'That was a close one, boss,' Willie remarked quietly.

'Yes, I got the impression that she'd tracked down a few battlefield relics and followed the trail as far as here. Still, I think we've seen the last of her, for now at least, but it goes to show that we can't let our guard down and it may well be time for Herself to move to a new home. Let's have Archie over sooner rather than later, shall we?' Replacing the curtain, the Colonel slid the sideboard back into place and the two of them made their way up the steps into the morning sunlight.

Two weeks later the *Washington Enquirer*, never a friend of the British, who the newspaper portrayed gleefully as a nation peopled with an asinine aristocracy and a brutal redcoat soldiery in the more fanciful Hollywood style, ran a major inflammatory story sure to create outrage. To the initial delight but ultimately deep chagrin of its Editor and a shocked Laura Benelli, the story was taken up by other publications before being rebuffed and ridiculed in the most embarrassing terms.

Accompanied by 'exclusive', if rather grainy and long-range, photographs of a 'secret location' – which turned out to be a pheasant-rearing field a few miles to the south of Glen Garron – the article told with breathless and righteous indignation of the scandal of grouse being reared in their tens of thousands to be turned out onto the hills of Scotland. There they would be gunned down by the chinless, well-heeled social elite, often on the very day of their release, having first been driven to exhaustion by gangs of servile bearded men wearing skirts decorated with the flayed skins of wild animals. Worse still, these shooting practices were destroying the fragile habitat of the seriously endangered Strongyle Worm, a species of international significance, and it was feared that the Upland Neep, a marsupial found only in Scotland, had been persecuted to near-extinction by gamekeepers over the last decade.

As a little careful enquiry might have made clear to a chastened Ms Benelli, the neep (or swede) is thriving alongside other root crops and it is difficult to think of anyone who might mourn the passing of the strongyle worm, a debilitating parasite of the grouse. Willie had regretfully decided not to add the Mountain Haggis, which would surely have given the game away, to his list of endangered species.

Furthermore, the red grouse is of course the one game bird that simply cannot be bred and reared in captivity for release onto the moors – not even in Glen Garron, where anything can happen and so very frequently does.

FURTHER READING

It's difficult to know where to start as there are so many worthy titles to choose from, so all I've done here is suggest a number which still give me pleasure, or which I reach for as trusted sources of information. Inevitably some may be out of print but an internet search should turn them up. As ever, a visit to Coch-y-Bonddu Books at www.anglebooks.com is a great starting point whenever looking for new or used sporting books.

Buckzacki, Dr S, *Fauna Britannica*
(Hamlyn 2002)
An ambitious, sweeping overview of British wildlife examining natural history, folklore and tradition. Authoritative, accessible, and packed with facts.

Coles, C, *Shooting and Stalking – A Basic Guide*
(Stanley Paul, revised 1988)
With sections written by experts in their respective fields, this book covers everything a newcomer to shooting sports needs to know. Chapters range across subjects including shooting and conservation, air weapons, game shooting, wildfowling, stalking and a host of others.

Corbett, J, *The Jim Corbett Omnibus*
(Oxford University Press 1991)
If you have never read Jim Corbett's adventures, you really are in for a treat.

Garfit, W, *Will's Pigeon Shooting*
(Quiller Publishing 2012)
Everything you need to know about pigeon shooting by an acknowledged master of the art. Full of tips, observations and sound advice, as well as being beautifully illustrated.

Jones, David S D, *Gamekeeping – An Illustrated History*
(Quiller Publishing 2014)
Written by The National Gamekeepers' Organisation's own archivist and historian, this is a meticulously researched and engrossing history of gamekeeping from the origins of the profession in the seventeenth century to the present day.

Marchington, J, *The Natural History of Game*
(Boydell Press 1984)
A comprehensive review of the game species. There may be more recent volumes, but this is still one of the best.

Martin, Brian P, *Sporting Birds of the British Isles*
(David and Charles 1984)
Another older but still magnificent book from a prolific countryside author, this one covers game birds, wildfowl, waders and 'pest' species such as pigeons and crows. It includes the added bonus of paintings by Rodger McPhail.

Ruark, R, *The Old Man and the Boy*
(Henry Holt & Co 1957, many reprints since)
No matter which part of the world you hail from, every sportsman will identify with this account of a young boy's sporting education at the hands of his grandfather in 1920s North Carolina. Ruark's foreword 'Anybody who reads this will realize I had a fine time as a kid' sums it up. This is one that I return to time after time – a true classic written with warmth, wit and wisdom.

Finally, you might try anything by Denys Watkins-Pitchford or 'BB', who wrote some sixty books as well as illustrating many others; my generation will remember his regular articles for *Shooting Times* up until his death in 1990. A passionate countryman and wildfowler (his *nom de plume* of BB was taken from his goose shooting loads), he was a keen observer of the natural world who many maintain had no contemporary equal as an outstanding descriptive writer or illustrator. For starters, consider *Wild Lone, the story of a Pytchley Fox* or *The Countryman's Bedside Book*, or if you have children there is *The Little Grey Men* which tells the story of the last four gnomes in England: 'honest-to-goodness gnomes, none of your baby, fairy-book tinsel stuff, and they live by hunting and fishing, like the animals and birds, which is only proper and right.'

A verse taken from a Cumbrian gravestone prefaced all of his works, and I make no apologies for closing with it as sound advice to sportsmen and women of all ages:

The wonder of the world
The beauty and the power
The shapes of things,
Their colours, light and shades
These I saw,
Look ye also while life lasts

Revelation

I hope that, among the rocket pistols, triple-barrelled shotguns and zombie-killing ammunition, you managed to spot the entirely fictional gunmaker John Aubrey and his equally fictional *Polychrest* choke system (page 184). Readers of Patrick O'Brian's wonderful seafaring novels will no doubt recognise where the names came from. The medical definition of a polychrest, by the way, is actually correct. Otherwise, although there have indeed been some very wild concepts in firearms design, a choke that splits the shot charge into two or more parts has never existed, and it would certainly be a very foolhardy individual who attempted to fire any gun with an obstruction, deliberate or otherwise, at the end of the barrel.